SHIP

B/W

MEMBERS OF THE COMMITTEE

Bernard Williams Esq

B Hooberman Esq

His Honour Judge John Leonard QC

Richard Matthews Esq CBE QPM

David Robinson Esq

Ms Sheila Rothwell

Professor A W B Simpson

Dr Anthony Storr

Mrs M J Taylor

The Right Reverend John Tinsley

Miss Polly Toynbee

Professor J G Weightman

V A White Esq MBE

OBSCENITY AND FILM CENSORSHIP

AN ABRIDGEMENT OF THE WILLIAMS REPORT

EDITED BY
BERNARD WILLIAMS
Provost of King's College, University of Cambridge

CAMBRIDGE UNIVERSITY PRESS
CAMBRIDGE
LONDON NEW YORK NEW ROCHELLE
MELBOURNE SYDNEY

Published by the Press Syndicate of the University of Cambridge
The Pitt Building, Trumpington Street, Cambridge CB2 1RP
32 East 57th Street, New York, NY 10022, USA
296 Beaconsfield Parade, Middle Park, Melbourne 3206, Australia

This abridged edition first published by Cambridge University Press 1981

Printed in Great Britain
at the University Press, Cambridge

Library of Congress catalogue card number: 81–10247

British Library Cataloguing in Publication Data
Obscenity and film censorship. – Abridged ed
1. Obscenity (Law) – England
I. Williams, Bernard II. Great Britain
Committee on Obscenity and Film Censorship
Report of the Committee on Obscenity and Film Censorship
344.205′274 KD8075

ISBN 0–521–24267–3 hard covers
0–521–28565–8 paperback

CONTENTS

Part 2—Principles

Part 3—Proposals

PREFACE

The Committee on Obscenity and Film Censorship, of which I was Chairman, was appointed in July 1977 by the then Home Secretary, the Rt Hon. Merlyn Rees, and reported in October 1979. This book is a reprint of our Report, originally published by HMSO (as Cmnd. 7772) in 1979. It is unchanged except for the omission of eight appendices, on such matters as the history of the criminal law in these areas and of film censorship, the law in other countries, and bibliographical and statistical issues. We are grateful to the Home Office and to the Stationery Office for giving permission for this reprint.

A Departmental Committee of this kind, like a Royal Commission, ceases to exist after it has reported. Responsibility for this Preface cannot therefore be ascribed to the Committee. Still less, of course, can it rest in any way with the Home Office, and it must be simply my own.

There are other and more general effects of the fact that such a Committee ceases to exist. It cannot do anything collectively to influence or comment on its Report's reception. This is no doubt inevitable, but it can put the Committee and its Report at some disadvantage against its critics, who, particularly in the case of organisations and pressure groups, have (quite legitimately) continuing opportunities to comment on it.

It would be inappropriate for me to comment here on the reception of our Report or on criticisms which it has received. However, I can perhaps say something about the kind of Report it is, and what it tries to achieve. For reasons that we explain in Chapter One, we did not think that this was a subject on which we could usefully commission or suggest new research. There is already a gigantic amount of research material on these subjects; much of it is admittedly not very helpful, but what would be needed to improve on it would be inspiration, not simply more labour or Departmental support. What we sought to do was to clarify the issues involved and to develop some shared understanding of such things as the nature of pornography, an understanding which we hoped would be at any rate rather less superficial than that often displayed in controversy. We were also very determined to direct our discussions towards a workable law, and to make recommendations that would be practical for this society at this time.

The people who were members of the Committee are certainly very various, and we did not start with shared conceptions of the problems, nor with the same prejudices about where we might come out. After a great deal of discussion, we arrived at a unanimous report, and I can honestly say that this was not a unanimity of compromise – in the sense of one person's giving way on one point if someone else gives way on another – but a unanimity of conviction, to the effect that our recommendations indicated the right way in which to proceed.

It is central to the recommendations of this Report that they identify two different kinds of objective that can be served by legal action on pornography, one of which calls for suppression while the other calls only for restriction. This second concern, that of the offensiveness of public display, had already, at the time of our Report, motivated a number of Bills to curb indecent display, all of which had failed. At the present time, however, another Bill, introduced by Mr Tim Sainsbury M.P., has passed through the House of Commons and is almost certain to become law during 1981. We have argued in the Report that the 'indecent displays' approach to this problem is likely not to be very effective, but I am sure that the Committee would welcome the measure so far as it goes, and wish it success in curbing offensive public displays. Even if it is successful, the Bill, as Mr Sainsbury himself has emphasised, addresses only some of the difficulties raised by the present hopeless state of the law on pornographic and similar publications, and, of course, there remain in addition the various problems that the Report identifies concerning the cinema.

There is one matter on which this Report has attracted misunderstanding, and it may be useful if I briefly explain in this connection what we were trying to say. We recommend that neither suppression nor restriction should be applied to any publication which consists entirely of the written word (or, to put it rather more precisely, the offensive element in which consists of the written word). Some have concluded from this that we must suppose literature to have a less significant effect on people than photographs do. I think that it should have been clear, though evidently it is not, that no such idea is implied by our recommendation. That recommendation is based on the consideration that merely *in the matter of immediate involuntary offensiveness*, which it is the principal aim of restriction to prevent, written material has less effect than photographs do: quite simply, to be offended by written material requires the activity of reading it. On the question of suppression, again, the criterion that we recommend for that (harm to participants) does not apply to written material at all. The recommendation about written material may be controversial, but I hope that the ideas behind it will not, at any rate, be misunderstood.

There is a great tendency for public debate on an issue of this kind to regress to stale formulae and well-worn patterns of controversy. I hope that the republication of this Report will encourage fresh discussion not only of its recommendations, but of the arguments and distinctions that surround and support them. Discussion of the Report up to now has tended to concentrate on a few issues, and there are several other important questions which have been so far largely neglected. The conclusions of Chapter Eight, for instance, about artistic merit and the 'public good defence', have been very little discussed, but if they are sound, they are of some consequence for any future comprehensive legislation about obscenity.

BERNARD WILLIAMS

Cambridge
May 1981

PART 1—BACKGROUND

CHAPTER ONE

THE COMMITTEE'S TASK

1.1 We were appointed on 13th July 1977 by the then Home Secretary "to review the laws concerning obscenity, indecency and violence in publications, displays and entertainments in England and Wales, except in the field of broadcasting, and to review the arrangements for film censorship in England and Wales; and to make recommendations". The Government had already announced its intention to set up a Committee to examine these matters. On 14 December 1976 the Minister of State at the Home Office explained in the House of Lords (on the Second Reading of the Criminal Law Bill) why the Government had decided not to legislate on the basis of Part III of the Law Commission's Report on Conspiracy, which concerned public morals and decency. Legislation along such lines, said Lord Harris, "would be bound to raise more fundamental questions about the general law of obscenity" than it had been the Law Commission's task to examine and it was the Government's view that a broader look should be taken at the subject before legislation was brought forward.

1.2 We held our first meeting on 2 September 1977 and have met 35 times in all. Immediately after our first meeting we issued a general invitation to members of the public to write to tell us of their views. We sent letters to over a hundred organisations who we thought would have a special interest in the subject, and we placed an advertisement in every national daily newspaper, seeking the views of their readers. Later on, we recognised a gap in the evidence we had received: there had been a very small response to our invitation from the women's movement, despite the strong views held about pornography by many who are active in the movement. We took further steps, and it was made known in *Spare Rib* and the Women's Page of *The Guardian* that we wanted to hear from women. As a result of all these measures we received written submissions from something like 150 organisations and groups and from nearly 1400 individuals. We are most grateful to all those who took time and trouble to help us in this way.

1.3 We should like to acknowledge very warmly at this point the invaluable help that the Committee has received from its secretariat. Mr Jon Davey has been the Committee's Secretary throughout its work, and no-one could possibly have been more patient, tactful, clear-headed and hard-working than he has been. To him, to the Assistant Secretary Mr Roger Creedon, and to the other members of the Home Office staff who have helped us, we express our most sincere thanks.

1.4 One limitation of our terms of reference must be mentioned at this point; it was one that many of our correspondents found hard to accept. Broadcasting was specifically excluded from our remit. The main reason was that the whole field of broadcasting had been the subject of review by the Annan Committee, which reported only in February 1977[1], and the Government considered it wrong to submit the control of broadcast programmes to yet another review so soon. From the point of view of legal control, broadcasting is easily separated from the matters we were asked to consider, since the controls imposed on programmes do not rely on the law of obscenity, for example, but on obligations placed on the Governors of the BBC and the Independent Broadcasting Authority to ensure that their programmes do not offend against good taste or decency and are not offensive to public feeling. However, some of our witnesses argued that it was wrong for us to be excluded from making proposals affecting radio and television, which they considered should be subject to the same legal controls as apply to the other media. Many of those who wrote to us expressed more concern about what is shown on television than in publications and films. Beyond recording this strength of feeling, we have not concerned ourselves with the field of broadcasting.

Exploring our subject

1.5 One thing that is certainly true about this subject is that people have differing conceptions, not merely of what should be done about obscene publications, but of what the material in question is even like. When we started our enquiries, we ourselves needed to form some clear and shared idea of what, quite literally, we were talking about. We arranged to see a range of magazines of this kind which were then widely on sale, and others, less freely available, which had in many cases been seized when being smuggled into the country. We also looked at publications which had been in trouble with the law in the past, and saw how certain magazines had in recent years been extending the range of what they considered they could show. We saw a number of films which are sold for home viewing or are shown in some of the smaller film clubs. Some of us visited such clubs and shops specialising in pornography and some of the live entertainment offered to adults in London. As a result of these experiences, we gained a reliable impression of what is available, and were able to place this in some kind of perspective in relation to the past.

1.6 We also needed to study how the law operated and what its effect was, in practice, on the various kinds of material. We took evidence from those who enforce the law, and from other people with a professional or practical interest in the law and its effects. We held discussions with a number of those who made written submissions to us, as well as with other people to whom we thought it would be helpful to talk on the subject.

1.7 Since we were also concerned with the arrangements for film censorship, we needed to find out how the present arrangements operated and how film censorship works. Mr James Ferman, the Secretary of the British Board of Film Censors, readily agreed to explain the Board's policy and practice to us and he spent four afternoons with us giving an illustrated guide to the ways in which the Board censors films. In the course of those four afternoons we saw extracts from 90 different films, sometimes in "before" and "after" versions, which illustrated the attitude taken by the Board towards the protection of

---

[1]Report of the Committee on the Future of Broadcasting. Cmnd 6753.

children who go to the cinema, towards the depiction of violence, the depiction of sex and towards sexual violence and sadism. We are much indebted to Mr Ferman for the trouble he took to familiarise us with the operation of film censorship: for his four talks, for meeting us on several occasions, and for receiving us at the Board's offices and letting us see the Board at work. There were several films we thought we should make a special point of seeing in their entirety. Some had been the objects of concern and controversy after they had been approved by the Board: films such as *Straw Dogs, A Clockwork Orange* and *The Language of Love* (which had been the subject of unsuccessful proceedings for indecency). Others were films to which the censorship had withheld a certificate, and had been criticised by some for doing so: these included *The Story of O*, Pasolini's *Salò*, Oshima's *Empire of the Senses* (*Ai No Corrida*) and Malle's *Pretty Baby*. In addition to these, Mr Ferman showed us *Manson*, which had been refused a certificate in 1972 for reasons slightly out of the normal run—it had been thought that it could incite to violence, though it was not itself violent. Last, in view of some concern expressed to us about some sex education material, we took steps to see Dr Martin Cole's *Growing Up*, which had attracted some controversy. In all, apart from our private cinemagoing, we saw as a Committee 110 films, trailers or extracts from films.

1.8 Our next aim was to find out what people perceived to be the defects—and the strengths—of the present law and practice, and how they thought the law and practice could best be amended. As well as studying the wealth of written material submitted to us and reading many of the books published on this subject, we invited a number of people to talk about the subject with us. Some have an official role to play in the administration of the criminal law or the film censorship system; others have jobs which inevitably involve them in the operation of those laws; others possess a wide variety of knowledge, experience and concern for the welfare of society and the well-being of individuals. Those who helped us in this way are listed at Appendix 8 and we are extremely grateful to them. These discussions helped us to an understanding of how the law works and of the difficulties it causes to those it affects; to a greater knowledge of the way the trade is carried on and of the nature of the market; to a deeper perception of the nature of the issues involved and of the factors on which we should base our conclusions; and also to a fuller awareness of the strength of the feelings which the subject arouses.

Research

1.9 Needless to say, we discussed the effects of pornographic and violent material with a number of psychiatrists and psychologists, of various outlooks. At an early stage in our work we considered, very carefully, whether this was a matter on which it would be useful to commission fresh research. We were able to take into account two reviews of the existing literature, one on the effects of pornography which had been undertaken by Mr Maurice Yaffé in 1972 for Lord Longford's Committee[1], and which Mr Yaffé brought up to date for our benefit, the other on the effects of screen violence by Mr Stephen Brody of the

---

[1]Appendix V to *Pornography: the Longford Report*, Coronet Books, 1972.

Home Office Research Unit[3]. Both of these drew attention to the considerable amount of research which had already been undertaken, and also to the difficulties of studying human behaviour and of drawing conclusions about its motivations. Yaffé, for example, stated that "there is no consensus of opinion by the general public, or by professional workers in the area of human conduct, about the probable effects of sexual material" and Brody said that "social research has not been able unambiguously to offer any firm assurance that the mass media in general, and films and television in particular, either exercise a socially harmful effect, or that they do not".

1.10 Such conclusions as we have been able to draw from the vast amounts of research that exist we shall set out later in this Report (Chapter 6). It will be seen that such research tends, over and over again, to be inconclusive. This is certainly not an accident, but rather reflects basic features of this subject, or perhaps of any social research into subjects of this kind. It would be stupid to claim that no future research could shed more light on these questions than past research has done. But we do strongly suspect, in fact, that what these questions need are not so much new facts, as new ideas; and further, that enquiries which will be helpful are more likely to be those directed to the study of human personality as a whole, rather than to specific questions about violent or sexual materials and their supposed effects. However that may be as a general issue, one thing that became clear was that this Committee, in the brief period of its work, was neither going to invent nor galvanise others into inventing, the fruitful research ideas which have eluded so many able, industrious and well-funded researchers over so long a time. What we did do, besides studying the literature and trying to think about it, was to discuss the problems with a range of people who have professional experience in the study of human behaviour.

Public opinion

1.11 A different question was that of research into public opinion. Obviously the body of people who took the trouble to write to us do not constitute a cross-section of the public. Many of those who did not write may be indifferent to the whole subject—and this is one of those questions on which indifference is itself an attitude. There are in any case problems about the ways in which public attitudes are relevant to our task. Few people suppose, for instance, that the mere fact that a lot of people dislike something is, just in itself, a good enough reason for suppressing it (it is interesting that some people who have very populist sentiments in other connections do not have them on subjects such as obscene publications or capital punishment: and conversely). But does it make a difference if the dislike is not merely dislike but outrage? How much difference would it make if it were not the material, but displaying it in public, which was to be suppressed? These issues of principle we shall come to in Chapters 5 and 7. However, without prejudging them, and without supposing

[3]*Screen Violence and Film Censorship.* Home Office Research Study No 40, Her Majesty's Stationery Office, 1977.

that findings about public opinion could properly determine our recommendations, we could agree that it would be interesting and important to know more about public opinion on the matter, if possible, especially since large claims are sometimes made about what that opinion is.

1.12 The obvious way to assess public opinion is through an opinion poll, and we therefore looked at the possibility of commissioning a survey of public attitudes. It was helpful to us in considering this to study the results of a poll undertaken by Opinion Research Centre in 1973, summarised in the *Sunday Times* of 30 December 1973, and also the report of an exploratory study of public attitudes towards film censorship conducted by Social and Community Planning Research in 1974 for the Greater London Council. We also looked at the results of an attitudes survey conducted in the United States of America for the Commission on Obscenity and Pornography; and, at a later stage, we had submitted to us the findings of a Gallup poll conducted in January 1979 on attitudes towards pornography. We found it very difficult to gain a clear idea from these polls of what people thought: contradictions and inconsistencies were evident in all of them. For example, in the 1973 ORC poll 79 per cent of respondents agreed that all films shown in public cinemas should be passed by a national censorship board, but 46 per cent agreed that there should be no censorship at all for films shown to adults. Again, still on the subject of film censorship, the 1979 Gallup poll found 70 per cent against the abolition of the censorship on sexual grounds of films, and 65 per cent against sex being filmed, but 48 per cent in favour of allowing ordinary people to decide for themselves what is fit for them to see. The 1974 pilot study by SCPR found that some people who said they were opposed to film censorship in principle were quite prepared to suggest that particular scenes should be cut or banned; while others who pronounced themselves believers in censorship found it difficult to think of an exercise of censorship powers with which they agreed. It seemed clear that even if questions were framed with considerable care, the answers could not be accepted at their face value.

1.13 This is not to say that previous surveys have been lacking in any lessons. For example, the 1973 ORC survey found people apparently much more prepared to take a libertarian line with publications than with films, 74 per cent (as against 46 per cent for films) saying that they were in favour of the freedom of adults to buy whatever literature they wished, and the same distinction emerged in the United States survey. As regards public displays, the 1973 survey showed a majority (54 per cent to 34 per cent) in favour of a new law against indecent displays, despite the fact that the relevant question was loaded with references to the police being given wide powers of search and arrest, and despite the fact that 71 per cent of respondents claimed, in a separate response, never to have been seriously upset by an indecent public display. The survey also permitted the conclusion that men are less likely to take a restrictive attitude than women, the young less likely than the old and, to a less significant extent, middle class people less likely than working class people. In showing where the line ought to be drawn in restricting displays the survey was a good deal less definite. Questions about what people found to be indecent produced only confusing results and certainly were of no help to us in deciding what the law should attempt to restrict.

1.14 It seemed to us in studying these earlier surveys that there were severe practical difficulties in mounting any survey the results of which would be useful to us. There are a number of reasons for this. One is that it is clear that many respondents would be answering questions about a subject of which they had little or no knowledge, both from the point of view of law and practice, and (as we have already said) with respect to the nature of the material under discussion. Quite apart from this, the quality of the response is doubtful because of the potentially embarrassing nature of the subject; the sex, appearance and demeanour of the interviewer and the nature of the surroundings will all affect the answers given. The findings also tend to be distorted, as the United States survey found, by the fact that those who prefer not to discuss such a subject exclude themselves; and even by the fact that interviewers tend to retire from the enquiry rather rapidly, because of the distasteful nature of the subject, and have to be replaced.

1.15 The major problem, however, seemed to us to lie in obtaining some kind of shared understanding between interviewer and respondent about what it is that the questions relate to. This is not merely a matter of avoiding such general terms as "pornography" and "obscenity", of which individuals often have different conceptions. Even if one tries to define the subject matter more closely by verbal descriptions—as in "material depicting sex organs"—one cannot eliminate different interpretations of the words, so that one person may have a mental picture of putting fig leaves on statutes, another a serious sex education manual and another a highly explicit pornographic magazine. As SCPR commented in their pilot study, "survey research cannot adequately convey the context and the manner of presentation of scenes which is essential to obtaining meaningful responses". The only way to overcome this kind of misunderstanding is to present the respondent with specific examples and ask such questions as "Is *this* acceptable to be displayed in public places?" or "Should material of *this* kind be permitted for those adults who wish to buy it?" Leaving aside any questions of law, however, there are clearly ethical arguments against thrusting examples of pornography or other extremely distasteful material before unsuspecting members of the public, and the results of such a bizarre transaction would have little evidential value; while if such a study were undertaken with volunteers only, that pre-existing bias would cast doubt on its findings.

1.16 The 1973 ORC survey seemed to recognise the problems we have mentioned, and the need to focus the response on particular examples. It tried to meet both by showing its respondents three photographs, but of a comparatively innocuous kind with which the law on indecent displays was unlikely to be concerned. One was of Rodin's *The Kiss*, another a costume sketch for *Scheherazade*, of a reclining nude, by Leon Bakst, and the third a front cover of *Men Only*. In the event 7 per cent thought *The Kiss* indecent, 30 per cent thought the Bakst sketch indecent and 28 per cent thought the *Men Only* cover indecent. These comparatively high figures for material unlikely to be indecent at law suggest that more outrageous material might well have aroused overwhelming hostility. It seemed to us that it was simply not possible, in the words of the *Sunday Times* report on the poll, to "find out what the nation considers indecent" by showing pictures of a relatively inoffensive character, let alone to conclude from the response that, as the headline put it, "it isn't easy to shock the British". This poll tended to confirm us in our view that it would be a mistake to expect very much assistance from the commissioning of a survey of public attitudes. In view of the various difficulties we have mentioned, we decided against commissioning a fresh survey. We paid attention to the evidence of ordinary people's views submitted to us, and took into account some broad indications which emerged from the surveys already undertaken.

Foreign experience

1.17 It seemed to us that there was something to be learnt from the way other countries deal with these matters. We were interested in their experience of trying to suppress pornographic and violent material or, alternatively, allowing its circulation; and also in the ways in which they had tackled such problems as the legal definition of any material controlled by the law. We therefore put in hand enquiries about the legal restrictions and the arrangements for film censorship in other European countries, in America and Canada, and in Australia and New Zealand. In the light of the information we received, we decided that we should find out more about the situation in Denmark, where pornography was legalised in the late nineteen sixties, and in France, where a more recent liberalisation, particularly in relation to film censorship, led to problems which prompted a Government control of a new kind. Small parties of members made short visits to Copenhagen and Paris to study those developments, to discuss them with Government officials and others and see for themselves what the present situation was. We summarise in Appendices 3 and 4 respectively the results of our foreign enquiries about obscenity law and about film censorship.

Previous reviews of our subject

1.18 Our review is the first there has ever been in this country of such a comprehensive kind. There have, however, been Reports before. The Obscene Publications Act 1959 had followed the Report of a Select Committee of the House of Commons, and the Theatres Act 1968 was based on the recommendations of a Select Committee of both Houses of Parliament. Most of the other laws we had to consider were older, but we found waiting for us two reports recommending changes in certain aspects of the law. One was the Report of the Home Office Working Party on Vagrancy and Street Offences which, since its task was to review the Vagrancy Acts 1824 and 1838 which contain provisions about indecent display, had already looked in detail at the control of public displays. That Working Party had made preliminary recommendations for a modernised offence of making an indecent public display and had seen them embodied in Part II of the Cinematograph and Indecent Displays Bill which was introduced into Parliament by the Government in the autumn of 1973, but fell because of the General Election of February 1974. The final Report of the Working Party[1] was published in 1976 and recommended certain modifications to the original Bill, and we took account of that work.

---

[1] Report of the Working Party on Vagrancy and Street Offences, Her Majesty's Stationery Office, 1976.

1.19 The other report of which we had to take account was that of the Law Commission on Conspiracy and Criminal Law Reform[1], which in Part III had examined conspiracies relating to public morals and decency, including various other individual common law offences. The Law Commission, as part of its long term objective of codifying the criminal law, recommended that the whole of the common law in this area should be abolished and replaced by certain new statutory offences and that, to a large extent, those new offences should be within the context of the existing statutory law on obscenity. As we have already explained, the Government's view was that the obscenity law itself should be more fundamentally examined before it was extended in this way; we describe in Appendix 1 how, nevertheless, certain interim amendments to the law were made. It was a considerable help to us to have the benefit of the Law Commission's thorough review of the common law in our field.

1.20 The film censorship system had never been the subject of a thorough review since it first evolved—a word we use because, as we shall explain in Chapter 3, it was never formally instituted. The system has come to receive a substantial degree of acceptance and support, though it has gone through times of strain, as it had in the three years before we were appointed. The particular problem of the influence of the cinema on children had been examined between 1948 and 1950 by the Wheare Committee on Children and the Cinema[2].

1.21 There have also been, of course, a number of unofficial studies of our subject of which we have had to take account. One was by what is commonly referred to as the Arts Council Working Party, more strictly the Working Party set up by a Conference convened by the Chairman of the Arts Council, on the obscenity laws, whose report was published in 1969[3]. Another was by a Sub-Committee of the Society of Conservative Lawyers under the chairmanship of Sir Michael Havers in 1971[4]. Another was by the Committee which Lord Longford gathered about him "to see what means of tackling the problem of pornography would command general support", whose report was published in 1972[5]. We also could not ignore the Report of the United States Commission on Obscenity and Pornography, which caused something of a stir when it was published in 1970 and instantly rejected by President Nixon; and that on *Violence in the Media* by the United States Commission on the Causes and Prevention of Violence, published in 1969.

1.22 We turn now to the present situation as we found it; and first, to the law as it stands.

---

[1] Law Com No 76. Her Majesty's Stationery Office, 1976.
[2] Cmd 7945.
[3] *The Obscenity Laws,* Andre Deutsch.
[4] *The Pollution of the Mind,* Society of Conservative Lawyers.
[5] *Pornography: The Longford Report,* Coronet Books.

CHAPTER TWO

THE PRESENT LAW

2.1 The statute which has been at the centre of our review is the Obscene Publications Act 1959. There had of course been law about obscenity before that Act, but it was in fact the first statute to lay down the offence of publishing obscene articles. Before 1959, obscenity offences rested on the common law, which meant that the law had been established and developed by the courts. We deal in Appendix 1 with the way in which the body of law on obscenity came into being and developed, the origins of law on related matters, and the details of what the present law provides. In this chapter, we shall bring out the main features of present law and how they came to be as they are, and shall discuss how they have been interpreted and applied.

The "tendency to deprave and corrupt"

2.2 The common law offence of obscene libel was first established in 1727, but does not appear to have been frequently prosecuted until the nineteenth century. It was not until 1868 that the definitive test of obscenity was laid down in Chief Justice Cockburn's judgment in *R* v *Hicklin*, in which he defined obscenity, in the now celebrated phrase, as the "tendency to deprave and corrupt those whose minds are open to such immoral influences and into whose hands a publication of this sort may fall". That test remained as the basis of common law prosecutions and was eventually adopted, with some modifications, as the statutory definition of obscenity when the 1959 Act was enacted, and when plays, by the Theatres Act 1968, and films were later brought within the scope of statutory control on obscenity.

2.3 This famous test—the *deprave and corrupt* test, as we shall call it[1]—has, as we shall show, brought a certain confusion into the interpretation of the law. The confusion does not stop there, however, for the *deprave and corrupt* test is not the only test which English law applies in deciding what is obscene. It does not, for example, apply to material which is banned from importation under the Customs Acts. Those Acts prohibit articles which are "indecent or obscene", but that description is not further defined by the statute. The same phrase appears in the statutes prohibiting the transmission of certain material through the post and the display of material in public places. The law therefore operates at two distinct levels, leaving aside for the moment certain other statutes which also fall within our terms of reference: one class of articles is banned from being published or sold, and another rather larger class is banned from being imported, displayed publicly or sent through the post, and the *deprave and corrupt* test is used in the one case and not in the other. We shall look more closely at each of these classes in turn.

2.4 The Obscene Publications Act 1959 provides that an article shall be treated as obscene "if its effect or (where the article comprises two or more

---

[1] Our use, throughout our Report, of this handy abbreviation, does not mean that we have forgotten that the test refers only to the *tendency* to deprave and corrupt and contains other qualifications on its application, as set out in paragraph 2.4.

distinct items) the effect of any one of its items is, if taken as a whole, such as to tend to deprave and corrupt persons who are likely, having regard to all relevant circumstances, to read, see or hear the matter contained or embodied in it". In those cases tried at the Crown Court, it is usually left to the jury whether an article has a tendency to deprave and corrupt, without a direction from a judge as to what the words mean, though various glosses have been put on the words in different cases over the years. In the *Hicklin* case itself, for example, Chief Justice Cockburn referred[1] to the offending pamphlet as one which would suggest to the minds of people "thoughts of a most impure and libidinous character"; something similar, though perhaps a little more demanding, was offered by the House of Lords in 1972[2] when it was emphasised that the words "deprave and corrupt" refer to the effect on the mind, including the emotions, and that it is not necessary that any physical or overt sexual activity should result.

2.5 In the famous case involving *Lady Chatterley's Lover* in 1961[3], the jury were at least helped by reference to the dictionary, the judge telling them that "to 'deprave' means to make morally bad, to pervert, to debase or corrupt morally. To 'corrupt' means to render unsound or rotten, to destroy the moral purity or chastity of, to pervert or ruin a good quality, to debase, to defile". A similar summing-up was approved in a subsequent case, but judges were discouraged from attempting to go any further, the Court of Appeal holding[4] that where a statute lays down a definition in plain English, it is rarely necessary and often unwise for a judge to attempt to improve on it or redefine it.

2.6 The implication of the *deprave and corrupt* test and of the judicial comments on it is clearly that for an article to be found obscene a court should be satisfied that it is likely to have some kind of deleterious effect on an individual, even if the nature of the effect is hard to specify. Obscenity, defined in this way, is a *causal* notion: this is an important point of principle, and we shall come back to it, as such, in Chapter 5. It is on the basis of claiming those deleterious effects that the law is supposed to work. It is much less clear, however, that that is how the law works in practice. We noted the comments of Lord Wilberforce in *DPP* v *Whyte*[5] that although the words "deprave and corrupt" appeared in Chief Justice Cockburn's formula they had in fact been largely disregarded in common law obscenity cases: the courts simply considered whether the publication was obscene in some everyday sense and the tendency to deprave and corrupt was presumed. Lord Wilberforce went on to say that the Obscene Publications Act 1959 had changed all this. However, we gained the clear impression from the evidence we received that much of the time the law has continued to work as Lord Wilberforce said it worked before 1959.

---

[1] (1868) L.R. 3 Q.B. at p 371.
[2] *DPP* v *Whyte* [1972] 2 All E.R. 12.
[3] 1961 Crim L.R. 177.
[4] *R* v *Calder and Boyars Ltd.* [1968] 3 All E.R. 644.
[5] [1972] 2 All E.R. 12.

2.7 For instance, it is one thing to claim that a publication tends to deprave and corrupt, and a different thing to claim that it offends against current standards of what is acceptable. Yet we heard evidence that it is on this second basis that the law is sometimes applied, and indeed that that is how the House of Lords has expected it to be applied. In the *Knuller* case in 1972[1], Lord Morris of Borth-y-Gest said that it was a difficult task to decide what tends to deprave and corrupt "but Parliament has fairly and squarely assigned such a task to a jury. Doubtless it has done so with the knowledge that there is every likelihood that the collective view of a body of men and women on a jury will reflect the current view of society". In the same case, Lord Reid said that although the question whether matter is corrupting is for the jury, "they should keep in mind the current standards of ordinary decent people." The indication given by these statements of the role that the jury is expected to fulfil seems to us to accord with the role that it has in fact been fulfilling, as is shown by the way in which the law has actually worked.

2.8 If the question whether something tends to deprave and corrupt is taken seriously, as a matter of genuine psychological causation, then there is no reason at all to suppose that articles which possess this tendency should rapidly lose it: the presence of that tendency would be a relatively unchanging matter of fact. Yet experience in recent years has been of an astonishing contraction in the range of what juries determine to be obscene. To relate that shift to the words of the statute requires the conclusion that it is the perception of what is capable of depraving and corrupting that has changed rather than what is actually capable of such an effect. It may be, for example, that defence counsel have been able to encourage a general scepticism in the minds of juries about the ability of publications to affect an individual in a harmful way, or that juries are in any case applying a more critical eye to the meaning of the words of the statute and looking in vain for evidence to support the allegation of a tendency to deprave and corrupt. But, although what goes on in the jury room rarely comes to wider notice, it is equally plausible that the words of the statute did not introduce a radical shift in the way obscenity is decided, in the way Lord Wilberforce suggested, and that "the tendency to deprave and corrupt", literally interpreted, has still not played a dominant role in decisions about obscenity; rather, the literal sense of the words has in practice been subordinated to an assessment of current standards of acceptability, as suggested in the *Knuller* judgments we have quoted.

2.9 It is hardly surprising that this should be so. Lord Wilberforce in the case of *Whyte* said that such words "provide a formula which cannot in practice be applied", and this criticism is borne out by much of the evidence we have received. The courts, it was emphasised to us by many witnesses, need more detailed guidance as to the basis on which they should decide what contravenes the law; at the moment, they simply do not know what is meant by "deprave and corrupt" and are at a loss to know how such a test should be applied. In this connection (as opposed to the question of the "public good" defence, which we come to later, in paragraph 2.19), the jury are not allowed to look to expert witnesses for help, and have to reach a decision on their own.

[1] *Knuller* v *DPP* [1972] 2 All E.R. 898.

This, itself, is odd enough, if the test means what it says: the question whether a given publication possesses this tendency is one to which expert psychological or sociological evidence might be expected to be relevant, and to be helpful to a jury if the jury is to answer it, and feel sure of their answer. The result of all this, the Criminal Bar Association told us from their experience, is that juries "would rather acquit than guess their way to a conviction".

2.10 So far as the *deprave and corrupt* test is concerned, then, it seems to us that there are two different factors at work, probably equally important, in the way the obscenity laws have in recent years left unchecked an increasingly wider range of material. The first is that the literal sense of the statutory test of obscenity has been ignored, and the courts have applied their own assessment of what the public at large are prepared to accept and tolerate. The second is that the courts have been increasingly pressed to consider the actual words of the statute, and that when they have done so, they have become increasingly confused about how the statute should be applied, and increasingly reluctant to convict. As we explain below, the *deprave and corrupt* test is applied, in many cases, not by a jury but by a magistrate. It may be that the second factor we have just mentioned has affected juries more than magistrates and that this is a reason why, even though magistrates' standards have themselves shifted with changing public attitudes, it is considerably easier, as many of our witnesses told us, to obtain a finding of obscenity in a magistrates' court than before a jury.

The "indecent or obscene" test

2.11 The separate test of "indecent or obscene" contained in the Customs Acts, the Post Office Act and the Acts relating to public displays fixes the boundary of the legal at a different point from that imposed by the Obscene Publications Acts. This is immediately obvious by the inclusion of the word "indecent", which is usually taken to be a weaker term than "obscene"; but in addition the courts have held that the word "obscene" itself, where coupled with "indecent", has its dictionary meaning rather than the meaning of "tending to deprave and corrupt".

2.12 One consequence of this different placing of the legal boundary is that it is unlawful to import or to send through the post some material which may quite lawfully be published or sold within the country. HM Customs and Excise themselves made the point to us that there were many British-produced publications on sale in Britain which would have been seized if they had been imported. They recognised the difficulty of sustaining a control which involved a discrepancy of this kind, and they made it clear to us that they tried to apply a commonsense approach so as to avoid the more ludicrous consequences of [illegible] divergence of tests. Nevertheless, this anomaly was severely criticised and [illegible] indefensible by other witnesses. The general effect of the *indecent or* [illegible] is thus much wider than the *deprave and corrupt* test; however, [illegible] a sense in which the Customs and postal prohibition does [illegible]braced by the Obscene Publications Acts. This could in [illegible]icle did not offend against current standards of [illegible]decency, but was nevertheless of a nature which tended to deprave and corrupt. However, we received no evidence to suggest that this possibility was of much significance; as we have already made clear, the staple fare of Obscene Publications Act proceedings is sexual pornography which would just as easily infringe the *indecent or obscene* test.

2.13 The other important point which was made to us about the two tests was that the *indecent or obscene* test was far simpler to apply than the *deprave and corrupt* test. This has been the burden of some judicial pronouncements, and certainly the *indecent or obscene* test has avoided the kind of criticisms, of being impractical, that we have quoted in relation to the *deprave and corrupt* formula. Representatives of HM Customs and Excise made it clear to us that they considered their task would become well-nigh impossible if the import prohibition was based on the test in the Obscene Publications Acts, with all the doubt and confusion that it entailed; at present, on the other hand, it was reasonably straightforward, they claimed, for customs officers to decide what was "indecent or obscene" and for the courts to reach a similar decision in disputed cases. Lord Denning has observed in pointing to the comparative simplicity of the Customs and Post Office Acts compared with the Obscene Publications Act, "customs officers and the Post Office know pornography when they see it, and they act accordingly"[1]; Lord Denning's remark may be right, but it does to some degree change the subject: *pornography* is a notion different from both "obscenity" and "indecency", and (we shall suggest in Chapter 8), clearer than either.

2.14 The *indecent or obscene* test had some defenders; the *deprave and corrupt* test, the basic idea of the most important present law, had virtually none, and almost all of our witnesses wanted it abolished. Many witnesses saw that if there is to be a law against the kind of material against which the present definitions uncertainly work, then there has to be some other definition, and many different formulations were put to us, some invoking such notions as "contemporary standards of decency or humanity", others simply listing certain acts which it would be unlawful to portray. Other witnesses, again, on grounds either of principle or practicality, thought that there should be no such law at all.

Forfeiture proceedings and the right to trial

2.15 Among the difficulties of the present law, the question of the test of obscenity was widely agreed to be the most severe. However, other criticisms of the law were also put to us. Some of these concerned the choice of the manner of proceeding offered by the Obscene Publications Act 1959. Under section 2, a person may be charged with the criminal offence of publishing an obscene article or having it for the purpose of publication for gain, and this gives an accused person the right, if he so wishes, to have the issues decided by a jury at the Crown Court. We heard evidence that this is a right to which importance is attached by many people, not least by those themselves charged

---

[1] *R* v *Commissioner of Police of the Metropolis, ex parte Blackburn* [1973] 1 All ER 324.

with offences, since the experience has been that juries are less likely to convict than magistrates. Under section 3 of the Act, proceedings may be instituted in a magistrates' court for the forfeiture of obscene articles seized by the police and although the person from whom they were seized may defend the proceedings in the usual way, he is not himself at risk of any criminal penalties. It is section 3 under which most proceedings are brought.

2.16 The main criticism we received about section 3 proceedings was that since they are triable only in a magistrates' court their use (increasingly frequent) by the prosecuting authorities has the effect of denying to publishers and others the opportunity of taking their case before a jury where, as we have already pointed out, they have a rather greater chance of a favourable decision. This is a criticism of long standing. We were told that it was urged strongly at the time of the passing of the Obscene Publications Act 1964 (which was intended simply to correct certain deficiencies in the 1959 Act) and that it led to an assurance being given by the Solicitor General, with the approval of the Attorney General, in the following terms:

> " . . . if an article is seized under a warrant from a retailer or printer and if, before it is brought before the justices under section 3(3) of the 1959 Act, the publisher indicates his intention to continue publishing, whatever the result of any forfeiture proceedings may be, then, in the absence of any special circumstances, and subject to satisfactory evidence of an offence being available, it will ordinarily be the policy of the Director of Public Prosecutions to proceed against the publisher by way of prosecution rather than to pursue the forfeiture proceedings."[1]

2.17 The Director of Public Prosecutions commented to us that it seemed certain that both the Solicitor General and the House of Commons at the time had in mind only literate works consisting entirely of text, such as *Fanny Hill* and *Lady Chatterley's Lover*. Nevertheless, he adopts the policy of regarding the undertaking as applying also to the many monthly magazines now produced by English publishers, which were unknown in 1964; but at the time of his evidence to us there had been only one case in which an English publisher had sought to take advantage of the undertaking, and in that case the request had been turned down because it did not satisfy the condition of having been made before the magistrates' court proceedings had been instituted. The Solicitor General's assurance does not satisfy critics of the law, in particular because there are no arrangements for informing publishers that their publications have been seized from retailers; this means that they often do not know about pending proceedings until it is too late, under the terms of the undertaking, for them to intervene.

2.18 A second major criticism of section 3 is that there is a lack of justice in a procedure which allows the large scale seizure of goods and their detention for some time pending the outcome of proceedings. Even if the defendant wins the case he may suffer an effective and substantial penalty.

---

[1] House of Commons, Standing Committee F, 16 June 1964. Official Report 1963-64, Vol IV, Col 77.

Mr David Sullivan, a publisher, told us that it was grossly unfair that he should have been deprived of an entire magazine issue for four months only to have the copies returned to him after the magistrates had found they were not in fact obscene; they were then out of date and useless to him and he had suffered a loss of £19,000 despite a court finding in his favour. It was not totally clear to us how a magazine of the kind in question became out of date, but an issue of justice remains, and Mr Sullivan's point was supported by others with a less direct interest, such as the Law Society, who expressed to us the view that an unjust means of enforcing the law brought the law into disrepute. On the other hand, it was put to us that this summary procedure of dealing with bulk pornography provided a far more effective weapon against an illegal trade than any other and that its increasing use in recent times had been crucial in deterring publishers from flouting the law. The publication of potentially obscene magazines was now on such a massive scale that seizure and forfeiture was the only practical remedy, and was both justified and successful in protecting the public interest.

The public good defence

2.19 A further feature of the 1959 Act which is problematical is the "public good defence" that it provides, which has been controversial from its use in the trial of *Lady Chatterley's Lover* onward. The Act lays it down that even though an article is found to have a tendency to deprave and corrupt, both criminal proceedings and forfeiture proceedings fail if its publication is found to be for the public good on account of its literary, artistic or scientific merit. The public good defence stemmed from the recommendation of the House of Commons Select Committee that it should be a defence to show that the literary or artistic merit of the work in question was such that the publication of the work should be allowed to continue without an offence being committed. What most people had in mind at that time was the book by a serious author offered to the public by a reputable publisher; experience had shown that such books could be brought before the courts for alleged obscenity, and the acquittal of *Lady Chatterley* was widely regarded at the time as a vindication of the "public good" provision. We found a widespread sympathy for the idea that works of literary or artistic merit should not be liable to suppression, but many witnesses were uneasy about the way in which the Act tries to bring this about. Needless to say, many pointed out to us the assumption embodied in the present law, which they found extraordinary, that there could be a work which tended to deprave and corrupt those who read it, but that, at the same time, it was for the public good that that work be published — as though it could be for the public good that readers be depraved and corrupted, so long as it was by art. Some witnesses told us that what tends to deprave and corrupt should be suppressed whatever other merits it might have; others preferred to say that what was of genuine artistic or literary merit could never be capable of depraving and corrupting. It seemed to us that this anomaly was another reflection of the point we have already made about the test of obscenity, that the *deprave and corrupt* test was not traditionally expected to be taken literally and has in practice often taken a subsidiary role in determining whether an article is obscene. (We shall come to general issues about art and obscenity in Chapter 8.)

2.20 In any case, the position under the Obscene Publications Act is indeed that the court considers whether the publication is for the public good only after it has reached the conclusion that the article is obscene. This two-stage decision process was affirmed by the House of Lords in *DPP* v *Jordan*[1]. However, although the decision is supposed to be dealt with in two stages, the evidence on both issues is heard before the court comes to deciding the initial question whether the article is obscene, and it is not usually clear whether an acquittal of an offence (or a decision not to order forfeiture) is based on the view that an article is not obscene, or rather on the view that, although obscene, its publication is nevertheless justified as being for the public good. It is hard to resist the conclusion that the expert evidence which is permitted to support a public good defence has been allowed to reflect on the issue of obscenity, where expert evidence is not allowed, and that the questions have not been separated as it has been held they should be. This was specifically stated to have been the case in the *Oz* trial[2], where the Lord Chief Justice said that thc expert evidence "bore no relation to" the public good defence but was "directed to showing that the article was not obscene". More recently, the Court of Appeal drew attention to a judge having erred in not directing the jury that evidence called under section 4 was not admissible on the issue "obscene or not" under section 1[3].

2.21 We have already drawn attention to the judicial view that the *deprave and corrupt* test provides the opportunity for a jury to apply the standards of the community in deciding whether an article is obscene. A slightly different view was offered in *R* v *Calder and Boyars Ltd*[4] where the Court of Appeal suggested that it was in balancing the strength of the public good against the strength of the obscenity that the jury "must set the standards of what is acceptable, of what is for the public good in the age in which we live". So the public acceptability test here seems to be attached more to the issue of public good—though it is less clear that this means the interests of literature or art—than to the issue of obscenity. We are not convinced that this interpretation is any more in line with the actual words of the statute than those to which we referred before; rather, we see it as another example of the courts trying to make sense of a confused and confusing enactment.

2.22 The public good defence has been used to defend material which has no pretensions to artistic or literary merit. Two comparatively recent decisions have limited this use of it. The issue in *DPP* v *Jordan* was the use of the words "other objects of general concern" to argue that pornographic material was psychologically beneficial to persons with certain sexual tendencies by relieving their sexual tensions and possibly diverting them from anti-social activities, and that its publication was therefore for the public good. The House of Lords held that section 4 had been diverted from its proper purpose, and indeed abused, when it had been used to enable evidence to be given that

---

[1] [1976] 3 All ER 775.
[2] *R* v *Anderson* [1971] 3 All ER 1152.
[3] *Attorney General's Reference (No 3 of 1977)* [1978] 3 All ER 1166.
[4] [1968] 3 All ER 644.

pornographic material may be for the public good as being therapeutic to some of the public, and ruled that expert evidence to this effect was not admissible. The closing of this avenue of defence encouraged defendants to find another, and this resulted in the Attorney General referring to the Court of Appeal a point of law about the true meaning of the word "learning" in section 4, in particular whether evidence was admissible to show that an article had merit in the field of sex education or value in teaching or providing information about sexual matters. The Court ruled[1] that "learning" meant in the context of section 4 "a product of scholarship", and accordingly that evidence of the educational effect of sexually explicit material was not admissible. These decisions seem to have stopped the controversial practice of certain medical practitioners and psychologists being allowed to give evidence on behalf of the kind of material which the Obscene Publications Acts must clearly have been aimed at if they were to have any effect at all. The decisions have done much to mitigate the criticisms of the public good defence, which had been tending to fall into disrepute. At the same time, however, some of our witnesses have urged that the benefits described in that evidence ought to be taken account of in the law—but that is a question to which we should return later.

Restrictions on the right to prosecute

2.23 Another matter of controversy is that the law lays down certain restrictions on who may bring proceedings. There is a confusing patchwork of different restrictions, or lack of restrictions, which we summarise in Appendix 1. The provision which has perhaps aroused most antagonism among certain of our witnesses is that contained in the Theatres Act 1968, which prevents any prosecution being brought without the consent of the Attorney General. From the evidence given to us, it seemed likely that had it not been for this restriction more prosecutions would have been brought under the Act, not by the Director of Public Prosecutions but by private prosecutors. As it is, the Act has been used only once. The Director told us that in the ten years since the Act was passed only 28 cases of alleged offences under the Act had been referred to him; he thought that this indicated that there was no great problem in this field. The one case under the Act was heard at Manchester Crown Court in May 1971, when four defendants pleaded guilty in respect of a play staged at a Manchester theatre club and were sentenced to varying periods of imprisonment. The play was described in the Court of Appeal as "filth for filth's sake", with the comment that no other plea than guilty was remotely possible. We have received some complaints that other plays have been allowed to go unchallenged, but otherwise concern about the theatre formed only a very small part of the evidence we received.

Seizures by the Customs and Post Office

2.24 The procedures involved in the Customs and Post Office prohibitions received less attention in the evidence we received. The Customs procedures operate by seizing at the port of entry imports which appear to infringe the prohibition; the owner is given the opportunity to contest forfeiture in the

---

[1] *Attorney General's Reference (No 3 of 1977)* [1978] 3 All ER 1166.

courts if he wishes. The Post Office Act does not provide such a formal procedure, but simply empowers the Post Office to detain and dispose of any prohibited articles in postal transmission.

2.25 Representatives of the Post Office made it plain to us that this prohibition was not enforced to any significant extent, because it was simply not possible to do so. A sealed postal packet rarely announces itself as containing prohibited material, and although the 1953 Act (in section 8) gives the power to open and dispose of any postal packet posted in contravention of the prohibition, this power does not extend, in the Post Office view, to the opening of packets *on suspicion* that they contain prohibited material. Cases which do come to light, numbering no more than about 50 a year, are usually those where a packet bursts open in the post or has to be opened because it is not capable of being delivered. Material coming from overseas is a special case because there is a specific provision allowing for mail to be opened for customs examination; but the Post Office emphasised to us that they felt unable to overstep their powers where the inland post was concerned and would not even accede to any police requests to detain and open mail which was the subject of an investigation into mail-order pornography. (This does not mean, of course, that the offence is not prosecuted: the police may obtain evidence of offences under the Act by means other than the opening of packets in the post.)

2.26 Up to 1978 the Post Office had regularly seized indecent or obscene material coming from overseas, which came to light in the course of customs examination. However, the Post Office told us that they had misgivings about removing items from the post in this way, on the basis of their own judgment—which they did not feel competent to make—of the material concerned, rather than the judgment of a court, and relying on a legal provision which was less than entirely clear in the way in which it sought to extend a domestic control to material posted beyond the jurisdiction of United Kingdom law. Accordingly, since the law gave a power rather than imposed an obligation, the Post Office determined that they would no longer, on the strength of the Post Office Acts, dispose of indecent or obscene material coming to this country from overseas. This decision meant that the customs authorities, who had formerly dealt with commercial consignments under their own powers but left the Post Office to deal with prohibited material in small quantities, were forced into the position of either seizing more material themselves or allowing into the country what they judged to be prohibited imports. For the last eighteen months or so, therefore, HM Customs and Excise have accepted this larger burden.

Indecent public displays

2.27 Provisions about indecent public displays derive from nineteenth century legislation and are often in archaic terms. For example, under the Vagrancy Act 1824 a person making an indecent display is dealt with by being deemed to be "a rogue and vagabond" and it is not surprising that one of the points reported by the Vagrancy Working Party was that the courts in certain areas tend to dislike proceedings brought under such outdated statutes as the

1824 Act. Certainly the number of prosecutions brought under these statutes is smaller than one might expect from the strength of feeling about public displays that was revealed in the submissions we received. The test applied is that of "indecent or obscene", interpreted, as with the customs and postal controls, in terms of offence against recognised standards of propriety, and in those proceedings that have been brought, it seems to have given rise to very little practical difficulty. One needs to bear in mind, however, that for a purely summary offence, the opportunities for a case to get before the Court of Appeal or the House of Lords for judicial comment are naturally small. The law on this subject would of course have been brought up to date if the Bills introduced by the Government in 1973, or by back-bench Members since then, had become law. Parliamentary consideration of the Bill introduced by Mr Hugh Rossi in 1978-79 was cut short by the last General Election; as we submit our report, another Bill, introduced by Dr Brian Mawhinney, is awaiting consideration.

The Protection of Children Act

2.28 Of the various statutes we have not so far mentioned we should perhaps single out the Protection of Children Act 1978, which was enacted by Parliament while we have been sitting. This was introduced as a Private Member's Bill and approved by Parliament to meet a public demand for action to prevent the use of children in pornography. The need for fresh legislation for this purpose was always in some doubt. Certainly no evidence was put to us that child pornography was a growing problem — indeed, the Director of Public Prosecutions told us that he had no evidence that there was any new problem, or one of any significance, and he considered that the existing law was adequate to deal with it. However, Parliament was well disposed to the proposed legislation, which made it an offence to take indecent photographs of children or to distribute or show such photographs, and the Bill, though with substantial amendments moved by the Government, became law in July 1978. It was made clear by Government spokesmen that they regarded the Act as an interim measure to plug any possible deficiency in the law pending our conclusions, and that it should be reconsidered in the context of our review and in the light of the way it had worked since it came into force. In fact, the information given to us is that the Act has been used in only a very few cases.

The chaos of the present law

2.29 The summary of the present law which we give in Appendix 1 makes it clear why one of the courses commonly urged on us was a rationalisation of the law into a comprehensible and coherent whole. The law is scattered among so many statutes, and these so often overlap with each other and with the various common law offences and powers which still exist in this field, that it is a complicated task even to piece together a statement of what the law is, let alone to attempt to wrestle with or resolve the inconsistencies and anomalies to which it gives rise. Even while we have been examining the law, its complication has been increased by measures amending the law on films and providing fresh powers against child pornography; in addition, two attempts have been made to amend the law on indecent displays. What we have so far in this chapter described as the broad effect of the law is a considerable over-simplification: for example, in suggesting that there is one standard of obscenity, the *deprave and corrupt* test, applying to what cannot be sold and another applying to what may not be imported, sent by post and publicly displayed. In fact, as we describe in Appendix 1, the sale of goods, irrespective of their display, is also susceptible to control in certain circumstances by the Metropolitan Police Act 1839 and the Town Police Clauses Act 1847, which apply the *indecent or obscene* formula, and also by the common law offences of conspiracy to corrupt public morals and conspiracy to outrage public decency, where the tests are different again. The law, in short, is a mess.

Territorial limitations

2.30 Our remit has obliged us to review the laws concerning obscenity, indecency and violence in *England and Wales.* This introduces another difficulty: our terms of reference thus coincide with the application of the most important statute we have had to consider, the Obscene Publications Act 1959, but other statutes go wider. Naturally, the Customs Acts and the Post Office Act apply throughout the United Kingdom; and the same is true of the Vagrancy Acts and the Indecent Advertisements Act 1889. On the other hand, the Judicial Proceedings (Regulation of Reports) Act 1926, the Children and Young Persons (Harmful Publications) Act 1955, the Theatres Act 1968 and the Unsolicited Goods and Services Act 1971 all apply in Scotland but not in Northern Ireland, while the Protection of Children Act 1978 does not apply in Scotland but has been extended to Northern Ireland, where English common law also applies.

2.31 The limitation of our terms of reference has avoided the need for us to study the completely different system of obscenity law and procedure applying in Scotland or the more familiar law in Northern Ireland, based as it still is on English common law. We have received some expressions of view from Scotland and Northern Ireland, but we have conducted our review in the context of the law in England and Wales only. We consider, however, that the validity of our conclusions is not confined to England and Wales, and we assume that consideration will be given to extending any implementation of our proposals to Scotland and Northern Ireland. Certainly, it would be impossible for customs or postal controls to be amended other than on a United Kingdom basis.

International obligations

2.32 It has also been necessary for us, in reviewing our domestic law, to bear in mind that the United Kingdom has certain international obligations which have some relevance. These are of three kinds. One comprises the various instruments which lay down the basic rights due to the individual citizen and the limits within which the State may properly interfere with them: these are contained in the European Convention on Human Rights, the International Covenant on Civil and Political Rights and (although it has a less formal status) the Universal Declaration of Human Rights. The second embodies international agreement about measures to be taken against pornography or other obscene or indecent articles: the International Agreement for the Suppression of Obscene Publications, the International Convention for the Suppression of the Circulation of and Traffic in Obscene Publications and the Universal Postal Convention, fall into this category. The third are the obligations we assumed as a member of the European Economic Community. Fuller details of these international obligations are set out in Appendix 1.

CHAPTER THREE

THE CENSORSHIP OF FILMS

The legal basis of the censorship system

3.1 Parliament has never legislated for the censorship of films: it is purely a matter of accident that the film censorship system was able to find some statutory support when it first struggled into existence just before the First World War. Although the system has for many years been taken for granted, it had very uncertain beginnings and did not become firmly established until about fifteen years after the first moves towards censorship had taken place. Its having been taken for granted for so long obscures the fact, which any closer examination of the subject brings home, that it is undeniably odd. It is its constitution, rather than its operation, that is odd: the then Mr Herbert Morrison told the House of Commons when he was Home Secretary in 1942, "I freely admit that this is a curious arrangement, but the British have a very great habit of making curious arrangements work very well, and this works"[1].

3.2 We describe in Appendix 2 how the censorship system as we know it today developed. It is an interesting story, which makes it clear that the system we now have was in no way inevitable. Indeed, we came very close in 1916 to having a Government-established system of film censorship, as many other countries have. (Information about the practice of film censorship in other countries is set out in Appendix 4.) We shall deal in this chapter first with the legal powers under which censorship is exercised in England and Wales—though effectively the system applies throughout the United Kingdom—and secondly with the way in which it operates in practice.

3.3 The Cinematograph Acts 1909 and 1952 provide a control of the premises in which cinematograph exhibitions are given. A cinematograph exhibition is defined in the 1952 Act as "an exhibition of moving pictures produced on a screen by means which include the projection of light", a definition which has the result that it is possible to give a cinematograph exhibition without using a film. Subject to certain exemptions, section 1 of the 1909 Act provides that no cinematograph exhibition shall be given elsewhere than in premises licensed for the purpose, and section 2 enables a district council—though under the London Government Act 1963 the Greater London Council is the licensing authority for the London area—to grant licences to such persons as they think fit to use the specified premises for such purposes, subject to such terms and conditions and under such restrictions as the council may determine.

Cinema licensing conditions

3.4 It is the invariable practice throughout England and Wales for licensing authorities to use the conditions of the licence as a means of controlling the films which may be exhibited, and this practice is reinforced by the provision in section 3 of the 1952 Act that it is the duty of licensing authorities to impose

---

[1]19 November 1942; Official Report, Vol 385, col 504.

conditions prohibiting the admission of children to films designated, by the authority or another body, as unsuitable for them. The licence conditions may be in different terms, but the general effect is similar. Those authorities who adopt the Home Office model conditions will stipulate to their local cinemas that:—

(*a*) no film, other than a current news-reel, shall be exhibited unless it has received a certificate of the British Board of Film Censors or is the subject of the licensing authority's permission;

(*b*) no young people shall be admitted to any exhibition of a film classified by the Board as unsuitable for them, unless with the licensing authority's permission;

(*c*) no film shall be exhibited if the licensing authority gives notice in writing prohibiting its exhibition on the ground that it "would offend against good taste or decency or would be likely to encourage or incite to crime or lead to disorder or to be offensive to public feeling";

(*d*) the nature of the certificate given to any film shall be indicated in any advertising for the film, at the entrance to the cinema (together with an explanation of its effect) and on the screen immediately before the film is shown;

(*e*) displays outside the cinema shall not depict any scene or incident not in the film as approved;

(*f*) no advertisement shall be displayed at the premises if the licensing authority gives notice in writing objecting to it on the same grounds applying to the prohibition of films.

3.5 The general effect of these conditions is that there is a presumption that a certificate from the BBFC renders a film acceptable; but the local authority reserves the right to permit a local showing to a film refused a certificate by the Board, to forbid the showing of a film despite the grant of the Board's certificate, or to vary the age restriction attached to a film by the Board's certificate. By far the most usual practice is for the local council to rely entirely on the Board's judgement of particular films. During the time that we have been reviewing the operation of the system, the most frequent exception to this has been that certain councils have prohibited the showing in their area of particular films certificated by the Board: the Cinematograph Exhibitors' Association drew our attention to a long list of films which the Metropolitan Borough of Sefton had either banned or ordered not to be shown without the Council's express consent. Each of the other courses, however, has been followed from time to time.

3.6 The Greater London Council is an example of a licensing authority which adopts licensing conditions in a slightly different form, providing that

"No film shall be exhibited at the premises—

(1) which is likely—

(*a*) to encourage or to incite to crime; or

(*b*) to lead to disorder; or

(*c*) to stir up hatred against any section of the public in Great Britain on grounds of colour, race or ethnic or national origins; or

(2) the effect of which is, if taken as a whole, such as to tend to deprave and corrupt persons who are likely to see it; or

(3) which contains a grossly indecent performance thereby outraging the standards of public decency".

The GLC conditions do also provide for the Council to notify the licensee that it objects to the exhibition of any film, but the provisions we have quoted above are in the form of a prohibition, which is not the case with the Home Office model conditions. The latter merely give the licensing authority the power to object on certain grounds, and unless such an objection is made it cannot be said that a cinema breaches the conditions of its licence— it does not do so merely by showing a film which, for instance, offends against good taste or decency.

3.7 The Greater London Council's grounds for objection were originally more limited than those of the Home Office conditions, and this gave rise to legal proceedings in 1976, in which the Court of Appeal ruled[1] that where a licensing authority decides to exercise its discretion to censor films, its rules must not be so framed as to permit the public showing of unlawful films. That decision arose from proceedings instituted by Mr Raymond Blackburn after a film which had been granted a local certificate by the Greater London Council was found by a jury at the Central Criminal Court to be indecent. The Council had not previously imposed a condition relating to indecency; a cinema film had never before been proceeded against and it had not been tested whether the common law offence of indecent exhibition was capable of applying to films. The Blackburn decision was of course before the criminal law relating to indecent and obscene films was amended by the Criminal Law Act 1977 in the way we describe in Appendix 1. As a result of that decision, the Council altered its licensing conditions to include the new requirement contained in subparagraph (3) of the condition quoted above, though now that the Criminal Law Act 1977 has changed the legal test applicable to the showing of films from indecency to obscenity, that is no longer strictly required under the terms of the Court of Appeal's judgment.

3.8 Under section 6 of the 1952 Act, a person aggrieved by the refusal of a licence or by particular conditions imposed in a licence may appeal to the Crown Court against the licensing authority's decision. In the recent past—as the Cinematograph Exhibitors' Association pointed out to us—this has most frequently been done by licensees where licensing authorities have wanted local cinemas to be required to give advance notice of the proposed showing of films of a certain class, in particular those to which the BBFC have given an "X" certificate. Cinema interests have resisted such conditions as being impracticable in the present circumstances of the industry and therefore unreasonable, and we were told that where appeals on these grounds had been taken to court they had been successful.

---

[1] *R* v *Greater London Council ex parte Blackburn*, [1976] 3 All ER 184.

3.9 It is an offence under section 3 of the 1909 Act for the occupier to allow premises to be used in contravention of the Act or of the Regulations made under it or of the conditions attached to a licence. This makes it possible to penalise acts of various kinds, such as the showing of films in unlicensed and non-exempt premises, the showing of uncertificated or banned films in licensed cinemas, admitting children or young people to films banned to them, as well as breaches of safety requirements and obstructing the entry of police or local authority officers. Despite the wide scope of the offence, prosecutions are infrequent; in the five years 1974 to 1978 there were only fifteen. The maximum penalty on conviction of an offence is £200.

Exemptions from censorship

3.10 Various exemptions from the licensing system are allowed under the Acts, and some of these have important implications for the censorship system. Section 7 of the 1909 Act provided that the Act should not apply to any cinematograph exhibition given in a private dwelling house to which the public are not admitted, whether on payment or otherwise, and also removed the necessity to obtain a licence for premises used for cinematograph exhibitions on not more than six days a year, provided that notice was given to the licensing authority and any conditions imposed by the authority complied with. The 1952 Act widened the exemptions, to cover

(a) exhibitions to which the public are not admitted;

(b) exhibitions to which the public are admitted without payment; and

(c) exhibitions given by "exempted organisations" (defined as organisations holding a certificate from the Commissioners of Customs and Excise certifying that the Commissioners are satisfied that the organisation is not conducted or established for profit), so long as such exhibitions are not held on more than three days in a week.

3.11 The exemptions do not apply to an exhibition organised wholly or mainly as an exhibition for children who are members of a club whose principal object is attendance at cinematograph exhibitions, unless the exhibition is given in a private dwelling house or as part of the activities of an educational or religious institution. There are certain other reservations about the application of safety requirements but no censorship requirements apply to exhibitions exempted in any of these various ways.

3.12 We received no evidence that the exemption for free shows is of much significance, at least in the context of film censorship, but that for "exempted organisations" is rather more widely used. We were told that most exempted organisations are either film societies or working men's clubs, which are thus able to disregard the censorship system. Film societies find this of benefit because it means that they are able to show foreign language films of such limited commercial appeal that the censorship fees might be prohibitive (though the British Board of Film Censors have recently introduced concessionary rates which could apply in such cases). However, in the matter of film societies, it is not the exemption for "exempted organisations" that is most important. Such status will be of benefit to film societies which admit members of the public as paying customers. But those film societies which present films to members only are exempt from licensing, and hence from the censorship arrangements, under the provision applying to exhibitions "to which the public are not admitted". This is the exemption that is most significant.

3.13 When this exemption was enacted in 1952, it was designed to perpetuate a distinction which had arisen in practice under the 1909 Act. That Act was framed only in terms of inflammable film. The commercial cinema was using 35 mm film which was inflammable and which therefore rendered the premises liable to licensing and hence the films liable to censorship; but 16 mm film had for some time used a non-inflammable base, and those using it were therefore not covered by the censorship arrangements. The introduction of 35 mm non-inflammable film made it necessary, certainly if powers of film censorship were to continue, to widen the scope of the 1909 Act, but the Home Secretary made it clear to Parliament that he did not wish in doing so to alter the existing exemption for "non-commercial exhibitions organised by film societies and educational and scientific bodies"[1]. What was not then foreseen was the growth of commercial film clubs designed solely for the exhibition of films which would not be passed under the censorship arrangements. Such clubs are able to take advantage of confusion as to the meaning of "to which the public are not admitted", and to adopt "membership" procedures often flimsy in the extreme, to the extent that many clubs will admit any passing stranger who fills in a membership form with a false name and address. The courts have not established what should be the minimum requirements for a club in this context and it appears that it has not been easy to take successful proceedings for the offence of using premises for a public cinematograph exhibition without a licence.

3.14 Cinema clubs have frequently been seen as an abuse, against which new powers are necessary. This is not only because they exist to circumvent the censorship system, but also because, in escaping censorship, they also escape the safety requirements laid down under the Cinematograph Acts. The result, the Greater London Council told us, is that uncensored films are often shown in premises that do not and could not meet the technical and safety requirements of a licensing authority. This is not true throughout the country, since some local authorities outside the London area have taken their own powers through local legislation to control the premises used for public entertainments of various kinds, even where the 'public' are members of a club. The City of Manchester, for example, requires the registration of the premises of any entertainment club and can either refuse to register premises which fail to provide sufficient standards of safety or impose conditions on registered premises as to the maintenance of public order and safety, fire precautions and means of escape, opening hours and the prevention of nuisance to local residents, but not as regards the content of any films to be shown there. The Association for Cinema Club Standards, formed since we were appointed, suggested to us in the course of evidence that controls of this kind have been applied in most of the country outside London and emphasised that their own code of conduct required cinema club operators to comply strictly with fire and safety regulations even though they were not legally binding.

---

[1]House of Commons, 21 October 1952. Official Report, Vol 505, col 870.

3.15 Steps were taken to place more restrictions on cinema clubs when the Cinematograph and Indecent Displays Bill was introduced into Parliament in 1973. That Bill sought to alter the present exemptions from cinema licensing so that any cinematograph exhibition "promoted for private gain" would be subject to the control of the licensing authority. In addition, the Bill would have made any film exhibition still exempt from local authority control subject to the Obscene Publications Acts. The Bill failed to become law and has not been reintroduced, but in the meantime film exhibitions generally, including those in cinema clubs, have been brought within the scope of the Obscene Publications Acts instead of being subject to the common law. So far as we have been able to perceive, this has not had much effect on the activities of cinema clubs.

The practice of film censorship

3.16 The law gives to local licensing authorities the only film censorship powers which exist; but in practice, as we have made clear, only a minority of local authorities take an interest in the exercise of these powers. There are theoretically 370 licensing authorities in England and Wales, but some of these have no cinema within their area, so for practical purposes the number is rather fewer, probably of the order of 330. The Cinematograph Exhibitors' Association told us that about 72 authorities take an interest in film censorship with some degree of regularity, actively reviewing or previewing films and from time to time prohibiting a film's exhibition. But of course even these authorities, along with those who take no interest of their own, are content to place the primary responsibility for film censorship on the British Board of Film Censors.

The British Board of Film Censors

3.17 Lord Denning, in his judgment in the proceedings brought by Mr Blackburn against the Greater London Council[1], described the British Board of Film Censors thus:

> "The British Board of Film Censors is not a legal entity. It has no existence known to the law. It is but a name given to the activities of a few persons".

The Board was formed by the film trade associations and still operates under the aegis of the Incorporated Association of Kinematograph Manufacturers: this is a trade association representing the manufacturers of cinema equipment, the providers of laboratory services etc, and therefore the only trade association whose members have no direct financial interest in the censorship of films. The Board is non-profitmaking and its income is entirely derived from the fees it charges film distributors for the censorship of films (calculated on the footage of each film), supplemented by the proceeds from the annual subscriptions paid by those licensing authorities who receive the Board's monthly report, which gives details of its decisions.

3.18 The President of the Board since 1965 has been Lord Harlech, and he is involved in decision-making on all matters relating to broad public policy.

---

[1] [1976] 3 All ER 184.

The day-to-day responsibility for the operation of the Board, for the formulation of detailed policy and for the supervision of the examiners rests with the Secretary, a post occupied since 1975 by Mr James Ferman. One of the examiners works as the Board's Assistant Secretary, and there are four other examiners—three women and one man—who all work part-time, and a small administrative and technical staff. The whole operation, in the Board's modest offices in Soho Square, struck us with its economy and its lack of technological sophistication.

3.19 All films intended for public exhibition in Britain, including full-length features, trailers, short films and advertisements but excluding newsreels, are normally submitted in the first instance to the Board. The Board's practice is for each film to be viewed by two examiners, who will reach an overall view of the category of certificate appropriate to the film and a view on whether any of the scenes in the film would be inappropriate to that certificate. The certificates used since 1970 have been the following:

"U" —Passed for general exhibition

"A" —Passed for general exhibition, but parents/guardians are advised that the film contains material they might prefer their children under fourteen not to see

"AA" —Passed as suitable only for exhibition to persons of fourteen and over. When a programme includes an AA film, no persons under fourteen may be admitted

"X" —Passed as suitable only for exhibition to adults. When a programme includes an X film, no persons under eighteen may be admitted.

3.20 If a film causes problems it may be seen again by different examiners and by the Secretary and, if necessary, by the President. It is not unusual for difficult films to be seen four or five times. A film may fall naturally into one of the categories set out above, but if there are some scenes which would move it into a category different from that called for by the film as a whole, the film distributor will normally be given a choice: between say, an "AA" certificate for the uncut film or an "A" certificate subject to certain cuts being made. In this way, the decision to cut a film to secure a less restrictive classification is shifted by the Board to the film company and, in any event, any cutting will be done by the company rather than the Board, with the film being reexamined by the Board to ensure that its final form is acceptable. Information about the numbers of feature films seen by the Board, the categories in which they were passed and the number of films refused a certificate is set out in Table 1. Table 2 gives more information about the numbers of films cut before a certificate was issued.

Table 1

British Board of Film Censors:

Classifications Awarded to Feature Films

Year	*Films Submitted*	*Certificate*				*Rejected*
		U	*A*	*AA*	*X*	
1954	537	347 (65%)	154 (29%)		28 (5%)	8 (1%)
1958	541	261 (48%)	197 (37%)		71 (13%)	12 (2%)
1962	456	171 (38%)	168 (37%)		102 (22%)	15 (3%)
1966	370	132 (36%)	114 (31%)		111 (30%)	13 (3%)
1967	389	130 (33%)	133 (34%)		112 (29%)	14 (4%)
1968	403	99 (24%)	124 (31%)		169 (42%)	11 (3%)
1969	445	91 (20%)	114 (26%)		219 (49%)	21 (5%)
1970	502	104 (21%)	84 (17%)	77 (15%)	212 (42%)	25 (5%)
1971	502	98 (20%)	77 (15%)	77 (15%)	228 (46%)	22 (4%)
1972	488	78 (16%)	81 (17%)	77 (16%)	222 (45%)	30 (6%)
1973	504	62 (12%)	78 (16%)	85 (17%)	249 (49%)	30 (6%)
1974	540	72 (13%)	80 (15%)	93 (17%)	268 (50%)	27 (5%)
1975	424	74 (17%)	96 (23%)	73 (17%)	164 (39%)	17 (4%)
1976	402	53 (13%)	73 (18%)	74 (18%)	187 (47%)	15 (4%)
1977	375	39 (10%)	86 (23%)	78 (21%)	164 (44%)	8 (2%)
1978	324	35 (11%)	81 (25%)	66 (20%)	138 (43%)	4 (1%)

Note: The meaning of the certificates has not been constant over the period of this table. Until 1970, the "A" certificate required children under 16 to be excluded unless accompanied by their parents or *bona fide* adult guardians; since 1970, it has involved no restriction, being advisory only. Until 1970, the "X" certificate excluded anyone under 16; since 1970, it has excluded persons under 18. The "U" (universal) certificate has had the same effect throughout, and the "AA" (no one under 14) has been unchanged since its introduction in 1970. The changes came into force on 1 July 1970.

Table 2

British Board of Film Censors:

Feature Films Certified After Cuts

	Total	*U*	*A*	*AA*	*X*
1969	176 (42%)	20 (22%)	50 (44%)	—	106 (48%)
1970	166 (35%)	9 (9%)	31 (37%)	29 (38%)	97 (44%)
1971	165 (34%)	7 (7%)	22 (29%)	25 (32%)	111 (49%)
1972	179 (39%)	5 (6%)	25 (21%)	23 (30%)	126 (57%)
1973	201 (42%)	4 (6%)	24 (31%)	25 (29%)	148 (60%)
1974	218 (42%)	5 (7%)	23 (29%)	21 (23%)	169 (63%)
1975	147 (36%)	5 (7%)	32 (33%)	12 (16%)	98 (60%)
1976	135 (35%)	3 (6%)	17 (23%)	10 (14%)	105 (56%)
1977	105 (29%)	1 (3%)	18 (21%)	8 (10%)	78 (48%)
1978	73 (23%)	2 (6%)	15 (19%)	8 (12%)	48 (35%)

Trends in recent years

3.21 The most noteworthy feature of these statistics is probably the significant drop over the last five years in the number of films examined. Cinemagoing has of course heavily declined as a popular pastime, and the reduction in the number of films released has obvious consequences for the Board. As we have said, the Board's only source of income, apart from subscriptions to its monthly report, lies in the censorship fees it charges for examining films. The Board has not laid stress in its evidence to us on its financial position, but it must be clear that it has difficulty in meeting costs on the income derived from examining a body of films which is over two hundred fewer in total than five years ago. The Board has of course increased its fees, so that a ninety-minute film would be charged £276 and a two-hour film about £355. But to load the costs of a censorship system on to a decreasing number of films must inevitably introduce strains of its own.

3.22 Another noteworthy feature of the statistics lies in the distribution of certificates and in the proportion of films cut before receiving a certificate. It was the increasing proportion of films appropriate to the "X" category and the increasing proportion of "X" films which needed cutting before being passed which led to the introduction of the "AA" certificate in 1970, with the age limit for "X" films being raised at the same time from sixteen to eighteen. The idea was that if the "X" certificate became a more specifically adult category more films could be passed uncut and greater freedom could be given to what an adult audience could see if it wanted to. At the same time, the system was to be much more flexible by introducing a new category to prevent children seeing material unsuitable for them, and abolishing a rule which required children seeing an "A" film to be accompanied. Even after these changes, however, a high proportion of films were still assigned to the "adults only" category and an increasing number of these still had to be cut. In 1974, over half of all the films seen were considered unsuitable for showing to anyone under eighteen and two-thirds of those were considered unsuitable to be seen in their entirety even by adults.

3.23 In the last five years, however, there has been a noticeable change in the trend. Fewer films are being refused a certificate; fewer are being placed in the "X" category; and fewer are being cut before a certificate is issued. Some people might leap to certain conclusions about these changes: that, for example, censorship has been liberalised and that what was formerly disallowed is now passing without hindrance. Clearly, there must be some truth in those suggestions, since we were told by the Board that in the field of nudity and sexual activity their practice was governed not by what they considered ought not to be shown, but by what they judged was not currently acceptable to the cinemagoing public (or perhaps more strictly to the majority of local licensing authorities whose confidence the Board has to retain) or to society generally through the law of the land. Therefore, as public standards of acceptability have evolved, so the Board have adapted their practice accordingly. At the same time, however, the Board made it clear to us that they are now less tolerant than before of violence and of material which exploits the sexual degradation of women, and we saw examples of scenes in films approved in the past which would not now be allowed.

3.24 The Board also emphasised that it would be a mistake to view the statistics simply in terms of the practice of censorship. The Board, after all, deals only with that part of what the worldwide film industry produces which British distributors consider will be marketable in this country. The censors examine only what distributors consider it is worthwhile submitting to them. An important factor in what appears as a reduction in censorship is, in the Board's view, that the Board's policy has become better known and understood in the industry, so that material which it is known will not be passed is no longer submitted. The Board points out, too, that many countries now permit hardcore pornography and that this had produced a *genre* of films which there would be little point in submitting to British censorship, at the same time probably decreasing the number of titillating, less explicit, films.

The role of the Board

3.25 It was put to us by Mr Ferman, Secretary of the Board, that the issue of a certificate to a film means only two things: that the film, in the Board's judgement, does not infringe the criminal law, and that it is likely to be acceptable to the majority of licensing authorities. We thought that this was an unduly modest view of the Board's work. Certainly one of the Board's guiding principles is that no film should be granted a certificate if it is believed to contravene the law of the land, whether it be the law of obscenity, the law relating to the protection of children or animals, or that on incitement to crime or racial hatred. But the suggestion that the Board's role is otherwise simply to judge what most licensing authorities will accept, while it is no doubt a proper statement of the constitutional position, seems to us from the study we have made of the Board's work to understate seriously the lead that the Board gives to licensing authorities. There are strong views within the Board about the social harms which might flow from certain kinds of material, and these have been developed on a more sophisticated level than we think would be adopted by almost any licensing authority. The Board does not hesitate to ask for psychiatric advice about the effect which some powerful scenes might have on a minority of disturbed people or about the degree of fear to which a young child might be subjected; it will refuse a certificate to a film or ask for cuts in it, if it displays what the Board feel to be an unhealthy glamorisation of violence or an exploitative degradation of women. *Manson* was refused a certificate because it portrayed the life-style of the Californian followers of Charles Manson in what the Board felt to be a dangerously seductive way. Other films have been cut because they illustrated techniques for stealing cars or for defrauding the telephone service.

3.26 The truth of the matter is that the Board takes on the role of professional adviser to the licensing authorities on the censorship of films, rather than merely prejudging what the reaction of the authorities to particular films would be. In the examples we have given, the Board is assessing neither whether the film would contravene the law—though it sometimes relies on a view of the tendency to deprave and corrupt which is rather more literal than we have suggested is the interpretation normally adopted by the courts—nor whether it would be unacceptable to licensing authorities. Mr Ferman said to us that the Board's role involved a certain 'political' element, in the sense that its activities needed to satisfy licensing authorities. It seems to us that this political role involves ensuring more that the Board's actions are acceptable to the licensing authorities than that the films themselves are. There is a significant difference. It means that the Board has a much more active function, but is still subject to the restraint that it operates only on the basis of the delegation of powers by local authorities. If it loses the confidence of those authorities its role vanishes. It must not reject films which most authorities, if appealed to, would allow, nor give certificates to those which most authorities would wish to ban.

3.27 A recent development in the Board's efforts to maintain the confidence of local licensing authorities is its monthly report. Between 1913 and 1937 the Board had published an annual report discussing its work in general terms, without reference to the action taken on individual films. The new series of reports, started on an experimental basis in November 1975 and available on subscription to licensing authorities, describes each film examined by the Board and explains the decision to give it a particular certificate and to require cuts, if any. The report is intended to meet misgivings about the secret operation of censorship by opening the Board's operation to informed public debate, and also to encourage in licensing authorities the confidence that censorship is being properly and sufficiently undertaken by the Board. We heard some criticism of the reports from within the film industry, generally on the ground that they might stimulate interest among licensing authorities in censoring films rather than the reverse; more particularly, it was complained that the reports were used as a vehicle for special pleading by the Board, especially in propagating ideas for changes in the system which the industry did not favour. The Board told us that concern on the first of these grounds had been misplaced. According to the Board's information, fewer councils had banned films in 1977 and 1978 than were doing so in the years 1972 to 1975 and more were now content to rely on the Board's decision. The second complaint is not baseless—the reports constantly press the idea, for instance, that changes in the age structure of the certification system would be desirable. We see nothing improper in the Board's using its report in this way: it is perfectly clear who issues it.

3.28 However great the confidence in the Board's work, it is not expected that all its decisions will be accepted by all licensing authorities. Attitudes vary in Britain, and what is acceptable in one area may be offensive in another. The Board has for some time attempted to find a middle way, recognising that some local authorities would want to allow more than the Board, while some others would allow less. The local option, it was put to us, enabled the Board to verify that the standards it was adopting were in fact in tune with most of the country and, on occasion, to shift its ground to take account of evidence to the contrary. An example of the Board's reconsidering its decision was in relation to *The Language of Love,* which was rejected by the Board in 1970 because its degree of sexual explicitness went beyond what the Board judged would be acceptable for screening in a public cinema. However, when it was submitted to individual licensing authorities—which is the only avenue of appeal from the Board's rejection—the film was passed by the Greater London Council and by some 127 other authorities. In the light of this evidence of its local acceptability, the Board felt able to give the film a certificate when it was resubmitted in 1973. But not all local authorities regard the film as acceptable: some still exercise their right to refuse to allow the film to be shown in their areas.

3.29 In recent times fewer local authorities have been prepared to take a line more liberal than the Board's. The Greater London Council, which has traditionally been one of the authorities prepared to allow a showing to some films which the Board regarded as unsuitable for a national certificate, has since we were appointed granted only one local certificate (to *The Beast*). As a result, the Board has suddenly found itself not occupying the comfortable middle ground, but out on the liberal wing, with most of the local variations from the Board's rule being in the direction of greater restriction. There is thus less chance of trying out reactions to films refused a certificate by the Board, and the Board clearly has felt less than easy in the new situation in which it has found itself.

Consultative arrangements

3.30 In establishing relations with the local licensing authorities, the Board has not confined itself to issuing its monthly report. Its Secretary has for many years been expected to meet and speak to authorities in different parts of the country and there have also been occasional conferences at which the Board has tried to illustrate some of the problems of censorship, and to obtain the views of members of local councils. Mr John Trevelyan, when Secretary of the Board, instituted a series of such conferences in November 1961, and Mr James Ferman, the present Secretary, organised the most recent in December 1976. But there are times when a more formal relationship is needed—when agreement is needed on new film classifications, for example—and such arrangements have, rather fitfully, existed over the years since the Board was established.

3.31 The Board's annual report for 1922 offered a view of the Board as a tripartite body consisting of the President, the examining staff and a Committee elected from the various branches of the film industry which met to discuss the principles and general policy of censorship. Although the Board was at pains to point out that this Committee did not interfere with the censorship of films, its existence reinforced the impression that censorship was being undertaken by the trade itself and that the Board was not independent (an impression, incidentally, which we found still existed among some people, although in our view it is totally baseless). That Committee did not survive. The first attempt at establishing a more formal machinery for bringing together the parties with an interest in film censorship was in 1931 when the Home Secretary set up the Film Censorship Consultative Committee to achieve greater co-operation between the licensing authorities and the Board. This lasted a few years but appeared to wither away and was not thought worth reviving until after the recommendations of the Wheare Committee on Children and the Cinema[1], which proposed a new Central Committee on Children and the Cinema. Many of the Wheare Committee's proposals were not taken up by the Government—though some were embodied in the Cinematograph Act 1952—but in the wake of the Committee a new tripartite Cinema Consultative Committee, embracing the Board, the film industry and the licensing authorities, was instituted in 1951. This in turn fell into abeyance, but was revived to discuss proposals for the reorganisation of the category system, which took effect on 1 July 1970. It was further resuscitated in 1973 and in 1977, when the Board wanted to propose that the categories be modified again, a proposal that was shelved pending our deliberations.

[1]May 1950, Cmd 7945.

3.32 The lesson seems to be that there are times when consultative procedures of this kind are necessary, but that there has not been sufficient continuing need for them to keep them in permanent existence. The practice of film censorship has been undertaken over many years without reference to formal consultative arrangements and with remarkably little controversy. The complaints we received about it were few. Although the system is a tenuous one, it has proved remarkably stable. There have been strains from time to time, and indeed the period before our appointment was one in which some stresses had been apparent, even to the point of raising the question whether the system could survive. These developments are part of the ground we shall cover in the next chapter.

CHAPTER FOUR

THE SITUATION

4.1 We shall describe in this chapter the recent events and developments which created the background to our appointment, and also the present situation which our study revealed. The subject always attracts controversy and an obscenity trial or a censorship decision is likely to be exploited by the media for its public interest. But this interest undoubtedly fluctuates over the years and the controversy rages more fiercely in some periods than in others. It may be that our appointment owes something to the fact that the preceding years had seen more frequent and more heated discussion of the subject.

The retreat of the law

4.2 For many years the obscenity laws have been in retreat. The Obscene Publications Act 1959 marked, of course, a conscious decision that the obscenity laws were affecting material which should be free of legal restriction and that the boundary should be changed; and the acquittal of the publishers of *Lady Chatterley's Lover* in 1960, after extensive use of the newly-provided defence of public good, seemed to show that the Act had brought about the change that its sponsors desired. That decision represented one stage in the retreat of the law from the written word. Another was perhaps the controversial prosecution involving *Last Exit to Brooklyn* in 1967, where the publishers were convicted by a jury but the conviction was quashed on appeal. A further, perhaps final, stage seems to have been reached with the prosecution of *Inside Linda Lovelace* in 1976. It was the trial, and acquittal, of the publisher of *Inside Linda Lovelace* which generated the most publicity for the obscenity laws in the years immediately before our appointment, and the view was expressed to us by representatives of the Metropolitan Police that the failure of that prosecution meant that the law was unlikely to be invoked again against the written word. Their view (which appeared from his summing-up to have been shared by the trial judge) was that it was difficult to imagine what written material would be regarded as obscene if that was not.

4.3 Here it is as well that we emphasise a point we have already made in Chapter 2, which is that, under the present law, an acquittal or a dismissal of a summons for forfeiture does not necessarily mean that the court finds the material concerned not to be obscene. First, obscenity is a relative concept. Obscenity proceedings are never against particular material itself and it is always the case, even when the proceedings are for forfeiture rather than in relation to a criminal charge against the person accused of publishing it, that it is the circumstances of publication, particularly in relation to the likely audience, that governs the finding of obscenity, not the content of the material alone. Second, the court's finding has to take account of factors other than obscenity. The decision might be that there was insufficient evidence that the defendant published it or that he had it for publication for gain; or the court might think that the material was obscene but that its publication was nevertheless justified as being for the public good. What we say in this chapter about court decisions on obscenity should be read accordingly. It is a useful shorthand to say, as was usually said to us, that material was found "not obscene" by a court, but it may not always be literally true.

4.4 So, the situation we found when we were appointed was that the law was effectively relevant only to pictorial material. There too, however, juries had been showing that reluctance to convict which we mentioned in Chapter 2. We were told of a succession of cases which had left the prosecuting authorities wondering where the boundary of the legal lay or even, sometimes, whether any boundary would soon be left. In April and September 1975, for example, juries at the Central Criminal Court failed to agree whether seized American magazines showing bondage and sado-masochism were obscene, although similar magazines had been certainly regarded as obscene up to that time. In October 1975 a jury at Portsmouth Crown Court was confronted with highly explicit pornography from Denmark (of a kind described to us by the defendant in that case as the "Rolls-Royce" of pornography) and found that only some of it was obscene and that, in particular, photographs of straightforward sexual activity between adults, whether heterosexual or homosexual and however explicit, were not obscene. Before that case, one of the certainties of life for the prosecuting authorities was that Scandinavian pornography was obscene; showing us examples of what the jury at Portsmouth decided was not obscene, the Director of Public Prosecutions commented that it was now quite impossible to be certain of securing a conviction by a jury of even what he considered to be a grossly obscene article.

4.5 If juries are reluctant to convict, the prosecuting authorities are likely to be less keen to institute proceedings. The main function of the Director of Public Prosecutions in advising on proceedings in this field is to decide whether an article is *prima facie* obscene, but since obscenity in law is what a court decides it is, the Director's decision is actually whether, in his view, a court is likely to find that the article is in breach of the Obscene Publications Acts. The decision of one court of trial is not binding on any other, so the fact that one jury has found particular material not to be obscene does not necessarily rule out future proceedings involving similar material: indeed the circumstances of publication, including the likely audience, might be different on another occasion. Nevertheless the results of earlier trials have an inevitable effect on the number of subsequent prosecutions. We have already referred to a trial and retrial in 1975 involving American bondage and sado-masochism magazines; another trial involving similar material at the Central Criminal Court in November 1975 also resulted in the jury failing to agree, but this time the Crown, instead of pressing the case as they had in the earlier instance, offered no evidence at the retrial. The next time similar material came before the prosecuting authorities, it would not be surprising if they thought twice about instituting proceedings at all. The Metropolitan Police told us that after the Portsmouth case the Director of Public Prosecutions ceased to advise a section 2 prosecution[1] when the magazines which had been found not obscene in that case were seized elsewhere, and they referred to an instance in December 1976 where prosecuting counsel at the Crown Court had offered no evidence in a case involving Scandinavian pornography, on the grounds that one of the magazines had been found not obscene at Portsmouth and that the others were of a similar nature.

---

[1]That is to say, a prosecution of a person, which gives him or her a right to a trial by jury: see Chapter 2, paragraph 2.15.

4.6 The examples we have quoted in the last two paragraphs (which are of course only a few of the cases brought under the Obscene Publications Acts) concerned a type of magazine which the Director of Public Prosecutions classifies as "Grade 3" material, that is, the most extreme of three categories of potentially offensive material. Most Grade 3 material is of foreign origin, and is sold only in shops specialising in pornography, and often covertly. It is what is often called "hard-core" pornography, although the Director finds, as we have found, that the distinction between "hard-core" and "soft-core" pornography is unclear and less than useful, particularly in a rapidly changing market. "Grade 2", in the Director's classification, refers to a range of the more explicit British publications often sold from street bookstalls, by some newsagents, and elsewhere. "Grade 1" material includes naturist magazines and other relatively mild publications, which even cautious newsagents might stock, but which, as our evidence has shown, are sometimes seized by the police in certain places as obscene.

4.7 It is clear from evidence we have received from the prosecuting authorities that while they have worked on the assumption that Grade 3 material is illegal (subject to the doubts introduced by the cases we have referred to), they have suffered persistent uncertainty whether they should proceed against Grade 2 material, and how best to do so. It is a noticeable feature of these magazines that their letterpress tends to be "stronger" than their pictures, sometimes offering the kind of prose characteristic of, say, *Inside Linda Lovelace*. Significantly, it was not so much this that caused difficulty, as the changing nature of the pictures in these magazines.

4.8 Following some unsuccessful proceedings in 1973, British publications were largely regarded by the authorities as keeping within permissible limits but, as we shall describe, from the end of 1974 a series of new magazines were launched which effectively tested the boundaries of the law. We have already referred in Chapter 2 to one case involving a magazine of this kind: having reached the conclusion that things were going too far, the Metropolitan Police seized in November 1975 the complete print of the latest edition of *Park Lane*, totalling 96,000 copies, but when forfeiture proceedings were heard at Tottenham magistrates' court in March 1976, the magazine was found not to be obscene. This decision may have discouraged the prosecuting authorities from proceeding against similar material, but as magazines continued to advance their limits, the question of enforcement action was constantly kept in mind. The Metropolitan Police told us that by the end of 1976 they were so concerned about the explicitness of some British magazines that it was agreed in conference with the Director of Public Prosecutions that further action should be taken. As a result, in the first six months of 1977 well over 300,000 copies of magazines were seized in the execution of six warrants alone. Court proceedings in these cases, again brought by way of forfeiture in magistrates' courts, were largely successful, though an appeal in one case resulted in 15,000 items out of the 72,000 seized being found not obscene. By that time, however, the number of highly explicit magazines in circulation was considerable and there were doubts as to whether the law could effectively control them.

Criticism of the law

4.9 The situation when we were appointed was therefore that the scope of the law was very much more limited than it had been a few years previously, and that this was the object of much criticism. It was suggested by many people that the law simply was not working as it should and that there was an urgent need to strengthen it. There was much comment to this effect following the acquittal of the publisher of *Inside Linda Lovelace* in January 1976, and it was still to be heard when we were appointed and in the evidence we received. There were perhaps three separate strands in this criticism of the law. The first concerned the test of obscenity and the way in which, as we have described in Chapter 2, the *deprave and corrupt* formula caused difficulty in deciding whether an article was obscene: these difficulties we have already discussed in Chapter 2 (paragraphs 2.3–10).

4.10 The second subject of criticism has also been mentioned in our discussion of the Obscene Publications Act in Chapter 2; this is the use that was being made of the "public good" defence, which sometimes, it seemed, was being deployed in order to undermine the finding of obscenity itself. One version of this criticism was that put to us by the Director of the Nationwide Festival of Light, who said that the defence provision had given clever lawyers the opportunity to pour scorn on the prosecution case and to sway the jury from the decision its natural commonsense would dictate. Another way of describing the situation would be to say that the expert witnesses had had the effect of putting into the jury's mind a doubt whether they really had reason to believe, beyond reasonable doubt, that the matter in question had the tendency to deprave and corrupt, however "obscene", in some more everyday sense, they might find it. In any case, there is no doubt about the fact that all the cases we have mentioned above as having been lost by the prosecution were defended by expert witnesses seeking to justify the publication as being for the public good. A rare case in which expert evidence was offered by the prosecution, when Dr John Court volunteered to give evidence at Snaresbrook Crown Court in February 1976, resulted in a conviction. The appearance of what became known as the "travelling circus" of medical and psychological witnesses to plead the benefits of sexually explicit material began to be regarded as an affront by those who wanted to see the Obscene Publications Acts effectively enforced. By the time we were appointed, however, some of these misgivings had been met by the House of Lords decision in *DPP* v *Jordan*, described in Chapter 2, which effectively ruled that the therapeutic benefits of pornography could not be argued as a "public good"; and the decision of the Court of Appeal on the Attorney General's reference about the meaning of the word "learning" (also described in Chapter 2) seems to have put an end to this line of defence.

4.11 There has been another feature of the operation of the law, not so far mentioned, which gave rise to criticism. This was the practice of using the defendant's right of challenge to prospective jurors so as to secure a jury which was thought to be more sympathetic to the publications figuring in the proceedings. The law allowed each defendant seven peremptory challenges, so that in a case involving more than one defendant the chances of getting a jury thought to be sympathetic were much increased. In the *Oz* trial, for example, in which there were four defendants, twenty-six potential jurors were challenged before the twelve members of the jury were finally chosen; and in the *Inside Linda Lovelace* trial, in which there were two defendants, the individual and his company, thirteen jurors were challenged. The argument against this practice was that if the function of the jury was, as envisaged by House of Lords judgments we have quoted in Chapter 2, to reflect a current view of society, then the manipulation of the system to secure, for example, a preponderance of young men and the exclusion of middle-aged women instead of a representative or random sample, means that that function cannot properly be fulfilled. Again, however, steps had been taken before we were appointed to meet these misgivings (which were not confined to obscenity trials), and section 43 of the Criminal Law Act 1977 reduced from seven to three the number of peremptory challenges allowed to each defendant. As a result, arguments about the composition of juries did not figure largely in the evidence we received.

4.12 The concern about the state of the obscenity laws which was widely expressed after the *Inside Linda Lovelace* decision led to a Private Member's Bill being introduced into Parliament, which was designed to meet particular criticisms we have mentioned and to reform the law in other ways. On 23 March 1976 Mr Tim Renton was given leave to introduce a Bill which would have abolished the *deprave and corrupt* test, leaving obscenity undefined; abolished the ability to plead the public good on any grounds other than the interests of science, literature, art or learning; altered trial procedure so as to separate the issues of obscenity and public good; set up an advisory committee to advise whether publication of particular articles would constitute an offence; restricted the reporting of obscenity proceedings; and brought television and radio within the scope of the law on obscenity. The Bill made no progress.

4.13 It was not only those who wished to see the law operate in a more restrictive way who were dissatisfied. Many of those engaged in the business of distributing or selling newspapers and periodicals, for example, argued that they had a right to be told what it was legal and illegal for them to handle and that the growing uncertainties of the law needed urgent correction. Those who saw the law as unnecessary or futile or positively harmful also joined the debate. The year 1976 saw the formation of the National Campaign for the Repeal of the Obscene Publications Acts, which brought together some people with traditional libertarian beliefs about the right of adults to choose for themselves what they read or saw, and others with what seemed to be a newer belief—or a belief that it was newly acceptable to express—about the liberating or therapeutic benefits of pornography, and the need for society to remove the stigma attached to pornography. The Campaign modified its name to refer to "Reform" rather than "Repeal" but made it clear to us that this did not affect its view that the Obscene Publications Acts 1959 and 1964 should be repealed.

Police Corruption

4.14 Those arguing against a law prohibiting obscene publications were able to draw support from the three major corruption trials in November 1976, March 1977 and June 1977 in which a number of senior and junior officers of the Metropolitan Police, in particular members of the Obscene Publications Squad, were charged with offences relating to the acceptance of bribes from those involved in selling pornography in the West End of London. For many people, the evidence which emerged from those trials—large sums of money systematically shared out between police officers, pornographers being "licensed to trade" or being given prior warning of impending raids or being invited to buy back publications which had been seized—provided a very clear illustration of the undesirability of penalising "victimless crimes" and of trying to impose a ban on a market which would inevitably continue to exist. Frequent comparisons were drawn with the futile attempt to ban liquor, as in the American period of Prohibition. The evils unleashed by the law were worse, it was said, than those it was intended to prevent.

4.15 Certain officers of the Metropolitan Police were carrying on corrupt activities in the years up to 1972. In that year Mr Raymond Blackburn instituted High Court proceedings for an order of *mandamus* against the Metropolitan Police Commissioner requiring him to enforce the law relating to obscene publications. Mr Blackburn pointed to the shops in Soho selling hard-core pornography quite openly, at £5 or £6 for each small magazine, and asked the question why the law which prohibited the sale of obscene publications was not being enforced against such shops. The full story why was to emerge only four years later. Whatever may have been the Commissioner's suspicions at the time—as we describe below, he was taking steps to reorganise this part of his force—his defence to the proceedings referred to other, no doubt genuine, difficulties. He referred to trials in which material had been found not to be obscene and to other cases in which a conviction had been obtained but only a small fine imposed, and he made the point that with limited resources he could not properly devote more effort to enforcing an aspect of the law which neither the public nor the courts appeared to take very seriously. Mr Blackburn's motion was dismissed by the Divisional Court and his appeal to the Court of Appeal was rejected, but much sympathy was expressed with his case and the judgments in the Court of Appeal in particular contained strong criticism of the Obscene Publications Acts and the way in which they had, in Lord Denning's view, "misfired".

4.16 Already, however, the new Commissioner, Sir Robert Mark, who was appointed in April 1972, was making reforms which were to remove the corrupt officers and to open the way to more effective enforcement of the law. The Obscene Publications Squad was reorganised with effect from 20 November 1972, and a glance at the statistics of searches and seizures which we were given and which are included in Appendix 7 shows the much increased police activity which followed. We were told that the material seized by the police in Soho in 1973 had a face value of over £1 million. It was clearly with some pride that representatives of the Metropolitan Police told us that the trade in foreign hard-core pornography had been considerably reduced since 1972 and that no shop in Soho would now dare to stock such material. Although Mr Blackburn made allegations to us of continuing and massive police corruption in the West End of London he gave us no evidence to support these allegations.

4.17 Mr Blackburn drew particular attention to the way in which cinema clubs still flourished in the West End, and, from our own observations, it did seem that cinema clubs had become less inhibited about the kind of films they were prepared to show. But this did not appear to us to be so because the police were inactive against clubs. Indeed, representatives of the Association for Cinema Club Standards complained to us that clubs were subject to harrassment by the police. One proprietor told us that his five cinema clubs had been raided by the police a total of 110 times in the course of one week in 1978, but that four cases in which proceedings resulted had all been dismissed by the court. Mr Blackburn and some others complained because they saw what they considered to be obscene material being made available; but if material of that kind has been taken to court, unsuccessfully, it is difficult to blame the police for failing to persist in taking action against it. We do not accept that the continued existence of clubs showing pornographic films in Soho is evidence that the police must have been bribed.

4.18 Metropolitan Police witnesses argued very strongly that their achievement in dealing with the Soho pornography market since 1972 showed that it was not true that pornography automatically led to the growth of corruption. Moreover, they do not accept the view, offered by some witnesses (and encouraged by the analogy to Prohibition) that the illegality of pornography itself encouraged the involvement of organised crime, which it was impossible, in such a field, to keep out. They claimed that where the law was relatively certain, as it still was in relation to imported hard-core pornography, vigorous police action and the imposition of severer penalties by the courts had meant that it was no longer worth the risk to deal in such material and individuals with links with organised crime had abandoned their interest in this field.

Trends in British publishing

4.19 This police action against foreign material left something of a vacuum, which has been filled by British publications. The growth and development of this market was remarkable. One of the leading figures in it, and perhaps the man with more responsibility than anyone for the direction taken by this section of the publishing trade, was Mr David Sullivan. Having started off by selling glamour photographs by mail order, he first instituted a magazine called *Private* and later, towards the end of 1974, one which he impudently called *Whitehouse*. In succeeding months, Mr Sullivan launched a series of new magazines which steadily became more explicit, and his success inspired competing publishers to produce other new magazines. Mr Sullivan explained to us that he went into riskier photographs after being visited by the police about the written matter in one of his magazines: he decided that if he was going to be at risk of prosecution anyway, there was no point in playing safe with the pictures. The publishers of these magazines competed throughout 1975 and 1976 to see how far they could go. Mr Sullivan told us that he had maintained an advantage over his competitors during this period by keeping one step ahead: part of the appeal of such magazines, he considered, was that people wanted to see things they had not seen before.

4.20 We have already mentioned the concern which the prosecuting authorities in London were feeling towards the end of 1976 about the content of these magazines, and the action which the authorities then took. But the publishing trade itself felt some concern. Competition in greater explicitness cannot go on for ever. There were clearly fears that many of these magazines were beginning to ask for trouble from the authorities and that any further advancement of the limits would be bound to provoke much harsher enforcement measures. It was suggested to us by one former publisher that anyway the trade was facing increasing difficulties because the market was becoming saturated and sales were beginning to decline, and foreign markets for unsold British magazines were disappearing because the abolition of censorship elsewhere meant that there was less interest in publications which still fell short of being totally explicit.

Self regulation by the trade

4.21 As a result of the alarm felt in the trade, a meeting was held in London on 29 May 1977, the outcome of which was the formation of a body called the British Adult Publications Association, which included nine out of the thirteen main publishers of sex magazines, nearly all the main distributors of such magazines, and a number of retailers. The main object of the Association was to regulate the content of magazines and to keep them within limits which were regarded as within the law as currently interpreted. The Association adopted guidelines of what they considered material unacceptable for this type of publication, based on what had been found in certain previous legal proceedings to be obscene or not obscene, and members of the Association agreed to observe these in the magazines they produced and sold from September 1977. The Association also set up a Publications Control Board to determine in individual cases whether or not material was in accord with the guidelines, and Mr John Trevelyan, the former Secretary of the British Board of Film Censors, accepted an invitation to be part-time President of this new Board. Mr Trevelyan told us in evidence in September 1978 that the sanctions operated by the Association against magazines objected to by the Board—namely that distributor members of the Association would not distribute publications which, after an initial determination by the Board, continued to flout the guidelines—had been implemented in four cases, and that certain magazines had ceased publication. He thought the guidelines were proving effective: publishing trends up to early 1977 had been halted and in some respects reversed.

4.22 Some of our witnesses considered that the institution of this self-regulation in the trade was a step in the right direction and was much to be welcomed; it was compared to the establishment of film censorship by the film industry, and Mr Trevelyan's appointment was perhaps intended to suggest such a comparison. But we also heard considerable cynicism, from those in the trade and outside it. Some people, including those in some parts of the distributing trade, dismissed the Association as a vain attempt to make respectable a part of the trade which could never deserve respect. Others saw the Association as a highly effective cartel, through which the interests of the big publishers could effectively squeeze out competition by denying non-members or small publishers an outlet for their publications. Others expressed scepticism about the effectiveness of the self-censorship imposed; the Director of Public Prosecutions was one of those who said to us that he saw little difference in the magazines published before and after the guidelines were introduced. Certainly, the fact that the Association's guidelines were being complied with was regarded by the prosecuting authorities as irrelevant for the purposes of deciding whether or not to proceed against a magazine under the Obscene Publications Acts.

Changes in enforcement action

4.23 Enforcement action against British magazines appeared, if anything, to become more vigorous. This was particularly so in Greater Manchester, where Mr James Anderton was appointed Chief Constable in July 1976. Mr Anderton made no secret of his view that pornography is sinful, and his force began to take more energetic action to enforce the law against it. Mr Anderton told us that in the sixteen months from 1 January 1977 his officers had conducted 355 raids under the Obscene Publications Acts and had seized nearly 200,000 items, with a value of almost half a million pounds. These seizures were predominantly from retailers, including Messrs W H Smith and station bookstalls. Mr Anderton himself made the point to us that what the Greater Manchester Police had done had had little effect on the production and publication of such material, particular since the publishers themselves were located outside the Greater Manchester area. But the police action appears to have had a significant effect on the availability in Manchester of publications of this kind: Mr Anderton told us that some retailers had changed their policy about which magazines they stocked and that there were now notably fewer outlets for such material. Because of delays in the judicial process, many of the proceedings arising from these seizures had not come to trial at the time Mr Anderton gave evidence to us, but he was able to say that every case in which proceedings had been brought had been successful. This was a striking record, and it seemed to contrast with other evidence we received about the difficulties of bringing successful proceedings under the existing law. It was put to us by other witnesses that the results were related to the fact that the decisions were those of magistrates' courts, usually in determination of a summons under section 3 of the 1959 Act (though the statistics given to us by Mr Anderton showed that 27 cases had been taken under section 2).

4.24 Because of the different circumstances in London, where most of the publishers are based, the policy of the Metropolitan Police had been to concentrate, where British publications at least were concerned, on publishers and distributors rather than retailers. This policy was reconsidered late in 1977, particularly in the wake of another trial at the Central Criminal Court in which the publishers of the magazines founded by Mr David Sullivan (Mr Sullivan by that time having sold out to concentrate on his film interests) were acquitted on most of the obscenity charges brought in respect of magazines seized in 1976, despite the fact that many of the same magazines had been found obscene both by magistrates and on an appeal heard only three weeks before. We have already pointed out that seizures from publishers and distributors earlier in 1977 were dealt with by way of forfeiture rather than criminal trial, and we drew attention in Chapter 2 to the argument put to us that the use of forfeiture proceedings had provided a most effective weapon in dealing with the trade in obscene publications. It was decided at the end of 1977 to extend police action in London to the retailers of British magazines, effectively taking a similar line to that already adopted in Manchester. The outcome was a very large number of raids on individual retailers throughout London in 1978 and the institution of forfeiture proceedings before local magistrates which were usually successful. One publisher told us that as a result of this "massive onslaught" on newsagents, his magazines had lost many outlets and were now harder to obtain.

The size of the market

4.25 Exactly what the size of the market is is difficult to establish. Some of the better-established magazines publish audited circulation figures, particularly those that take a moderate line which does not discourage the advertising agencies from using them for consumer advertising; but most of the magazines in this field do not publish figures. Mr Michael Brown, an independent marketing and research consultant, surveyed the available information for us and we reproduce his memorandum, summarising the data on the audience for sexually explicit periodicals, at Appendix 6. Audited circulation figures for the three largest men's magazines, *Mayfair, Men Only* and *Penthouse*, show a significant drop in circulation over the period 1974 to 1978, which may perhaps be explained by the increasing competition from the newer magazines. These newer magazines do not have an audited circulation, but most of the publishers gave us information either about the circulation of their magazines or about the number of copies that they printed each month. Some caution is necessary in translating print orders into UK circulation: we gained the impression that most publishers in this field printed many more copies than they expected to sell during the month concerned, offering them to the wholesale and retail trade on a sale-or-return basis and hoping that they would enjoy a long shelf life. One reason why most of these magazines can have a long period of sale is that the usual practice is not to date them but simply to allocate them issue numbers, so that the casual customer cannot readily tell how old they are; many have nothing of topical interest in them and some retailers offer for sale at any one time two or three issues of the same magazine. It seems that in some cases old unsold magazines have been re-covered, sometimes with a different title, and offered for sale again.

4.26 Putting together the audited circulation figures of those magazines which publish them and our own estimate of how much of the print order figures we were given by publishers represents a UK circulation, it appears that the total market for magazines of this kind in this country is of the order of 3 million copies every month. This estimate does not take account of fluctuations that there may have been while we have been sitting: it is hard enough to obtain any figure in this shadowy area without trying to operate a continuous monitoring of the size of the market. But if it is true, as we were told by sources within the trade, that the market reached its peak in mid-1976 and then suffered a decline, partly natural and partly due to increasing police action against retailers, we think it likely that the monthly market may have been larger than 3 million copies and could well now be smaller.

4.27 As with circulation, information about the readership of the newer and less restrained magazines is not available. The better established magazines are included in the National Readership Survey, the results of which indicate a growth in readership up to 1973, a decline from then until 1976, followed by an upturn in mid-1977 and a further decline. Extrapolating these results to the whole market would suggest that the gross audience for magazines of this kind is about 8 million adults in Britain, but this does not mean that 8 million adults in Britain read these magazines, because some read more than one. However, the indications are that about 4 million people have read one or more of these magazines during the preceding month. This is a significant section of the population. Moreover, the readership information available suggests that this audience is fairly broadly based, except that it is predominantly male. It is also younger than the population at large, with those under 35 much more likely to be readers of such magazines than those over 45. Readership spans all social classes, but is strongest among the skilled working class and weakest among the highest and lowest socio-economic groups. But interest is clearly not confined to any particular small group in the population: the common idea that this material appeals especially to the "dirty old man" is not supported by the evidence. These results agree with what our enquiries found about the kind of people who were customers for this material. One retailer specialising in such material told us that his customers were of all ages and from all walks of life, and a similar picture emerges from research studies which were undertaken for the United States Commission on Obscenity and Pornography.

Controlling public displays

4.28 We have so far concentrated on the way in which the obscenity laws have affected the publication and sale of magazines. A rather different aspect of the subject is the way the sale of such magazines impinges on the attention of the public. As we have explained in Chapter 2, there are existing laws preventing the public display of indecent material, but these are prosecuted only rarely. The Government's attempt in 1973-74 to modernise these laws, and similar later efforts, came to nothing. There had not been before our appointment any particular controversy about public displays, but views had been widely expressed, and formed a notable part of the evidence we received, that whatever might be allowed for willing adults to purchase, or to see in the cinema, there were strong grounds for controlling the exposure of such material to unwilling members of the public. A large proportion of our correspondents volunteered comments of this nature. These views were expressed in general terms, but they often mentioned the display of magazine covers in newsagents' shops and the display of photographs outside cinemas and other places of entertainment, particularly in the West End of London. In fact, of course, most magazine covers are already a good deal more restrained than their contents and there did not appear to be many public displays being mounted that by contemporary standards would be caught by the existing law against matter which was "indecent", or, indeed, by a modernised version of such a law. It seemed to us that the evidence we received on this subject was in fact making a more subtle point and that what people were objecting to, at least in many cases, was the display in public of matter they believed (for instance, in its inner pages) to be indecent, rather than a public display which was itself indecent. If so, this is one reason for thinking that merely to impose controls on what is displayed, in the sense of what is shown on the outside of things, is not a sufficient answer to these problems. We shall come back to this question in our more theoretical discussion in Chapter 7.

Applying the law to the showing of films

4.29 In discussing the operation of the obscenity laws we have not mentioned the showing of films. Those who were responsible for the Obscene Publications Act 1959 would not have been surprised at this. The Act was passed in a form which expressly excluded the exhibition of films; moreover, the assumption at that time was, as the Lord Chancellor said in the House of Lords on the proceedings of the Bill, that it was "unthinkable" that there should be prosecutions for obscenity against a form of entertainment already subject to its own censorship. Not for the first time, the unthinkable came to pass.

4.30 The assumption that the censorship system was a sufficient control on cinema films lasted for some years. But from the late nineteen-sixties an increasing number of films sought to deal frankly and explicitly with subjects which were distasteful or disturbing to some people. We noticed in the last chapter the increasing proportion of films given an "X" certificate, and the growing number needing to be cut before they were approved. Despite the cuts, some people felt more and more that additional controls should be applied to what was shown in the cinema. This was pursued in two ways: by invoking the criminal law and by encouraging the greater use of local authority powers to censor films.

4.31 Since the Obscene Publications Acts did not apply to films, those who wanted to place more curbs on them had to find other ways to invoke the law. The first course taken by private prosecutors was to invoke the Vagrancy Act 1824, and its offence of publicly displaying indecent material. However, a prosecution involving *Last Tango in Paris* was dismissed in Cornwall in February 1974 and another one involving *Blow Out*, brought by Mrs. Mary Whitehouse in London, was dismissed in April 1974. Both cases were rejected on the ground that a film shown inside a cinema was not a display in a public place, though the magistrate in the second case gave the prosecutors some encouragement by agreeing that the film was indecent. In March 1974 a different attack on *Last Tango in Paris* was mounted. Mr. Edward Shackleton of the Nationwide Festival of Light initiated a prosecution under the Obscene Publications Acts, not in respect of the showing of the film but in respect of its distribution. The case was committed for trial and an application for the indictment to be quashed on the ground that the publication of a film intended for public exhibition fell outside the provisions of the Acts was rejected by the Lord Chief Justice in May 1974. At the trial in November, however, the jury were directed to acquit on the ground that the only publication involved was by the distributors to the licensee of the cinema, and that there was no evidence that the film had tended to deprave and corrupt him. Although the prosecution was a private one, the apparent conflict between the views of the Divisional Court and the court of trial introduced some confusion into the law and the Attorney General instituted an appeal to resolve the point, the Court of Appeal confirming in March 1976 that the Obscene Publications Acts did not apply to cinema films.

4.32 In the meantime, however, a more successful means of attack had been identified. Mr Raymond Blackburn complained to the Director of Public Prosecutions about the film *More About the Language of Love,* which differed from the other films proceeded against in that it had been refused a certificate by the British Board of Film Censors and was showing in London by virtue of a local certificate issued by the Greater London Council. In the event, the Director of Public Prosecutions decided to institute proceedings against the exhibitors of the film, using the common law offence of indecent exhibition (which seems last to have been used in 1875 against a showman on Epsom Downs). At the trial in June 1975 legal arguments for the defence failed and the jury were unanimous in finding the film to be indecent. The exhibitors were convicted and fined.

Doubts about film censorship

4.33 This finding by a court against a film approved for public viewing by the Greater London Council was a blow to an authority which had already had severe doubts about its role as a censor of films. In 1972 it had asked the Government for a review of the law and practice relating to film censorship, and in 1973 had followed this with a plea that censorship should no longer be the responsibility of local authorities. In June 1973, under the influence of Mrs Enid Wistrich, the new Chairman of the Council's Film Viewing Board, the Council agreed on its own review of the practice of film censorship, the outcome of which was a recommendation to the Council towards the end of 1974 that since it was under no legal obligation to censor films, it should cease to exercise any powers in relation to the showing of films to persons over the age of eighteen.

4.34 The implications of this step were considerable. As we have made clear, film censorship exists only because there has been common consent that film exhibitions should be regulated, and every local authority in the country has supported the system. Suddenly, by far the most important licensing authority in the country, with a large proportion of the country's cinemas within its area, was talking about opting out of the system and effectively abolishing film censorship for adults. A lead from London would have been influential on other authorities and, without the support of local authorities, the role of the British Board of Film Censors would have become doubtful; the Cinematograph Exhibitors' Association put it to us that a state of "unprecedented anarchy" would have arisen. Moreover, the prospective abolition of censorship when, as we have indicated, many people thought censorship was too lax anyway, aroused great controversy and the debate of the proposal by the Council which took place on 28 January 1975 was the focus of much attention and lobbying. At its conclusion, the proposal was rejected by a majority of 50 votes to 44.

4.35 Since then, the Greater London Council has maintained its support for the film censorship system, but it proposed to us that a new statutory film censorship board should take over the role now given to local authorities, subject to there being a local involvement in appeals from the statutory body. In 1975, however, the doubts which had been introduced about the future of the system were kept alive by the legal action against *More About the Language of Love* and by the repercussions of it. Mr Blackburn followed it up with proceedings against the Greater London Council in which he sought an order preventing them from exercising their film censorship powers in such a way as to permit the public showing of unlawful films. As a result of this, as we described in Chapter 3, the Council amended its rules for censoring films.

Rethinking the control of films

4.36 These legal proceedings seem to have had a profound effect on the attitude of the film industry towards censorship. For the first time, the industry found that the exhibition of a properly certificated film in a licensed cinema was not immune from successful proceedings under the criminal law; moreover, the law applicable to the cinema employed a test of indecency, instead of the test of obscenity which applied to publications and plays. With the Greater London Council having just demonstrated the fragility of the censorship system, and the Law Commission indicating in its working paper on Conspiracies relating to Morals and Decency, published in December 1974, its preliminary view that that system might take the full weight of controls on the cinema once the common law was abolished, the industry reconsidered its policy. Its conclusion was that it would be better off if the law of obscenity were applied to the cinema rather than the law of indecency and that, if this were done, the powers of local authorities to censor films (which the industry had urged the Greater London Council not to abandon) could be abolished.

4.37 As we make clear in Appendix 1, the Law Commission also rethought its proposals in the light of the comments received on its working paper, and in 1976 recommended that the law of obscenity should be extended to cover the showing of all films, whether in licensed cinemas or not; and we explain how steps were taken to implement that proposal in the Criminal Law Act 1977, even though the decision had been taken that a Committee should be appointed to review the obscenity laws. That change in the law took some of the heat out of the situation, though there were people who regretted that films should be made subject to the *deprave and corrupt* test rather than the test of indecency which made it generally easier to get a conviction. Before the law was changed, Mr Blackburn, once again, instituted legal action against the film *The Language of Love* in an effort to prove that *More About the Language of Love* was not the only indecent film which had been allowed to be shown publicly, and he attempted to indict the President and Secretary of the British Board of Film Censors with aiding and abetting, by virtue of having given the film a certificate (in circumstances to which we referred in Chapter 3). However, that prosecution failed, a jury finding that the film was not indecent, and no other films shown in licensed cinemas have since been the subject of proceedings.

4.38 The film censorship system has attracted less controversy in the last few years. It survived the crisis that broke out when it looked as though the Greater London Council would initiate its disintegration; and the spate of very controversial films which brought the British Board of Film Censors under attack in 1971 and 1972 has passed. The system underwent a major change when the Local Government Act 1972 transferred cinema licensing functions from county councils to district councils, and cinema interests expressed vexation at the way in which groups like the Nationwide Festival of Light had used this opportunity to encourage the new authorities to take an interest in film censorship and to strengthen their local controls on the showing of films. This increased local activity—although, as we said in the last chapter, it is still confined to a minority of local authorities—was much criticised in some of the evidence we received and the weight of the views expressed to us, even on behalf of many local authorities themselves, was against powers of film censorship continuing to rest with local authorities.

The end of controversy?

4.39 We have suggested reasons why the atmosphere surrounding both the obscenity laws and the film censorship system has become calmer than it was four or five years ago. But we believe that another factor has been the existence of this Committee itself. The fact that formal steps are being taken to consider how the law and the censorship system should be reformed has itself reassured many people who believe, from very different points of view, that the present law is profoundly unsatisfactory and that the time has come for a reorganisation of film censorship. We have heard more than enough evidence to convince us that the controversy has not evaporated or been forgotten. The fact remains that few people regard the present state of the law as acceptable; the fact remains that the same groups responsible for instituting film censorship in the form we know it now wish to see it abolished so far as it affects films shown to adults. Our witnesses welcomed our examination of these matters. We are convinced that that examination requires us not to tinker with the existing framework, but to go back to first principles, and ask what the purpose of controls of this kind properly is. We turn to these principles in the part of our report which follows.

PART 2—PRINCIPLES

CHAPTER FIVE

LAW, MORALITY AND THE FREEDOM OF EXPRESSION

5.1 What sorts of conduct may the law properly seek to suppress? An answer to that question which is widely accepted in our society, as in many other modern societies, is that no conduct should be suppressed by law unless it can be shown to harm someone. It is one sign of how many people now accept this answer and the condition which it imposes on legislation—it may be called the *harm condition*—that almost without exception the evidence we received, insofar as it touched on these matters of principle, stated something like this condition or took it for granted. Submissions to us differed, very obviously, about what harms, if any, publications and films might cause. They differed also about what might count as a harm. Those who favoured the abolition or limitation of legal restraint tended, not surprisingly, to define "harm" in a narrower and more determinate way, while those who supported greater legal control admitted more generalised and less identifiable harms. Virtually everyone, however, whatever their suggestions, used the language of "harm" and accepted, so it seemed, the harm condition.

5.2 We accept the harm condition. As the variety of views in the submissions to us shows, however, that leaves many basic questions still to be answered.

Law and Morality

5.3 The harm condition has been very much discussed in recent years in the context of debates on the question whether prevailing morality should be made into law: that is to say, whether the fact that many people in society think something morally wrong is a good enough reason for there being a law against it. If the harm condition for legislation is accepted, then the answer to this question will be "no", since there are acts which are morally disapproved but are not harmful, and it will follow from the harm condition that there should be no law against these.

5.4 Some people hold that if society held correct moral views, this question should not arise, since even *moral* judgement should, correctly, be controlled by the harm condition. They will say that if certain conduct does no harm, then not only should there not be a law against it, but it should not be the object of any moral reactions either: if someone's behaviour does no harm, then it is nobody's business but his own, and no question of morality comes into it. This is clearly a liberal and tolerant outlook, and can be a beneficent one, but it does involve a very narrow view of morality. It tends to imply that everything that does not involve harm is simply a matter of taste or preference, as some people like spinach or detective stories and others do not. This is simply not true to the depth and complexity of one's possible reactions to other people's behaviour and to social phenomena. People can be distressed or contemptuous, admiring or impressed, more variously and more seriously than this model allows, and in ways which they think it important, for instance, to impart to their children. They still, following the harm condition, may not think that the matters which arouse these reactions are matters for the law, but they do care about them, and properly so, at a level which is not catered for by making "harm" the only notion relevant to morality.

5.5 In the matter of pornography, there exists real disagreement about how serious a matter it is, even among those who think that it does little identifiable harm. Some do, after serious consideration, think that it is entirely a matter of preference: some people like it, some people do not. Others think that it is, at any rate, a deeper matter than that and whatever one might think about the case of an individual person, the fact that a society was extensively given to the consumption of pornography would tell one something about it, and something discouraging. It would not be merely like learning, for instance, that a certain society had a tendency to consume an unusually large amount of pasta. At the individual level as well, some would take a similar view. There are many of our witnesses who might not perhaps react to those with a taste for pornography with "moral disapproval", but who nevertheless would regard such a person's state as a matter for ethical concern (if one may so put it) and think that such a person was in respect of his character and personality not as people desirably should be; and that we all had good reason to hope that our children would not develop into such a state, and to discourage them from doing so.

5.6 There is, then, a view that wants to apply the harm condition to both morality and the law. An opposed view, associated in recent years with arguments advanced by Lord Devlin[1], agrees with us that what is of serious moral concern can range more widely than the harm condition, but argues from this that even legislation should not be tied by the harm condition and can properly go wider, to express and affirm morality.

5.7 The shortest argument for the harm condition is simply that there is a presumption in favour of individual freedom: that the incursions of government into that freedom have to be justified; that the proper sphere of government is the protection of the interests of citizens; and so what is justifiably curbed by government is only what harms the interests of some citizens. But there is of course more to society than a collection of individuals under a set of rules which harmonize and collectively promote their self-interest. Society involves shared history, culture, and values, and there is more to being "at home" in it than knowing the language (that is already a lot) and remembering the way to the market. It is from this truth that Lord Devlin argued that the harm condition was not correct. Since a society rests on moral consensus, he claimed, what threatens moral consensus threatens society. But it is the business of the law to protect society; hence it can properly be used to protect the moral consensus.

---

[1] eg in *The Enforcement of Morals,* Oxford, 1959.

5.8 As Professor Hart[1] and other critics have argued, however, the conclusion that Lord Devlin wanted does not follow. One immediate point is that his position seems not so much to abandon the harm condition as to urge another and wider category of harms, those associated with society's moral disintegration; and indeed, as we shall explain in the next chapter, many of our witnesses did urge on us the existence and importance of harms of this very general type, supposedly associated with pornography and violent publications. Such witnesses were undoubtedly arguing in the terms of the harm condition. With Lord Devlin's argument, however, and the issues of principles it raises, there is an important, if perhaps rather fine, distinction to be made. On his view, there will be kinds of act which are not necessarily harmful in themselves, but are morally disapproved by (let us suppose) a majority of citizens. He argues, roughly, that if these acts are not discouraged by the law, certain harms will follow, of social and moral disintegration. On Lord Devlin's argument, however, those harms follow not simply from that type of act, but from that type of act when, in addition, it is morally disapproved by the citizens: in a society with a different moral fabric, containing no moral opinion against those acts, it is possible that no harms would follow from there not being laws against them. That kind of harm would not be admitted (except perhaps in extreme cases) by those who believe that legislation should be restricted by the harm condition. They are concerned with the harms that follow from the kind of act itself, leaving aside the citizens' moral opinion of those acts. They would say that to allow citizens' opinions to determine the matter in this way, is to sacrifice people's rights to do things that are otherwise harmless totally to majority prejudice. So even though Lord Devlin speaks in terms of harms, the harms of social disintegration, there is a difference between those who believe in the harm condition, and Lord Devlin or anyone else who believes, in the celebrated words of Lord Mansfield, referred to approvingly by a Law Lord in 1962[2]:

> "Whatever is *contra bonos mores et decorum* the principles of our laws prohibit, and the King's Court as the general censor and guardian of the public morals is bound to restrain and punish."

5.9 A substantial point against Lord Devlin's view is that it exaggerates the identity and extent of the moral consensus required by a society, and hence overstates the harms that supposedly follow if moral opinion is not made into law. Certainly society requires some degree of moral consensus, but moral opinion can, and does, change without the disintegration of society. One thing that can happen is that the society moves to a new consensus; another is that it supports, in some particular area, a real degree of variety and pluralism.

5.10 Of course, there are many people who would prefer, or believe that they would prefer, a society less pluralistic than modern capitalist societies, and embodying a stronger moral consensus and a higher level of moral conviction. This yearning for a morally more homogeneous society takes many

---

[1] H L A Hart, *Law, Liberty and Morality*, Oxford, 1963.
[2] For references, see Hart op. cit. pp 7–9. Lord Mansfield's dictum dates from 1774.

different forms, belonging, in political terms, both to the Right and to the Left. Some seek the recovery of a consensus which they believe once existed, others look to a new society yet to emerge.

5.11 We have been impressed by the extent to which submissions that we have received against pornography and obscene publications have been very obviously moved by sentiments not just about these phenomena themselves, but about certain underlying features of the modern world, and express in some cases nostalgia, in others an aspiration, for a world where not just sexuality but human relations more generally were controlled by a firmer and more effective morality. Some of these views, naturally enough, ascribe present evils to the decline of Christian belief.

5.12 Many of these submissions are evidently deeply sincere. some of them indeed speak more for "the party of humanity" than does a certain kind of "liberal" evidence which we have received, which complacently extols the high task of furthering enlightenment and human fulfilment which, it claims, is sustained by the more literate kind of porno magazine. Any Committee enquiring into this kind of subject is likely to encounter a certain amount of humbug. Perhaps the most striking example of it that came our way was the pretence that present day commercial pornography represents some fulfilment of liberal and progressive hopes.

5.13 Leaving aside those with a commercial interest in it, few but the incurably complacent are likely to be pleased by the present scene in parts of Soho, for instance. The distaste for that scene indeed goes beyond those who pine for a more extensive moral consensus, and is felt by many who want a very individualist society containing many different images of life.

5.14 There is indeed a question of how deeply significant, as opposed to distasteful, these phenomena are. But even if such things as obscene publications are significant expressions, as some of our witnesses passionately believe, of things wrong with our society, there would still remain another question of whether laws directed to suppressing those publications would be either justified or effective. To be the identifiable cause of harms is one thing, to be the expression of underlying ills in society is another.

Freedom of Expression

5.15 A particularly eloquent and influential advocate of the harm condition was John Stuart Mill, and he and his work *On Liberty* (1859), have been several times cited in submissions to us. Mill applied the harm condition to all proposals to coerce people's actions. He held, however, that where the actions in question were those of publishing a book or expressing oneself in speech or writing, there were special reasons against coercion and in favour of liberty. The freedom of expression is not for him just one more example of freedom from coercion but is a very special and fundamental form of freedom. It is clear that many of our witnesses share this view, some of them for Mill's own reasons, and we think it important to give those reasons some attention. Some of Mill's reasons we believe to be still very relevant today. Some of his arguments, however, were always flimsy and are yet more so in modern conditions. His basic thought was that human beings have no infallible source of knowledge about human nature or how human affairs may develop, and do not know in advance what arrangements or forms of life may make people happy or enable them to be, as Mill passionately wanted them to be, original, tolerant and uncowed individuals. Since we do not know in advance, we do not know what new proposals, ideas or forms of expression may contribute to the development of man and society.

5.16 From this Mill drew the conclusion that we have no basis for suppressing or censoring any of them. He did so, in particular, because he thought (and many others have shared this view) that the only way the truth could emerge was by a form of natural selection in a "free market" of ideas: if all ideas were allowed expression, good ideas would multiply, bad ideas would die out. This conception, if sound, would have very powerful consequences. It is important, for instance, that it would tell almost as much against restricting a publication as against suppressing it, since any constraint on a work's availability will reduce the chance of its message being heard. However, we do not find Mill's conception entirely convincing, anyway, and it is also far from clear how it applies (as it has been applied) to the sort of material which is the subject of our enquiry.

5.17 If the "survival of the true" notion applies to anything, it applies to publications which indeed contain *ideas*, which may be true or false. It can be extended more widely—to works of serious literature, for instance, the expressive powers of which contribute in their own way to the formation of images of men and of human possibilities. It is hard to see, however, how the argument can be extended to everything that is published. In particular it is hard to see how it applies to such things as standard photographic pornography, and we find it a rather ironical comment on the survival power of good ideas that some submissions to us have put forward in defence of the most vacant and inexpressive pornographic material the formulations which Mill hoped would assist in furthering ". . . the permanent interests of man as a progressive being".

5.18 It is interesting in this connection that the Supreme Court of the United States has for a long time followed a line—though both unclearly and controversially—of arguing that the First Amendment to the United States Constitution, which says that "Congress shall make no law . . . . . abridging the freedom of speech . . . .", does not protect hard-core pornography (at least), on the ground that such pornography is not, in a constitutional sense, "speech": the idea being that it lacks communicative content[1]. This is not an issue which, happily, we are under any obligation to pursue, but the fact that this argument can be influentially sustained does illustrate the point that there is something open to question in calling on the "market-place of truth" argument in defence of such items as standard photographic pornography.

---

[1]See F Schauer: 'Speech and "Speech"—Obscenity and "Obscenity": An Exercise in the Interpretation of Constitutional Language': 67 Georgetown Law Journal 899–933 (1979), which defends the argument. We are grateful to Professor Schauer for discussion and for information about US law.

5.19 Even in the area of ideas, the notion of a "free market" has to be regarded with some scepticism, and the faith in *laissez-faire* shown by the nineteenth century and earlier does not altogether meet modern conditions. If everyone talks at once, truth will not prevail, since no-one can be heard and nothing will prevail: and falsehood indeed may prevail, if powerful agencies can gain an undue hold on the market. Even in natural science, which Mill regarded as the paradigm, he neglected the importance of scientific institutions and the filter against cranks which is operated, and necessarily operated, by expert opinion, excluding from serious consideration what it sees as incompetence. Against the principle that truth is strong and (given the chance) will prevail, must be set Gresham's Law, that bad money drives out good, which has some application in matters of culture and which predicts that it will not necessarily be the most interesting ideas or the most valuable works of art that survive in competition—above all, in commercial competition.

5.20 Thus we cannot entirely agree that "the Truth certainly would do well enough if she were left to fend for herself"[1]; she may need more of a chance than that. This point can surely justify intervention. Intervention, however, need not be and should not be negative intervention: it can take the form of such things as state subventions for the arts, or policies of refusing to design television programmes solely on the basis of ratings, or subsidising institutions of critical enquiry. This is not just a point about the rights of minorities; it involves Mill's own basic idea (though differently applied) that progress involves a belief or a value being first a minority belief or value, which must be preserved if it is ever to reach further.

5.21 The fact that the market-place model is an inadequate basis for the value of free expression does not mean that one replaces the market with monopoly, and institutes a censorship by the State or by worthy citizens. There is certainly no reason to think that that would do better in the detection of error or the advance of enlightenment. The more basic idea, to which Mill attached the market-place model, remains a correct and profound idea: that we do not know in advance what social, moral or intellectual developments will turn out to be possible, necessary or desirable for human beings and for their future, and free expression, intellectual and artistic—something which may need to be fostered and protected as well as merely permitted—is essential to human development, as a process which does not merely happen (in some form or another, it will happen anyway), but so far as possible is rationally understood. It is essential to it, moreover, not just as a means to it, but as part of it. Since human beings are not just subject to their history but aspire to be conscious of it, the development of human individuals, of society and of humanity in general, is a process itself properly constituted in part by free expression and the exchange of human communication.

5.22 We realise that some may disagree with this basic idea because they think that fundamental human moral truths have been laid down unchangeably for all time, for instance in religious terms. Mill, certainly, thought that there

---

[1]A remark made, but perhaps not totally endorsed, by John Locke: see his *Letter Concerning Toleration*, ed. Gough (1948), page 151.

was no such revealed truth, and his arguments for freedom of expression and those of people who think like him are to that extent an expression of religious scepticism. We would suggest, however, that even those who believe that there are revealed truths of morality and religion should attend very anxiously to the argument for freedom of expression. First, the barest facts of cultural history show that any set of supposed revealed truths which have survived have received constantly new applications and interpretations, to which new moral perceptions have contributed. Second, every believer in some set of moral certainties has to share the world with other believers in some different set of moral certainties. If they share the same society, at least, and even if they could come to do so, they have some common interest in not accepting principles which would allow someone else's certainty to persecute their own. Third, many religious believers in moral certainties also believe that human beings have been created not just to obey or mirror those certainties, but freely to live by them, and that institutions of free expression can be in fact a more developed representation of the religious consciousness itself than authoritarian institutions. We have thus not been surprised, though we have been impressed, by the constructive concern for freedom of expression which has been shown by many of the submissions we have received from religious bodies, disturbed though most of them have been by the present situation.

5.23 Because we believe that the value of the freedom of expression is connected with the open future of human development, we do find a difficulty with certain proposals for obscenity law we have received, which both admit the fact of changing standards, and also invoke present standards to justify the actual suppression of certain publications. The Nationwide Festival of Light and others, following a formulation of Lord Longford's Committee, have recommended the suppression of what grossly affronts "contemporary standards of decency or humanity accepted by the public at large". But while some such provision might ground, as we shall ourselves suggest, a *restriction* of some material, to prevent its offending the public at large, the position of trying to justify suppression—which, if successful, is permanent—on the basis of what are acknowledged to be contemporary standards, seems to us to make, more than is justified, present views the determinant of the future.

5.24 We come back to the total emptiness of almost all the material we are concerned with. These arguments, it will be said, are all very well for serious works of art or for writings of intellectual content, but it is absurd to apply them to everyday, in particular pictorial, pornography. We do not claim that, directly, they do apply. But here we must stress two very fundamental points: first, that what the argument grounds is a general presumption in favour of free expression, and second, that censorship is in its nature a blunt and treacherous instrument. The value of free expression does not lie solely in its consequences, such that it turns out on the whole to be more efficient to have it rather than not. It is rather that there is a right to free expression, a presumption in favour of it, and weighty considerations in terms of harms have to be advanced by those who seek to curtail it. Methods of control, moreover, bring their own harms, and can readily involve other violations of rights. Once one has left on one side the suppression of what produces the most immediate and obvious and gross harms, it is quite unrealistic to suppose that institutions of censorship can be guaranteed not to take on a repressive and distorting character, whether simply in the interests of some powerful or influential group or in opposition to new perceptions and ideas. Most of what is in our field of discussion contains no new perception and no idea at all, old or new, and that cannot seriously be disputed. But even if there were a case for suppressing that material, it must never be forgotten that no-one has invented, or in our opinion could invent, an instrument which would suppress only that, and could not be turned against something which might reasonably be argued to be of a more creative kind. The Obscene Publications Acts sought to avoid this danger by the "public good defence", to prevent conviction of material which was creatively valuable. We have already given an account of its sad history; we shall later argue, in Chapter 8, that such a device is misconceived in principle.

5.25 The "slippery slope" difficulty, the vagueness of any test, is inherent in any proposals for legislation about obscene publications, and indeed for any censorship at all, and this itself constitutes an argument against attempts at suppression. We shall argue later that rather different considerations apply to the less drastic course of restricting, without suppressing, certain publications. In that connection we shall also argue that there are reasons for treating the printed word differently from pictorial matter, and considerations drawn from the present area of discussion also support that conclusion, since (without entering on the troubled waters of the Supreme Court's definition of "speech" to which we have already referred) there is no doubt that it is to the printed word that the argument about the survival of new ideas and perceptions applies most directly.

Harms

5.26 The presumption in favour of freedom of expression is strong, but it is a presumption, and it can be overruled by considerations of harms which the speech or publication in question may cause. The first question that arises is, harms to whom? (In this chapter, as elsewhere, we will speak generally of harms to persons, though sometimes it might be more natural to speak of harms to their interests.) In particular, in the case of publications, there is the question whether supposed harm to consumers—ie., those who voluntarily choose to read the material—is, just in itself, to count. Mill and many others who advance what we have called the "harm condition" for coercing behaviour would say that it did not. They say this because they accept the principle that, if one is dealing with adult persons, it is best to assume that each person is the best judge of whether he or she is being harmed. This additional principle makes an important difference. The harm condition by itself would not necessarily produce very liberal results. One might agree that laws should only suppress what does harm but think that disgusting books should be suppressed by law because their readers (though those readers would not themselves agree) are in fact harmed by them. With this other principle added, however, such paternalist laws would be ruled out.

5.27 Most people would admit some paternalistic principles—with regard to harmful drugs, for instance. Some would like to apply similar ideas to people's reading habits, and regard "harmful" publications in much the same light as dangerous drugs. It is worth noting that the very strong resistance from liberal opinion that this kind of analogy meets is not just due to the uncertainty that surrounds the "effects" in question, and whether literature produces them. It is also that in this case, but not (for the most part) in the case of drugs, there is a real question about "who is to judge" what counts as harm; since it is a question of moral harm, there is room for disagreement about what such harms are, and there is a danger that the moral opinions of some group, presumably some rather conservative group, should be made authoritative for the moral health of readers. In the proceedings against *Lady Chatterley's Lover* in 1960, the prosecuting counsel in his opening speech invited the jury to ask themselves "Is it a book that you would even wish your wife or your servants to read?", and this ingenuous and unforgotten remark has served for twenty years to remind people that questions of what one should read cannot be regarded just as questions of health, on which there are experts as there are experts on drug addiction, but are closely connected with issues of power and authority in society.

5.28 An important point connected with the issue of paternalism is whether there is some *independent* test of whether a given activity produces harm. The effects of drug taking are a bad physical and mental condition, and this condition would be bad even if it were caused by something other than drugs. But if the bad effects of reading dirty books were alleged to lie only in the fact that they produced a deplorable state of mind manifested just in wanting to read dirty books, that would not be much of an argument; though if the state produced were that of compulsively reading dirty books, against one's will (as one witness has claimed to us happend to him), that would be more of an argument.

5.29 In fact a lot of the argument about harm supposedly caused by publications lies in the area of claims that they cause harms not to consumers, or merely to consumers, but to those affected by consumers. The harms cited in these arguments are usually the kind of thing that is indisputably a harm. In evidence put to us it was claimed, for example, that crimes, particularly sexual crimes, are caused by exposure to pornographic or violent films or publications. There were other arguments about individual behaviour being modified or conditioned by what was read or seen in ways that were less specifically anti-social but which conflicted with perceived standards of morality or with the expectations of society. Some emphasised the aspects of pornography which degrade women in that much material is not only offensive, but encourages a view of women as subservient and as properly the object of, or even desirous of, sexual subjugation or assault. Others emphasised the exploitation of those who participate in the production of pornography and the damaging effects this was believed to have. At a rather more general level, some people saw certain kinds of material, in presenting a distorted view of human experience, as damaging to human relationships by hindering the full development of the human personality or corrupting the imagination. So we heard arguments about pornography leading to sex crimes, and violence in the media engendering crimes of violence, about pornography leading to marital breakdown by encouraging unusual and sometimes abhorrent sexual demands (usually by husbands of their wives) and arousing false expectations of sexual fulfilment, about the encouragement of promiscuity and sexual deviation, about the promotion of self-gratification and a contempt for discipline, about the engendering of hate and aggression, about the risk to the normal sexual development of the young, about people becoming desensitized or callous through a diet of violence.

5.30 These are the kinds of harm that we shall principally consider in the next chapter. Besides these, however, harms of a less definite and more pervasive kind have been alleged, which relate to general effects on society of pornography and violent publications and films, and which can best be summed up, perhaps, under the phrase, used by several witnesses, "cultural pollution". Such phrases certainly refer to something, and we take seriously what they refer to. In the case of such descriptions, however, there is often a real difficulty in identifying what the harmful effect of the material is supposed to be, and whether indeed it is really an *effect* of the materials circulating that is in question, rather than the circulation itself which is regarded as intrinsically an objectionable thing; as we have already mentioned, it may be an expression, rather than a cause, of an undesirable state of society.

5.31 In the next chapter we shall try to evaluate some claims that have been made about these various harms and their association with pornography. In evaluating these claims, there are two general principles that we think it important to bear in mind. One is the requirement, for legal purposes, that the causation of the harm should lie "beyond reasonable doubt".

5.32 Restrictions on freedom of publication in connections other than obscenity are, of course, accepted by every legislature: with respect to libel, for instance, or sedition. It is significant, however, that in such cases liberal states require that the harms in question should be of a clear and immediate kind. So in the law of the United States in respect of seditious matter, where Mr Justice Holmes in a Supreme Court decision of 1919 produced the famous formula

> " . . . The question in every case is whether the words used are used in such circumstances and are of such a nature as to create a clear and present danger that they will bring about the substantive evils that Congress has a right to prevent. It is a question of proximity and degree . . ."[1]

At least one United States Judge did attempt to apply the same test to the alleged effects of obscene publications. Judge Bok, of Philadelphia, dismissing in 1948 a case against a number of books that included Faulkner's *Sanctuary* and Caldwell's *God's Little Acre,* stressed the impossibility of "even reasonable precision" in assessing a reader's reactions to a book, and sought to establish the principle that no book should be suppressed unless it could be shown that

---

[1]*Schenck* v *United States,* 249 US 47.

there was a clear and present danger of the commission of a crime as a result of its publication[1]. Superior Courts upheld his judgment of the case, and his reasoning in other respects, but not this suggested principle.

5.33 The causal concept of obscenity, in terms of doing harm, has in legal practice proved very resistant to being given the precise application, and submitting to the canons of proof, required in general by the law; and, as we have already said in an earlier chapter, the courts seem often in fact to have been proceeding on a basis altogether different from that of the publications supposedly causing harm.

5.34 The second principle that should be borne in mind is the requirement that if a certain class of publications, say pornographic publications, is to be legally banned, then harms have to be ascribable to that class of publications. No-one can reasonably say—though one or two of our witnesses have incautiously said it—that no pornographic book has ever harmed anyone. But that is not the point. It may well be that reading the Bible, for instance, has harmed someone. The question is whether pornography constitutes a class of publications to which, as such, there belongs a tendency to cause harms. That is the question that we shall be concerned with in the next chapter.

5.35 We must not forget at the same time that arguments about the effects of pornography have also been advanced in the opposite direction, suggesting that sexual and violent material has positive benefits in the opportunity it offers for the release of sexual or aggressive tensions, for the removal of ignorance, fear, guilt and inhibition, for the relief and comfort of lonely, handicapped or frustrated people and for members of society as a whole to gain a more open acceptance of sex as a natural part of life. It will be appropriate to touch on these suggestions as well in the next chapter.

---

[1]*Commonwealth* v *Gordon*, 66 Pa.D. and C. 101 (Phila. 1949).

CHAPTER SIX

HARMS?

I: Effects on Sex Crimes and Violence

6.1 We start our review of the harms possibly caused by pornography and violent material with the area where the harms alleged are of the most definitely identifiable kind, and where it is suggested that the effects of the material are kinds of behaviour which tend to be noticed particularly because they conflict with the law.

6.2 The arguments here are that certain kinds of behaviour, particularly in the form of criminal offences of violence and of a sexual nature, are either directly provoked by exposure to particular stimuli—such as the reading of a sex magazine producing a state of arousal which is manifested in rape or sexual assault, or the viewing of a film producing imitative violence—or are at least more likely to occur in an atmosphere created by pornography and violent material. The arguments suggest, therefore, that the proliferation of pornography results in increasing sexual offences and that violence in the media leads to an increase in offences of violence.

6.3 Submissions made to us on this subject, where they considered it necessary to support simple assertions by some kind of evidence, rested on three different classes of information. One kind may be called (without disrespect) "anecdotal", and is drawn from particular instances in which an association between crime and pornographic material has been observed, and a causal connection, it is claimed, can plausibly be supposed. We consider in this context also considerations put to us by psychiatrists on the basis of clinical experience. A second kind of evidence is drawn from research, involving experiments or guided observations, into human responses to particular kinds of material. Such research, obviously enough, does not itself involve the subjects committing crimes (or at least none that does has been drawn to our attention). What it rather does is to enquire whether reactions in the experimental set-up are of a kind—for instance, of an aggressive kind—which would lead one to expect crime or other anti-social behaviour as a response to that material in ordinary life. The third kind of evidence—the kind that has commanded a great deal of attention and aroused a great deal of controversy in this subject—is that drawn from statistical analysis of trends in known crime relative to the varying availability of pornography.

6.4 The relations between the last two kinds of evidence we take to be the following. A positive result in the second, experimental, kind of enquiry might be expected to show up in the statistical enquiry, if that is reliable, since if greater availability of pornography in real life is not connected with more crime, then the experimental results cannot have the significance for real life that is ascribed to them. On the other hand, a positive result from the statistical enquiry would be compatible with negative results from the experimental enquiry, since it might be that crime and pornography were linked in real life, but not by any mechanism which was revealed under those experimental conditions.

6.5 We will consider these kinds of evidence in turn.

Anecdotal and clinical evidence

6.6 A number of cases was drawn to our attention, and our own enquiries brought others to light, in which particular publications or films or a general interest in pornography, had been connected with the commission of offences. We saw a number of press reports in which the defence had alleged on behalf of a man charged with sexual offences that the commission of the crime could be ascribed to the influence of pornography. To lay weight simply on what is said by the defence would be rather naive: offenders or their counsel are not slow to proffer an excuse which mitigates the seriousness of the offence or reduces the individual's responsibility for having committed it, and it was noticeable that there were fewer cases in which the trial judge offered his own comment on the influence of pornography. Two notable cases mentioned to us were those of the Moors Murderers and the Cambridge Rapist, in both of which it has been alleged (not by the trial judge in either case) that the corrupting effect of pornography played a role.

6.7 In the case of the Cambridge Rapist, the defence tried to emphasise the influence of pornographic films and magazines and the local Chief Constable stated at the end of the trial that the case had "proved the real danger of pornography". We do not believe that a study of the case permits such a simple conclusion. The offender was a man with a long history of mental disturbance and criminal activity, with psychopathic tendencies evident from an early age. He had shown an interest in pornography but there was nothing to suggest that the particular methods which he had chosen to use in committing his offences owed anything to the pornography he had seen or that he would not have committed the offences had it not been for the influence of pornography. Somewhat similar considerations applied in the case of the Moors Murderers, though in that case less emphasis was placed on the influence of the publications in the possession of the offenders, both during the trial and in subsequent comment. Both these cases seem to be more consistent with pre-existing traits being reflected both in a choice of reading matter and in the acts committed against others. It would be extremely unsafe, in our view, to conclude, even tentatively, that exposure to pornography was a cause of the offences committed in those particular cases.

6.8 The same point applied to the other cases which came to our attention (and indeed, the indications from research, as Yaffé has pointed out, are that sex offenders have had less recent exposure to sexual material than other groups). Although there was on occasion some evidence of a link between an offence committed and a previous exposure—in the form of some common feature, for example—even this is no evidence that the link is a causal one: as one of our witnesses put it to us, to give a person who is predisposed to commit crime an idea of a particular way in which to do it is really very different from instilling the disposition in the first place. We discussed these matters with a number of psychiatrists and psychologists, including some with special experience of the treatment of offenders, but we were struck by the fact that none of them was able to tell us of a case of which they had experience in which there was evidence of a causal link between pornography and a violent sexual crime. None of our psychiatric or psychological witnesses in fact saw very great harm in straightforward sexual pornography, and some, indeed, felt that cases more frequently occurred in which the effects of pornography were beneficial rather than harmful. Dr P L G Gallwey of the Portman Clinic was one of these, stressing the sense of security that was sometimes generated, particularly through a lessening of the sense of exclusion and by assuaging the violent feelings associated with exclusion. Professor H J Eysenck of the Institute of Psychiatry, despite his serious reservations, which we will consider later, about violent matter, agreed that, depending on how it was portrayed, sexual material could reduce violent activity. Dr A Hyatt Williams of the Tavistock Clinic told us that his experience was that the outlet provided by pornography could prevent the commission of offences and that an offence could result if a person dependent on that kind of satisfaction were deprived of it. It was also widely agreed that if published pornography was not available, some people would simply produce it for themselves: Dr Gallwey, for example, showed us a highly pornographic and very disturbing story written by a young offender he had treated and cited to us another instance of a man using what materials were available to him in prison—even *The Farmers' Weekly*—to construct pornographic pictures.

6.9 This does not mean that no harm was seen in pornography. Dr Hyatt Williams, for example, was less concerned about the possibility of initial corruption than about the way in which certain patients might have their recovery impeded if they were again exposed to pornography and he made the point that dependence on pornography, even when it had a cathartic effect on those otherwise disposed to commit offences, masked the need for the person concerned to seek treatment which might provide a cure. Dr Gallwey, too, made the point that for some people on the edge of psychosis pornography served to weaken their grip on reality. Our witnesses emphasised to us, however, that it was only a very small minority of people who were likely to be affected in this way and there was a general reluctance to suggest that the balance of advantage lay in attempting to place more severe restrictions on pornography in order to safeguard them.

6.10 Clinical opinion and our impression of the anecdotal evidence cohere: the cases in which a link between pornography and crime has even been suggested are remarkably few. Given the amount of explicit sexual material in circulation and the allegations often made about its effects, it is striking that one can study case after case of sex crimes and murder without finding any hint at all that pornography was present in the background. What is also striking is that if one tried to eliminate the stimuli in published material which may have some relation to sexual deviation or the commission of offences, the net must be cast impossibly wide. As an illustration of this point, Dr Gallwey mentioned to us a patient who had killed himself in the course of his masochistic practices which had started when, as a disturbed child of only 8 or 9 years, he had been excited by coming across a picture of a woman bound to a stake. The protection of the young raises special considerations which we shall come to later, but even so it is clearly impossible to suppress pictures of Joan of Arc. A glance at the list of books found in the home of

Ian Brady, the Moors murderer, makes the same point. There are people who will gain a perverted satisfaction from reading accounts of Nazi atrocities or of other historical happenings, or even passages in the Bible, but publications cannot be suppressed on that account. All kinds of literature can have a destructive effect. The case of Goethe's *Sorrows of Young Werther*, which was said to have made suicide fashionable, is famous, but equally we heard of a romantic novel linked to the drowning of a teenage girl and of an Agatha Christie story linked to a real-life poisoning. There can be no question of suppressing such works. Art galleries cannot be closed to those who find excitement in paintings of barbarous acts or semi-clad women; nor can such people be kept away from beaches or be prevented from reading daily newspapers. For those who are susceptible to them, the stimuli are all around us; but the main point we wish to make from our study of the anecdotal and clinical evidence is that there is very little indication that pornography figures very significantly among these stimuli.

6.11 Our expert witnesses had more reservations about violent material, though again we heard no direct evidence of cases in which it was considered that crime had resulted from a particular stimulus. But both Professor Sir Martin Roth and Professor Trevor Gibbens told us that it was pornography with a violent content which concerned them most. Some cases were brought to our attention by other witnesses in which such effects were alleged to have occurred, and perhaps the chief object of such allegations was the film *A Clockwork Orange* which after its release early in 1972 was cited in a few court cases as the cause of real-life violence perpetrated by young men. The film was undoubtedly a powerful one and it seems clear that aspects of the film were deliberately copied by some youths who engaged in violence. Whether that violence occurred only because they had seen the film is of course more difficult to say and Mrs Mary Whitehouse, in the evidence submitted to us by the National Viewers' and Listeners' Association, was perhaps not on the strongest ground when she attacked the film principally on the basis of a case in which a 16 year old youth had brutally murdered a tramp: the youth concerned, though certainly fascinated by the story, had not in fact seen the film. (Since the film was classified as unsuitable for persons under 18 years, if he had seen it, he would not have done so legally.) We came across just three other cases in which *A Clockwork Orange* had been mentioned. Another film mentioned for its disturbing and anti-social effects was *The Exorcist*, and we read about two cases in which young men took their own lives (in only one of these was the link with the film very strong), and three other cases in which sexual offences or murder were associated with the film. The case involving murder, which was brought to our notice by the Nationwide Festival of Light, illustrates what we said earlier in this chapter about such films being made an excuse. The young man concerned had said that he had committed the offence while possessed by an evil spirit, after seeing the film *The Exorcist;* but it seems, from the press reports, that he admitted on the last day of his trial that he had simply made up this story after seeing a copy of the book in the police car. In the two other cases the film did not, even superficially, appear to be the dominant influence in the offences.

6.12 With respect to violence, the same point arises as before. The net would have to be cast very wide to prevent actual events from being influenced undesirably by what people see. It was, for example, a televised version of *The Brothers Karamazov* which was said to have influenced a young man to attempt to kill his parents with a meat cleaver in 1976, and it was the American television series *Roots* which was alleged to have prompted a Jamaican in London to rape a white woman, saying that he was going to treat her as white men had treated black women. While we have been preparing this report, the IRA have planted a bomb in a manner modelled on an incident in a television crime series; a 12 year boy has been reported as shooting himself in Detroit while playing Russian roulette after seeing *The Deer Hunter*; and an 8 year old girl has jumped from a second-floor landing in Barcelona after telling her playmates she was *Superman*.

Research studies

6.13 A great deal of research work—more in the United States than in this country—has been undertaken into the effects of exposure to pornographic or explicit sexual material or material having a violent content. Unfortunately, no very clear impression emerges from the results of this work and, as we shall see, even those who have surveyed it cannot always agree about the conclusions which can be drawn from it. We had available to us two reviews of the relevant literature, by Mr Maurice Yaffé on the effects of obscene material[1] and by Mr Stephen Brody on Screen Violence and Film Censorship[2]. Besides the general evidence which was put to us on these matters, we also had the advantage of discussing the lessons of work in this field, particularly in relation to violence, with two other authors who had made a study of it and published the results, Professor H J Eysenck[3] and Dr Guy Cumberbatch[4].

6.14 Some serious reservations inevitably attach to research in this field. There is the absolutely general point that correlation experiments in artificial conditions are regarded by many competent critics as an unilluminating and unreliable way of investigating complex behaviour, even in many other species, let alone in human beings. But further, more specific, criticisms apply in the case of the kinds of behaviour that are in question here. Since criminal and anti-social behaviour cannot itself, for both practical and ethical reasons, be experimentally produced or controlled, the observations must be made on some surrogate or related behaviour, often expressed on a representational object, in some fictional or "pretend" context. This feature of the work can come close, in some cases, to simply begging the question. The fundamental issue in this field concerns the relations that hold between the reactions aroused in a subject by a represented, artificial, or fantasy scene, and his behaviour in reality. Fantasy and reality, and their relations, are the basic categories of the question. We can only express surprise at the confidence that some

---

[1]Appendix V to *Pornography: The Longford Report*, Coronet Books, 1972 as updated by Mr Yaffé for our benefit.
[2]Home Office Research Study No 40, Her Majesty's Stationery Office, 1977.
[3]*Sex, Violence and the Media*, by H J Eysenck and D K B Nias, Temple Smith, 1978.
[4]*Mass Media Violence and Society*, by D Howitt and G Cumberbatch, Elek Science, 1975.

investigators have shown in supposing that they can investigate *this* problem through experimental set-ups in which reality is necessarily replaced by fantasy. Such criticisms apply, of course, to the whole investigation, not to a particular kind of result; they are equally relevant to those whose results, derived from this kind of experiment, are supposed to deny correlations between pictorial stimuli and real-life violence, and those whose results tend in the opposite direction.

6.15 Besides observations of behaviour under experimental conditions, which particularly apply to questions of violence, the evidence considered in relation to sexual material is, as Mr Yaffé points out, basically of three kinds: retrospective personal history studies of exposure to the material, self-reports before and after experimental exposure, and physiological and biochemical measures of change in response to experimental exposure. The reliability of studies which depend on retrospective surveys or self-supporting is notoriously suspect and this is particularly true where they touch on highly personal and value-laden subjects such as sexual behaviour.

6.16 Survey studies have included several which have asked varying samples of people such as young male offenders, sexual offenders and various other groups in the population about their exposure to pornography and their sexual behaviour and other factors. Many of these were undertaken for the United States Commission on Obscenity and Pornography and their interpretation, quite apart from the difficulty of deriving any lessons from them, has given rise to some controversy. We do not propose to discuss these studies in detail: a summary, and a citation of the original work, appears in Mr Yaffé's survey. We noted that the American Commission, in the light of all the studies undertaken for it, concluded that "empirical research has found no evidence to date that exposure to explicit sexual materials plays a significant role in the causation of delinquent or criminal behaviour among youth or adults"; we noted also that this conclusion was criticised in a number of quarters as having been based on a partial examination of the evidence in which ambiguities and certain contra-indications were ignored. Without ourselves entering into the controversy about the Commission's methods, we make the comment that the effect of re-examining the original studies in the light of a hostile critique of the Commission's conclusions, such as that put forward principally by Professor Victor Cline, is simply to make one adopt rather more caution in drawing inferences from the studies undertaken. It is still possible to say, as Mr Yaffé points out in his updated review, that there does not appear to be any strong evidence that exposure to sexually explicit material triggers off anti-social sexual behaviour. We would add only that this is consistent with what we learned from the clinical experience of those experienced medical witnesses we consulted.

6.17 Studies of the effects of violent material have concentrated on laboratory experiments, a method which has figured less in research into the anti-social effects of sexual material, though laboratory techniques have of course been used in studying sexual arousal generally. Studies using adults have concentrated on men but girls as well as boys have been studied in experiments using children. A considerable amount of work has been done in relation particularly to television violence, which was not of direct relevance to our review, but it was the view of our witnesses that many of the results of this work could be applied equally to films. In the case of sexual material, we encountered disagreement about the exact weight of the evidence for different conclusions; with regard to violent material, we met flatly opposing views.

6.18 In his review of the literature, Brody concluded that "it can be stated quite simply that social research has not been able unambiguously to offer any firm assurance that the mass media in general, and films and television in particular, either exercise a socially harmful effect, or that they do not". He went on:

> "The most reasonable interpretation of the considerable quantity of research results so far available would suggest that some people—particularly young people—may be inclined both to actual aggressiveness (however this is manifested, and not necessarily in criminal behaviour) and to a preference for entertainment dealing with aggressive themes, for reasons which probably originate with the development of personality and character; but that watching violent action on the screen is unlikely in itself to impel ordinary viewers to behave in ways they would otherwise not have done. Research into the causes of crime has repeatedly indicated the enormous variety of possible contributing factors, all of which overlap in complex ways and are quite unpredictable for any one individual; in all these studies, incidentally, the mass media have warranted scarcely a mention. That potentially violent or anti-social persons may find their own sentiments and dispositions confirmed and perhaps reinforced by television and films is not a consideration to be ignored, but it is in the amplification of existing tendencies that the main influence is likely to lie, not in the moulding of social behaviour.'

Howitt and Cumberbatch had fewer doubts as a result of their comprehensive survey of research which, they suggested, had "shown effectively that the mass media—as far as it is possible to tell using social scientific methodologies—do not serve to amplify the level of violence in society". Eysenck and Nias, on the other hand, though following a less thorough review of earlier studies, also showed few doubts but in the opposite sense: "the evidence is fairly unanimous that aggressive acts new to the subject's repertoire of responses, as well as acts already well established, can be evoked by the viewing of violent scenes portrayed on film, TV or in the theatre".

6.19 Such contradictions between investigators present a problem. We do not have the space to discuss in detail all the studies from which such different conclusions can be derived but it may be helpful to examine just one as an illustration of how conflicting views can arise, and of the limitations which, as we have already suggested, are inherent in these ways of investigating these questions. A common tool in studying imitative violence is the Bobo doll, an inflatable toy with a weighted base which resumes an upright position after being knocked over, and a number of studies have observed the reactions of children towards such a doll after they have seen an adult assaulting it. For example, in the earliest such study by Bandura and others in 1961, a number of children between 3 and 5 years were split into three groups, one of which was left in the presence of an adult model punching, kicking or striking with a mallet a Bobo doll, accompanied by aggressive cries of "Sock him . . . pow" etc, another was left in the presence of an adult who spent the time quietly assembling toys and the third group left to play by themselves, though in later experiments the children saw similar behaviour which had been filmed. When later given a chance to play with various toys, including a Bobo doll and a mallet, the group who had seen the adult assaulting the doll displayed similar aggressive tendencies to a much greater extent than the other groups. Eysenck and Nias simply record this result and the fact that similar studies have invariably found that children do tend to imitate an aggressive model when given the chance, and presumably notch it up among the "fairly unanimous" evidence to which they refer.

6.20 Both Brody and Howitt and Cumberbatch, on the hand, discuss the severe criticisms which have been made of such studies as the basis for applying notions of imitated violence to the real world outside the laboratory. Bobo dolls, it is pointed out, are designed to invite knocking about and to extrapolate to social behaviour the way in which a child plays with them is quite unwarranted. This objection relates to the point we have already made, that in studying this issue, the investigation of violence towards a fantasy or surrogate object such as a doll comes close to begging the question. Various other arguments about the many differences between the laboratory situation and real life have been put forward, which in Brody's view seriously undermine any attempts to apply research results to the claim that films promote aggressive or violent behaviour by imitation. Howitt and Cumberbatch point out in addition that Bandura's studies involve exposing children to fairly novel kinds of toys and that if the children have prior experience of Bobo dolls the amount of imitative violence is reduced. They also draw attention to the point that the children classified by their teachers as more aggressive might have been expected to attack the doll more readily than the others, if such behaviour was adequate as a predictor of real-life aggression: this was not so, and that fact, in their view, points away from the conclusion that the findings may be generalised to real life. Howitt and Cumberbatch, therefore, discount such experiments in considering a link between media violence and violence in society.

6.21 Eysenck and Nias do not so much dismiss these objections, as ignore them. They leave the unsuspecting reader ignorant that such substantial reservations have been widely voiced about the implications of these experimental studies, and this, in our view, diminishes the value of their work as a contribution to the scientific literature. Their book is indeed aimed more at the popular market, drawing partly on press reports to illustrate the alleged effects of media violence (including the now celebrated *Clockwork Orange* murder, but again omitting the information that the young murderer had not actually seen the film); but we thought it a pity that the lay reader should be presented so incautiously with only one side of the story. It seemed to us right to be sceptical about attempts to apply the lessons of these laboratory experiments to real life and we therefore preferred the more non-committal view taken, in particular, by Brody. We consider that the only objective verdict must be one of "not proven".

Analysis of crime statistics

6.22 Part of the basis for the conclusion reached by the United States Commission, which we have already mentioned, was a preliminary assessment of the trend in reported crime in Denmark following the liberalisation of the Danish laws on pornography in the late nineteen-sixties. The controversy surrounding the Commission prompted some people to question the thesis that the legalisation of pornography reduced the incidence of sex crimes in Denmark; and in time a contrary thesis emerged, that there is in fact statistical evidence indicating that the free availability of pornography can be linked to an increase in sexual offences. This is an argument which rests heavily on work undertaken by Dr John Court, Reader in Psychology at the Flinders University of South Australia, and Dr Court was good enough to submit to us several papers on the subject. The Nationwide Festival of Light and the National Viewers' and Listeners' Association urged us to pay special attention to Dr Court's work; and others with a more specialised interest in the field of human behaviour, such as Professor Sir Martin Roth and Professor H J Eysenck, made reference to Dr Court's work in the course of giving evidence to us.

6.23 It was clearly right that we should examine this evidence in some detail and we also think it right that we should discuss it in some detail here[1]. It has not so far been subjected to close scrutiny and we think it important that the public should have the opportunity to assess what it shows. The issue of whether people are more likely to be sexually assaulted as a result of the circulation of certain kinds of publication or the showing of certain kinds of film is obviously a very important one. But we would not want to give the impression, by dealing with the issue at considerable length, that we think that it is the only or the decisive issue. We shall come in due course to other kinds of consideration, including other concepts of harm which have been put to us, and these are also important. A special feature of the argument about porngraphy and sex crimes is that the effects that have been suggested here are claimed to be statistically measurable.

6.24 But are they measurable? Here there are several sets of problems. The first set concerns the number of offences. Certainly we have detailed information about the number of sexual offences reported to the police over a long period. However, this is not the same as knowing how many offences occurred, since there is no means of telling how many victims decided not to go to the police to report what happened. It is often suggested that rape and sexual offences are peculiarly prone to non-reporting because victims often prefer to avoid the prolongation and reinforcement of the distress they have suffered which may result from questioning by the police and the giving of evidence and cross-examination at a trial. We cannot be sure, therefore, how many offences have been committed or what proportion never come to light. The particular difficulty in examining trends in offences is that there is no way of knowing whether the unreported proportion of offences is remaining constant—in which case the trend can accurately be assessed even though the

---

[1]We received assistance in analysing the statistics and the arguments based on them from the Home Office Research Unit, in particular in a paper prepared by Mr Stephen Brody.

incidence of offences is not fully known—or whether fluctuations are occurring in the proportion that are not reported: victims may at different times be more or less ready to report offences, because of changing social attitudes, or because of changes in the law or legal procedure or police practice.

6.25 It follows that even apparently detailed information about the number of offences reported to the police gives an imperfect picture of the number of such offences; it may not even reveal whether, or by how much, the number is increasing or decreasing from year to year. The problem gets worse if one tries to make international comparisons. Legal systems vary considerably between countries and differences in what constitutes a criminal offence—and what name is given to it—often mean that comparisons which seem straightforward are not in fact comparing like with like. Moreover, the form and reliability of criminal statistics varies widely from country to country. Finally, it is all too easy to look at statistics in isolation from the procedures and social climate in the country concerned which may affect, for example, the readiness of victims to report offences.

6.26 The second set of difficulties concerns the other side of the correlation: the availability of pornography. The imperfections of the information about the incidence of sexual offences are insignificant compared with the lack of information about the availability of pornography. There are two kinds of problems here. One relates simply to the quantity of pornography available, about which there is very little reliable information. The second raises the question of what kind of material we should consider for these purposes as pornography, and whether the differences between different kinds or degrees of pornography are likely to produce different effects, and so should be taken into account in trying to make correlations with the incidence of sexual offences.

6.27 Much of the evidence we received assumed that pornography had worse effects, the more extreme it was. Thus, mild pornography consisting of little more than "pin-up" pictures is often regarded as harmless, while the strongest and most explicit material is commonly regarded as the most corrupting. Yet in considering a hypothesis that sexual offences are linked to the widespread availability of pornography, it is not obvious, on reflection, that hard-core pornography should lead to the commission of offences in a way that soft pornography does not. Indeed, many people might think that if a potential sex offender were going to be triggered off by something he saw, that effect would be produced at least as well if not better by the titillating and erotically arousing than by the clinical close-up. So how should one set about quantifying pornography? How should an index of availability reflect changes in the type of material over a period of time? How should one compare one country where soft pornography is widely available, but hard-core material is banned, with another where hard-core pornography is available for anyone who wants it but where pornography generally appears to be less pervasive?

6.28 These difficulties seem to us very real, and it is a severe shortcoming of much of the work which has been put to us that the sometimes detailed study of criminal statistics is accompanied by only the most generalised and unsupported statements about the availability of pornography. If no measures exist for what is supposed to be the causal factor, it is impossible to make any progress in attempting to relate cause to effect.

6.29 The relation of cause to effect brings in the third, central, and best-known, problem. Even if it is possible to provide an accurate measure of two variables, the existence of a correlation between them is certainly no proof that one is influenced by the other. The causes of crime are undoubtedly complex and elude isolation. Many factors are at work and much stronger indications than a mere correlation between variables are necessary before the existence of a causal link can even be suggested, let alone proved. The difficulties of proving or even plausibly arguing for, causal relationships between general or diffuse social phenomena on a purely statistical basis are sufficiently well-recognised for us not to need to dwell on them further.

England and Wales

6.30 Having drawn attention to the general considerations which limit both the available information and the inferences which can be derived from it, we should nevertheless look at some of the information which exists and examine what our witnesses said about it. It is natural that we should start at home.

6.31 First, in relation to the availability of pornography in England and Wales, it needs to be said that no information exists to provide any kind of index. In the papers submitted to us, Dr Court did not attempt to provide such information. He does however treat Britain as an example of a "liberal" country in which the detrimental effects of pornography are to be seen, and he identifies two times at which, he suggests, pornography became increasingly available—first with a change in the law introduced by the Obscene Publications Act of 1964, and subsequently following the impetus of the American Commission Report on Pornography in 1970. Dr Court offers nothing to substantiate his statement and we find his explanation of the significance of these two dates less than convincing. As we have explained earlier, the Obscene Publications Act 1964 was a minor measure designed to strengthen the existing law by plugging two loopholes which had been found in the Act of five years previously. Dr Court cites as the only authority for his suggestion that pornography became more available after the enactment of the 1964 Act as an article by Mr Ronald Butt in *The Times* on 5 February 1976 which attacked what Mr Butt then found to be the ineffectiveness of the law in controlling pornography. Mr Butt argued that the intention of the 1959 and 1964 Acts had been systematically destroyed over the years by the exploitation of their letter, but nothing in his article supports the idea that the 1964 Act opened the way to the greater availability of pornography. Nor do we know of any authority for the suggestion that pornography became more freely available here after 1970 as a result of the influence of the Report of the US Commission. It seems to us that the choice of the years 1964 and 1970 as crucial in the increasing availability of pornography is purely arbitrary.

6.32 Our own enquiries have not placed us in a very much better position to assess the availability of pornography over a period of time. It is the experience of all of us that for very many years there has been a steady trend towards greater frankness in sexual matters and greater tolerance of the portrayal of nudity and sexual activity. This has been reflected in a wide variety of publications and films, including those which many people would regard as pornographic, but it does not help us to construct any kind of index with which to compare changes in the numbers of sexual offences. The Head of the Obscene Publications Squad of the Metropolitan Police told us that police activity in the last six years or so had resulted in a considerable reduction in the amount of hard-core pornography from overseas in circulation, at least in London, though the police were unable to quantify the amounts concerned. The same period, however, has seen a considerable increase in the publication of British magazines with an explicit sexual content which, particularly in the years 1975 to 1977, moved very quickly to adopt a character much less restrained than had previously been acceptable. These magazines were distributed throughout the country and clearly reached a much wider audience than the undercover trade in overseas pornography ever had; it was suggested to us by some witnesses that if sexual offences were indeed linked to pornography, a noticeable effect should have occurred over the last five years. However, as we have described in Chapter 4, there are indications that the circulation of these magazines reached a peak in 1976 and has subsequently suffered a decline, aided by increasing police action against publishers from early in 1977 and, in London, against retailers from early in 1978. The managing director of the largest publisher in this field stated in the trade press in June 1978, and confirmed in correspondence with us, that the effect of this action had been to reduce the sales of his magazines by 40 per cent. in the first quarter of 1978.

6.33 With that patently inadequate basis for assessing the availability of pornography, let us nevertheless turn to the information available about the incidence of sexual offences. Figure 1 shows the numbers of indictable sexual offences reported to the police in every year since 1946. This gives a longer perspective than Dr Court has offered and enables the point to be made that sexual offences (or reports of such offences) were significantly increasing long before pornography is alleged to have become more widely available and well before the "ineffective" Acts of 1959 and 1964 had a chance to exercise their influence. Indeed, it would appear that the number of reported offences levelled off between 1959 and 1966; though if the figures for 1964 to 1970 are taken in isolation, an increase becomes noticeable, even if it is less marked than that in the period 1946 to 1959. But what is perhaps even more significant is the trend since 1973: until the increase last year, there had been a steady fall in the number of sexual offences known to the police. In the light of the suggestion we reported in the preceding paragraph, this should be interesting to those who are impressed by such correlations: a period of apparently rapid increase in the availability of pornography seems to have been accompanied by a reduction in the number of sexual offences reported, which was reversed in the year in which increased police activity reportedly reduced the availability of sex magazines.

6.34 We have also used Figure 1 to make another point of some substance, which is that it is futile to seek to examine one class of offence in isolation from the trend in crime generally. In our society, as in others throughout

FIGURE 1: INDICTABLE OFFENCES RECORDED BY THE POLICE (ENGLAND AND WALES) 1946-1978

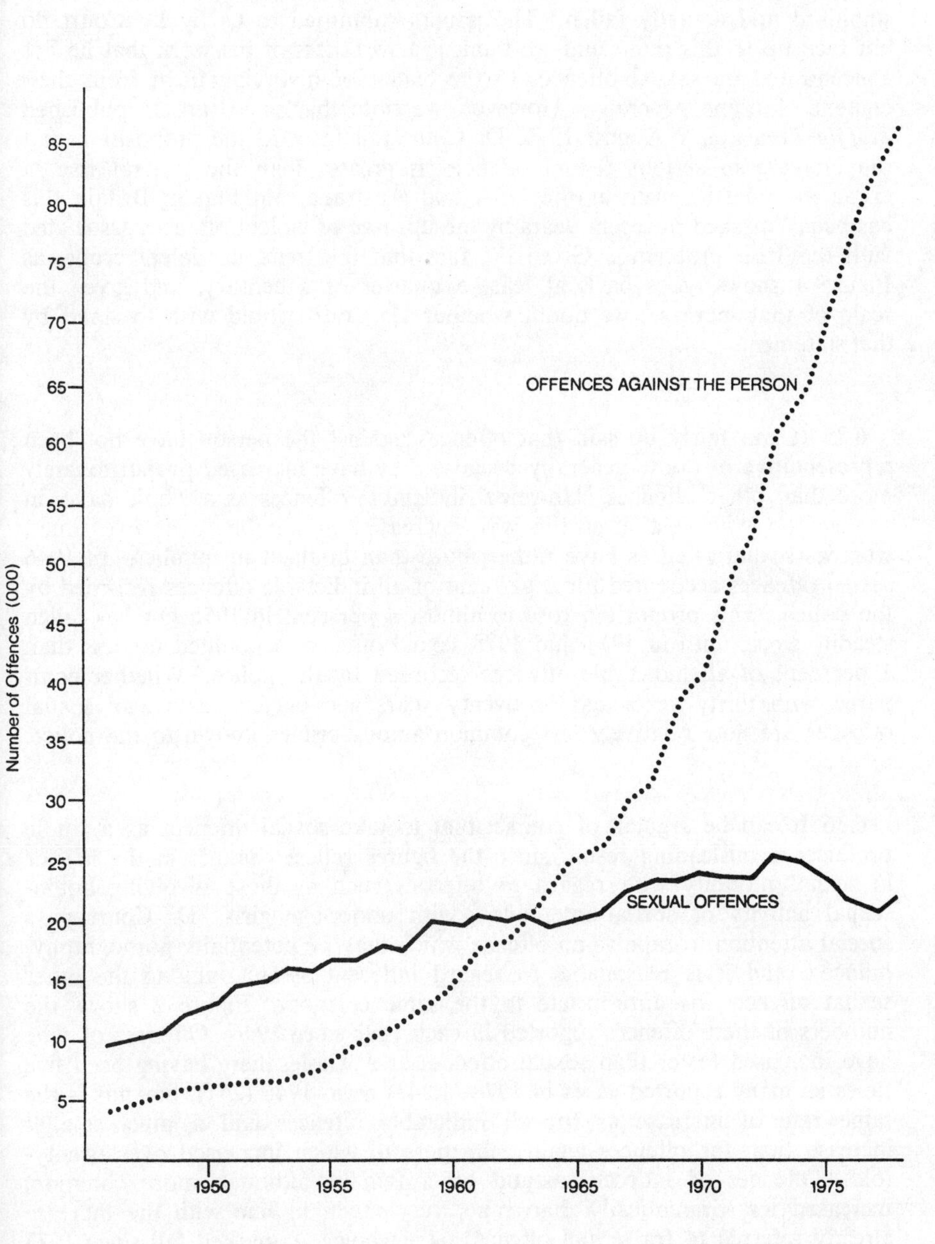

the world, rising crime has been a matter of much concern for many years and it is pointless to seek a special explanation for a rising trend in sexual offences if that trend merely reflects an increase in the general level of offences. But is that the case? In fact it is not, because sexual offences seem to have been significantly out of step with other offences, in that they have not shown anywhere near the same increase in numbers over the years. This is shown dramatically in Figure 1 by comparison with offences against the person, which have continued to rise steeply when sexual offences have stabilised and actually fallen. The papers submitted to us by Dr Court do not face up to this point and we think it a weakness of his work that he has concentrated on sexual offences to the extent of divorcing them from their context of crime generally. However, we note that in an article published in *The Times* on 7 August 1976, Dr Court put forward the proposition that the increase in serious sexual offences is greater than the general rise in crime in countries such as the USA and Australia, but that in Britain this has been "masked in recent years by the upsurge of violent offences associated with the Irish problem". Given the fact that the trend in violent crime, as Figure 1 shows, goes back at least a quarter of a century, and given the scale of that increase, we doubt whether Dr Court would wish to stand by that statement.

6.35 It can fairly be said that offences against the person have not been representative of crime generally because they have increased proportionately more than other offences. However, indictable offences as a whole have, in comparison with just after the war, increased in number over five times, whereas sexual offences have rather more than doubled in number. In 1946 sexual offences accounted for 2 per cent of all indictable offences recorded by the police. This proportion rose to almost 4 per cent in 1955 but has fallen steadily since, until in 1977 and 1978 sexual offences accounted for less than 1 per cent of all indictable offences recorded by the police. Whether compared with thirty years ago or twenty years ago or ten years ago, sexual offences are now relatively less common among crimes known to the police.

6.36 It can be argued, of course, that to take sexual offences as a whole produces a misleading result, since the figures reflect changes in the law or in sexual morality with regard to offences such as those involving homosexual activity or sexual intercourse with under-age girls. Dr Court pays special attention to rape as an offence which may be potentially pornography-induced, and it is reasonable to regard indecent assault, among the other sexual offences, as appropriate to the same category. Figure 2 shows the numbers of these offences reported in each year since 1946. Offences of rape have increased faster than sexual offences as a whole, there having been five times as many reported cases in 1978 (1,243) as in 1946 (251), but this is the same rate of increase as for all indictable offences and a much smaller increase than for offences against the person, which increased over twenty-fold. Offences of indecent assault on a female, although more common, increased less dramatically than rape, very much in line with the increase already referred to for sexual offences as a whole. A marked fall since 1973

FIGURE 2: OFFENCES OF RAPE, SEXUAL ASSAULT AND ROBBERY RECORDED BY THE POLICE (ENGLAND AND WALES) 1946-1978

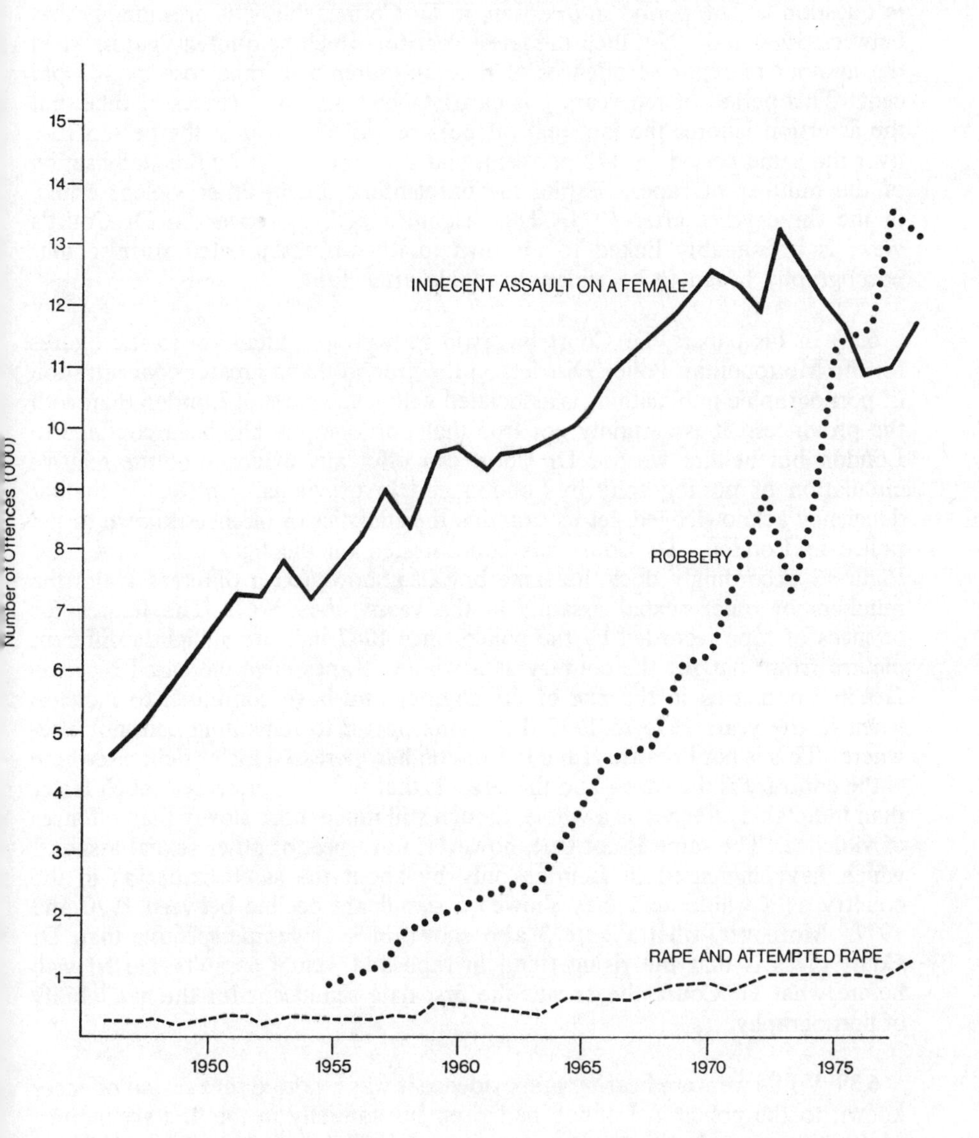

has been reversed in the last two years. As with Figure 1, Figure 2 also shows how the trend for another offence of the same order of frequency, robbery, is in contrast to that for the sexual offences examined.

6.37 Dr Court did not devote much attention to the situation in England and Wales. Yet he confidently observed in a published paper that "highly significant increases are apparent for rape and attempted rape for the period in question". The period in question, in Dr Court's thesis, is presumably that between 1964 and 1974, then the latest year for which he quoted figures, when the number of reported offences of rape and attempted rape rose by 103 per cent. This period of ten years was clearly a bad one for offences of rape, but the assertion ignores the fact that offences of violence against the person rose over the same period by 172 per cent, and it is not helped by the stabilisation of the number of rapes, despite the unrelenting rise in other violent crime, in the three years after 1974. The "significance", moreover, in Dr Court's view, is presumably linked to his own totally unsubstantiated surmise that pornography began to be widely available after 1964.

6.38 In his papers, Dr Court has paid rather more attention to the figures for the Metropolitan Police District, on the ground that a greater concentration of pornographic publications is associated with some parts of London than with the provinces. It is certainly not true that pornography has been confined to London but neither we nor Dr Court can offer any evidence of the relative circulation of pornography in London and in provincial centres. With that deficiency acknowledged, let us examine the statistics of offences known to the police in London. Dr Court has concentrated on the figures for rape, and Figure 3 accordingly does the same but also shows (on a different scale) the numbers of other sexual assaults in the years since 1947. The figures for offences of rape recorded by the police since 1947 indicate a slightly different picture from that for the country as a whole. Rapes have increased twice as fast in London as in the rest of the country and have continued to increase when in the years 1975 to 1977 they came nearer to remaining constant elsewhere. This is not because crime in London has increased faster than elsewhere—the contrary is the case—and the effect is that rape has increased much faster than indictable offences as a whole, though still much more slowly than offences of violence. The same is not true, however, in respect of other sexual assaults, which have increased in London only by about the same extent as in the country as a whole, and they showed a significant decline between 1970 and 1977. Moreover, what Figure 3 also shows in a longer perspective than Dr Court gives is that the rising trend in rape and sexual assaults started well before what Dr Court alleges was the first date significant for the availability of pornography.

6.39 While we were hearing oral evidence it was reported that sexual offences known to the police in London had risen substantially in the first six months of 1978 compared with the same period of 1977 (rapes from 75 to 122 and sexual assaults from 550 to 741). These reports prompted some of our witnesses to draw the conclusion that the rise was linked to the onset of a more active enforcement policy in the Metropolitan area, in which, from the beginning of February 1978, scores of raids on retailers by divisional police officers had

FIGURE 3: OFFENCES OF RAPE AND SEXUAL ASSAULT RECORDED BY THE POLICE (METROPOLITAN POLICE DISTRICT) 1947–1978

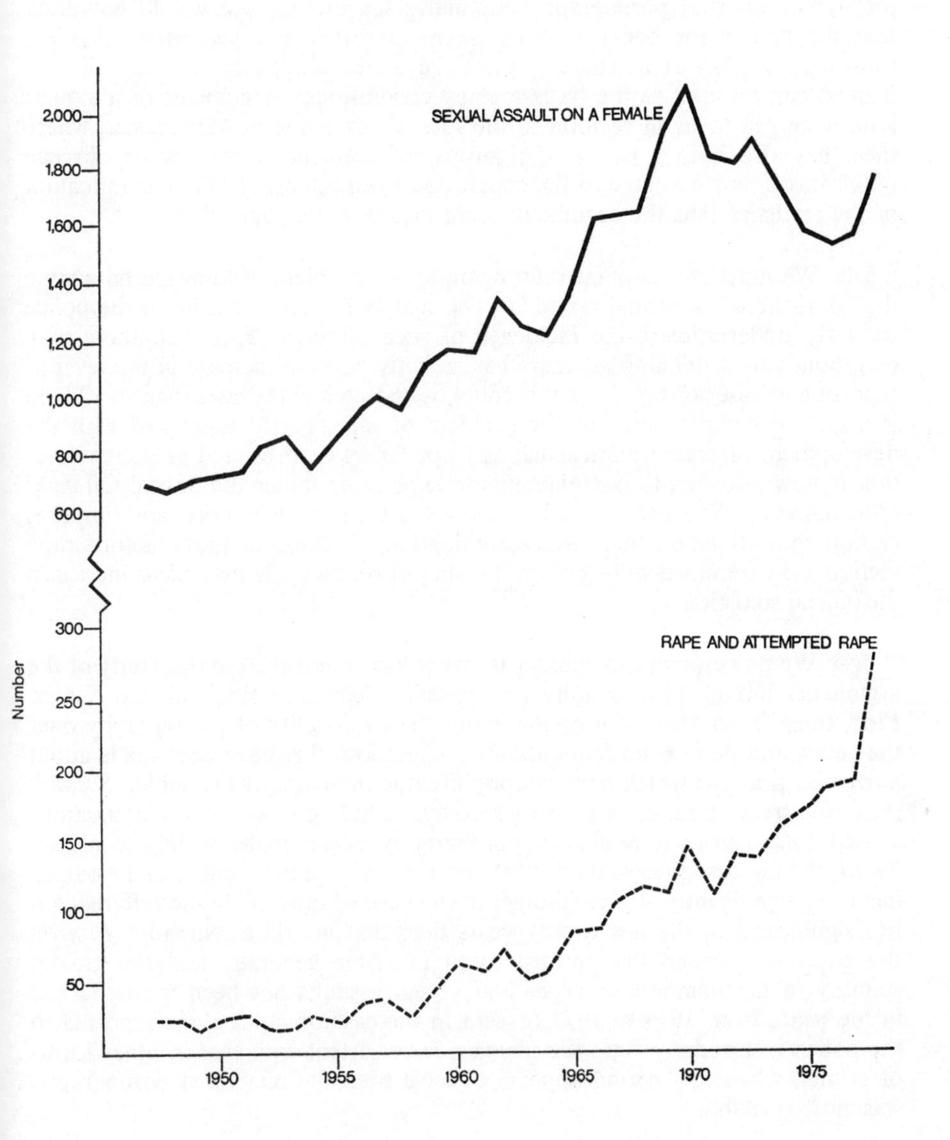

significantly reduced the amount of pornography available in London (we have already reported one publisher's statement of the effect on his sales). A reduction in sexual assaults during a period when pornography is widely available, followed by an increase when curbs are placed on the trade, hardly bears out the hypothesis that pornography stimulates sex crimes; but we do not think that the figures for one period of six months or for a year (now that the statistics for 1978 as a whole confirm the increase apparent in the half-year figures) can be used as the basis for any conclusions. Arguments of a similar kind were put to us in relation to the rate of sex crime in Manchester, where there has also been a policy of rigorous enforcement of the law on obscene publications, but we came to the conclusion from a more detailed examination of the statistics that the arguments were insufficiently supported.

6.40 We must at this point refer again to the problem of knowing how large the "dark area" of sexual crime is. The figures for rapes known to the police certainly underestimate the incidence of such offences. However, there may be grounds for thinking that there has recently been an increase in the level of reporting of cases of rape, and this could be reflected in the latest figures. There is a greater consciousness of the problem of rape, partly associated with the development of organisations such as Rape Crisis Centres, and greater protection is now afforded to complainants in rape cases under the Sexual Offences (Amendment) Act 1976 (which provides for their anonymity and imposes certain restrictions on their cross-examination); because of these factors, rape victims may be more willing to go to the police, and this may have increased the official statistics.

6.41 We now attempt to summarise what has emerged from this study of the arguments linking pornography and sexual offences in England and Wales. *First*, there is no firm information about the availability of pornography over the years, and there is no foundation to suggestions that have been made about particular times at which pornography became increasingly available. *Second*, the rising trend in sexual offences generally, including rape and sexual assaults, started long before it is alleged pornography began to be widely available. *Third*, the increase in sexual offences generally, and in rape and sexual assaults, has been significantly slower (though in the case of rape alone the difference is less significant) in the last twenty years than that in crime generally. *Fourth*, the contrast between the upward trend in crime generally and the greater stability in the numbers of rapes and sexual assaults has been most marked in the years from 1973 to 1977 (except in the case of rapes alone reported to the police in London where the increase is consistent with that in other forms of crime), when this period appears to have been the one when pornography was most available.

6.42 So, what conclusions can be drawn? We have already referred briefly to the extreme difficulty of identifying causal factors in the incidence of crime but, in the light of the findings we have set out above, we see no need to develop that argument. The case put to us by Dr Court, and by other witnesses who have looked to Dr Court's work for support, cannot on the basis of the situation in England and Wales, we believe, even survive as a plausible hypothesis. Each of the findings in the preceding paragraph stands opposed to it. Consider

FIGURE 4: RAPE AND SEXUAL ASSAULT AS A PROPORTION OF INDICTABLE OFFENCES RECORDED BY THE POLICE

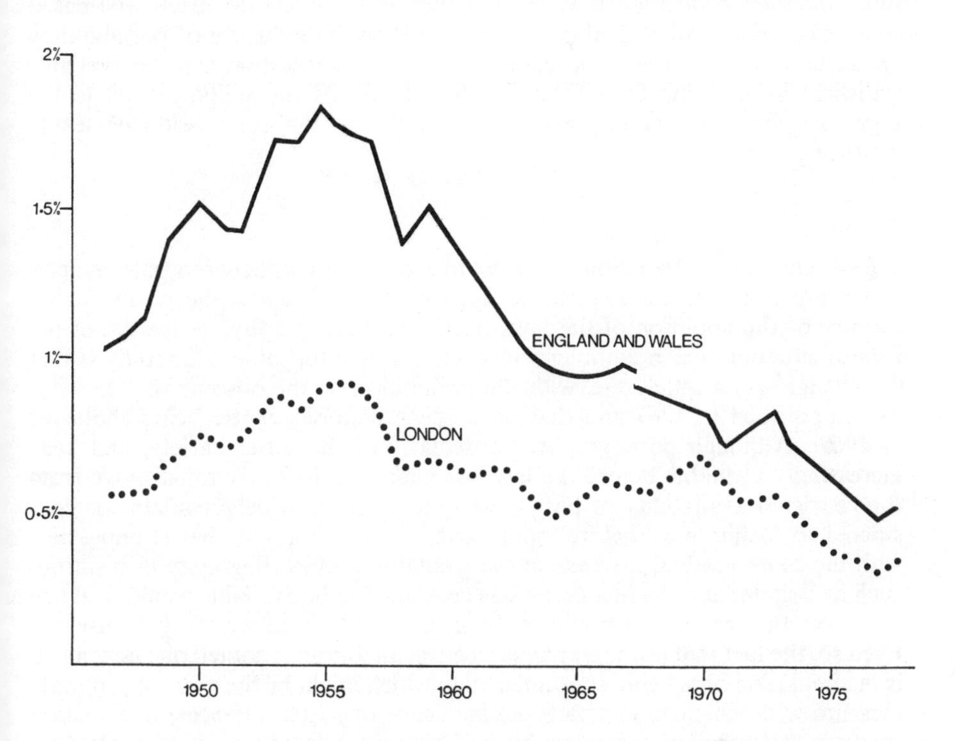

Figure 4, which shows the relative importance of the numbers of rapes and sexual assaults in the totality of crime. We think it unlikely that any fair-minded person would, on the basis of the information depicted in that graph, feel the need to construct a special hypothesis to explain the increase in sex crimes, still less that the hypothesis constructed would be that an alleged increase in the availability of pornography first after 1964 and secondly since 1970 (increases for which there is no independent evidence) provided a crucial influence in the growth in such offences.

6.43 We are not denying the possibility that pornography could be linked to the commission of sexual offences. Nor are we suggesting, on the other hand, as the data in Figure 4 encourage some to suggest, that the availability of pornography is associated actually with a decline (or at any rate a reduction in the rate of rise) in sexual offences. It might be, for example, that if only information were available about the amount of pornography in circulation some kind of correlation might be possible; it might be that whatever the factors are which have given rise to the substantial increases in most other forms of crime, they do not operate in respect of sexual offences and therefore some other separate explanation of the more modest growth in sexual crime has to be sought; it might be that there has been a substantial reduction in the willingness of victims of rape and sexual assault to complain to the police, so that the true number of offences, and the trend, is quite different from what appears in the criminal statistics. These are, we say, possible: but we do not think they are probable. It is not possible, in our view, to reach well-based conclusions about what in this country has been the influence of pornography on sexual crime. But we unhesitatingly reject the suggestion that the available statistical information for England and Wales lends any support at all to the argument that pornography acts as a stimulus to the commission of sexual violence.

Denmark

6.44 The main international interest in a possible link between pornography and sex crimes has centred on Denmark and on what was the result in that country of the abolition of the laws restricting pornography. A feature of the Danish situation which is thought to make it a helpful subject for study is that the change was a quick one, with the prohibition on the obscene written word being abolished in 1967 and that on obscene pictorial matter being abolished in 1969. Although pornography, particularly of the softer variety, had been increasingly available before the law was changed, the fairly rapid move from the restricted availability of pornography to its being widely available, is considered to facilitate a "before" and "after" study in a way that is impossible with the more gradual increase in the availability of pornography in countries such as Britain; and the fact that it has continued to be available would lead one to expect that any adverse effects there might be would manifest themselves. Even so, the fact that pornography is freely available does not tell one how much is in circulation or is being consumed, data which might be the more appropriate measure with which to compare the incidence of sexual offences; information suggests that sales of pornography in Denmark slumped drastically after an initial boom which accompanied the removal of legal restrictions. Nevertheless, it is reasonable to assume that one is in a better position in the case of Denmark to provide an index of the availability of pornography than one is in the case of England and Wales.

6.45 There has grown up something of a folk myth about the effect of the Danish liberalisation on the incidence of sexual offences. This may have resulted from the general way in which studies of the Danish situation were reported, before the studies themselves became available, in the Report of the United States Commission on Obscenity and Pornography in 1970. It is often said, and it was said to us, that the freeing of pornography in Denmark resulted in a decline in sexual offences, but this kind of unguarded statement is very vulnerable to attack. Authoritative claims about the Danish experience are a good deal more limited. The most detailed work has been undertaken by Dr Berl Kutchinsky of the Institute of Criminal Science at the University of Copenhagen, a preliminary study by him having been commissioned by the United States Commission in 1969. That study permitted only first impressions to be given of the results of the changes made in 1967 and 1969, though we think it right to make the point that even Dr Court, who has sought to detract from Dr Kutchinsky's work, made it clear to us that he regards those reports as careful, detailed and appropriately cautious about the conclusions which might be drawn. Dr Kutchinsky has continued his work since 1970, and we had the opportunity of discussing it with him, but the more detailed assessment he has been preparing of the effect of Denmark's legal changes on the incidence of sexual offences has not yet been published. This means that most of the debate has so far been based either on a thorough study of statistics up to 1970 or on a more superficial examination of statistics since that date.

6.46 It is useful first to identify some of the problems involved in making comparisons. First, various changes were made to the Danish law on sexual offences at about the same time that pornography was legalised; this has led Mrs Mary Whitehouse to make the point that of course sex crimes will diminish very significantly if eleven categories of sex crime are removed from the statute book. Dr Court makes a similar point in a more discreet way by suggesting that "some of Kutchinsky's data apparently were influenced by legislative changes", while admitting that "it is true to say that the reported decline does not arise from legislative change". Dr Kutchinsky assured us that he had been most careful in excluding from his figures any offence in respect of which any liberalisation had occurred, in order to avoid the obvious pitfall identified by Mrs Whitehouse. There are of course other disadvantages in leaving out of account offences in respect of which there have been legal changes, since it can be suggested (as by Dr Court) that this itself may lead to serious effects being masked; but there is really no alternative, from the methodological point of view, to omitting figures for offences where there can be no proper comparability.

6.47 Second, it can be suggested that there has been an alteration in the rate of reporting of certain offences because of the different atmosphere itself partly caused by changes in the law. Dr Kutchinsky has recognised this possibility and Dr Court has commented that he has made a commendable attempt to measure changes in the readiness to report offences. Part of Dr Kutchinsky's study has been of public attitudes towards the criminality of certain acts, which, for example, demonstrated a generation shift in attitude towards physical indecency with women, but no similar change in attitude towards the molestation of children. A study was also made of the relative seriousness of reported offences, the detailed results of which indicated that for such offences as physical indecency with women the less serious offences were now much less likely to be considered worth reporting, while there had been no similar change in the seriousness of the reported offences of molesting children. Dr. Kutchinsky's conclusion from this is that a drop in the number of reported assaults on women is at least partly explained by the fact that fewer women bother to report them, but that, with regard to sexual offences against children, the fall in the number reported to the police does in fact represent a falling-off in the number of such offences actually committed.

6.48 It seemed to us, however, that there was still a need for caution in interpreting these findings. Another factor, for example, to affect the rate of reporting of offences against children might be a growing belief that a child could be further harmed by the court procedures involved. This factor might affect the reporting of offences of all degrees of gravity, and if so, would not be reflected in any changes in the seriousness of reported offences. Dr Kutchinsky's extensive studies do go some way to meet this point: they include a survey of attitudes towards readiness to report, which appears to show that this factor was of some effect, but that the decrease in readiness to report offences against children was less, relatively, than it was with other offences studied.

6.49 According to Dr Kutchinsky, the incidence of reported sex offences before the liberalisation of pornography had remained steady for twenty years, at about 85 cases per annum per 100,000 of the population. In 1967 this dropped to 67 and continued to fall to a level of about 40. This was very much an urban phenomenon, offences in the capital having decreased by 75–80% compared with very little change in the already lower level in rural areas. Ordinary heterosexual crimes unaffected by changes in the law dropped consistently, most noticeably after 1966, from just over 100 per 100,000 to less than 30 in 1973, and then levelled off.

6.50 This overall trend, however, conceals a variety of changes in relation to particular types of offence, and it is more instructive to examine what happened to different types. Dr Court has, as in respect of other countries, concentrated on rape. Figure 5 shows offences of rape and attempted rape reported to the police in Copenhagen, based both on figures for the years since

FIGURE 5: RAPE AND ATTEMPTED RAPE REPORTED TO THE POLICE IN COPENHAGEN

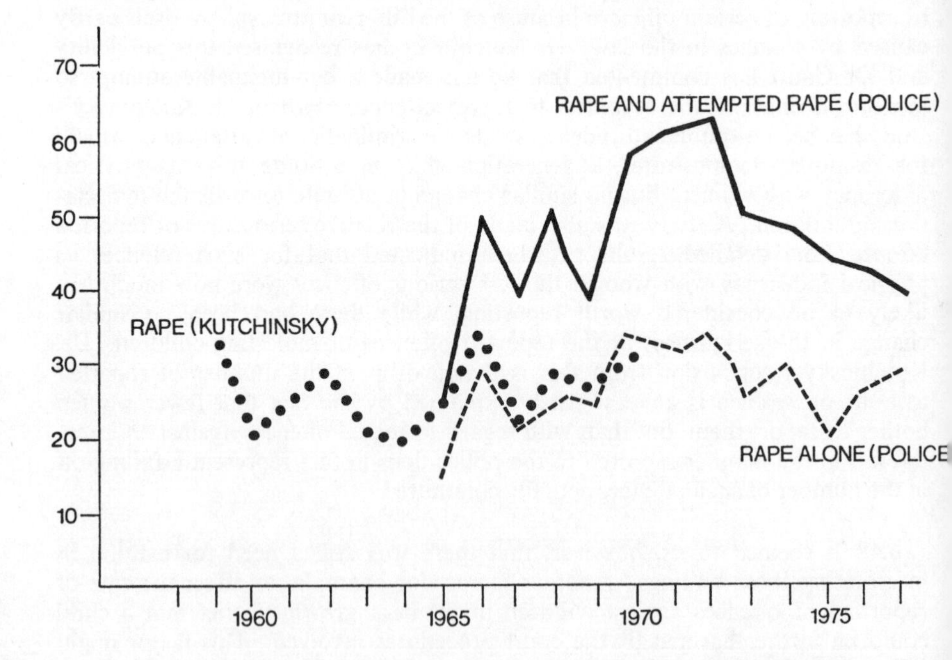

1965 given to us by the Police Commissioner for Copenhagen, and on figures published by Dr Kutchinsky in 1973. Even these are not the only figures which have been quoted, and Dr Court has commented that the incidence of rape in Copenhagen over the past 15 years is more difficult to establish than might be supposed. The variation evident in Figure 5 arises from reservations which Dr Kutchinsky has had about the recording practice of the police. His workers have examined police records to reassess against agreed criteria the nature of every reported case, including those where complaints had been withdrawn or where the police had decided that no offence had been committed. As a result, Dr Kutchinsky has a statistical record of sexual offences which differs from that issued by the police, but which he regards as more accurate and reliable. This explains the discrepancy in the figures up to 1970 which Dr Kutchinsky has already published, and which he will be bringing up to date when he publishes his forthcoming book.

6.51 Whichever set of figures is regarded as the more reliable, it is impossible to discern a significant trend in rape which could be linked in any way with the free availability of pornography since the late nineteen-sixties. Dr Kutchinsky emphasises that he has never suggested that such a link exists, and said to us that be believed that the availability of pornography had not affected the incidence of rape, one way or the other. Dr Court sees the figures as evidence that generalised statements about the "sudden fall-off in sex crimes" are based on an illusion; but he has gone further, and, lacking the figures for recent years which we have included in Figure 5, has stated that by 1974 at least "the trend towards an increase in reports of rape and attempted rape was clear"—a statement which he has not supported with figures. Figures for the years since 1972 show that there is in fact no such trend, and although Figure 5 stands as a reproof to those who have drawn a conclusion that serious sex crimes have declined since pornography became widely available in Denmark, it certainly provides no support at all for the thesis put to us by Dr Court.

6.52 Dr Kutchinsky has made a particular study of four types of offences which were among those showing the largest decline in numbers since 1965. These are: peeping, exhibitionism, indecent assaults on women and indecent assaults on young girls. The preliminary conclusions which Dr Kutchinsky reported to the United States Commission—which he emphasised to be only tentative—were that changes in the readiness of women to report sexual assaults were apparently large enough to account for the decrease in reported offences of that type during the nineteen-sixties; that the reduction in reported cases of indecent exposure could also be explained by a decrease in readiness to report, but that this reduction seemed to parallel more closely the availability of pornography, something which might possibly be explained by the effect of pornography having been that fewer women were so shocked by real-life exposure as to think it worth reporting; and that the reduction in reported cases of peeping and of indecent assaults on children could not be explained by lower reporting rates, but reflected an actual drop in the number of such offences committed, and that this could be tentatively explained by the effect of pornography being available.

6.53 Since peeping does not even constitute an offence in England and Wales (those indulging in the practice are sometimes bound over to be of good behaviour), the most significant of these tentative findings for us is that concerning offences against children. We discussed it with Dr Kutchinsky who confirmed that his later work has supported his view that there has been a real and significant reduction in indecent assaults on female children, and that this very closely correlated with the availability of pornography. The dramatic reduction of two-thirds in the number of sex offences against children between 1967 and 1969 was difficult to explain other than in relation to the availability of pornography, and it was also notable that 1973 was the last year in which a significant increase occurred in the availability of child pornography, and was also the year after which the drop in offences levelled off.

6.54 In looking for an explanation of this perceived relationship, Dr Kutchinsky suggests that the literature concerning this type of offender indicates that those who interfere with children typically do so not because they are irresistibly attracted to children, but as a substitute for a preferred relationship with a woman which they find difficult to achieve; but if there is another substitute available in the form of pornography, then that serves the purpose just as well. The fact that the reduction was most significant in offences involving younger children and less so in relation to more "normal" offences against older girls supported the hypothesis.

6.55 We find it difficult to draw any firm conclusions about these more specific matters. While we were impressed by the thoroughness with which Dr Kutchinsky had studied the situation and the restraint with which he sought to derive lessons from his findings, the fact remains that correlation studies are a weak research tool, partly because of the difficulties of measurement—which still exist in relation to both the availability of pornography and the incidence of offences in Denmark, in spite of Dr Kutchinsky's considerable efforts to overcome them—and partly because of the impossibility of translating a correlation into cause and effect. A common explanation of a correlation between two sets of social data is that each is affected by some third, possibly unknown, factor and no matter how strong a correlation, it can never, bearing in mind all the other factors and influences that are also present, "prove" anything. We recognise, however, that Dr Kutchinsky has identified a very dramatic reduction in reported offences against children which coincided with the sudden upsurge in the availability of pornography and which, in consequence of the careful studies undertaken by Dr Kutchinsky, cannot readily be explained by any other likely factor. While Dr Kutchinsky's explanation cannot be conclusive, we have to admit that it is plausible.

6.56 Dr Court has not commented at all on this finding of Dr Kutchinsky, other than in making general criticisms of Dr Kutchinsky's work, some of which are patently mistaken and others apparently unjust, and in stressing that a direct causal relationship, given the nature of the problem, could never be demonstrated. It seemed to us that because the Danish experience is in Dr Court's description "counter-intuitive", his faith in his intuition has led him to the view that it "must be assumed to be false". In these circumstances he has sought to cast as much doubt as he can on the findings, even when that has meant attacking secondary reporting rather than the original work, persisting in allegations of error which we were assured he had been told were false, quoting polemicists as if they were scientific sources, and resorting to a general broadside on Dr Kutchinsky's figures as being "utterly misleading". We have examined with some care the work of both Dr Kutchinsky and Dr Court in relation to the situation in Denmark and have to say that Dr Kutchinsky's is in every respect more impressive: it is comprehensive, detailed and scrupulously careful. Dr Court has made no pretensions to a study of equal thoroughness and, having looked at each of the points he has made about Dr Kutchinsky's work, we find that the one to which most weight attaches concerns just the absolutely general difficulty of trying to draw conclusions from the examination of statistics of this kind. However, the conclusion which is inevitable from reading the voluminous papers by Dr Court and Dr Kutchinsky is that it is Dr Court who has felt the less inhibited by the argument and who has based far broader conclusions on a much more rudimentary framework of information. If Dr Court were to be bound by the restraints which he urges the reader to apply in judging Dr Kutchinsky's work, his case would collapse entirely.

Other countries

6.57 We have discussed the incidence of sexual offences in England and Wales and in Denmark at greater length than Dr Court has in any of the papers he submitted to us because we think it important that more light should be thrown on the subject so that the objective reader may reach his own conclusions about Dr Court's case. Dr Court has additionally referred to a number of other countries, such as Australia, the United States of America, New Zealand, Sweden, South Africa, Japan and Singapore, but we do not think it necessary to deal in detail with the situation in all of these countries. His reference to Sweden, for example, appeared to be based on nothing more in the way of evidence than one sentence from an article published in 1962 in *The Spectator*; and all his other references were subject to the same severe criticisms that we have already mentioned, in that he produces no evidence on which an index of the availability of pornography may be constructed; his treatment of statistics of criminal offences is superficial and fluctuations in the figures for rape are never viewed in the context of trends in crime as a whole; and he shows an unscientific readiness to associate any rise in rape statistics with the influence of pornography.

6.58 A fellow South Australian writer who has criticised Dr Court[1] has drawn attention to the fact that, although Dr Court picks out Singapore as illustrating the association between the restriction of pornography and a stable rate of rape, in order to contrast it with a city such as London where a permissive attitude towards pornography is coupled with an increasing incidence of rape, rapes are, on the figures quoted by Dr Court, actually more common in Singapore than in London. Dr Court may retort that to make

[1] P Cochrane, *Sex crimes and pornography revisited,* International Journal of Criminology and Penology 1978, 6, 307–317.

such a comparison ignores the difficulties in assuming a similarity of legal definition, cultural attitudes, police strength etc, but it seems to us that it is equally hazardous to take the statistics of rape for an unfamiliar country and to attempt to relate them to a vague idea of the extent to which pornography is and has been available in that country, again in total isolation from cultural traditions, the state of the law and social developments. Dr Court has made no attempt to place the developments he briefly chronicles in their social context.

6.59 We are satisfied that Dr Court's publications about pornography are more successful in expressing condemnation of pornography than they are in giving the study of its effects a sound scientific basis. We discount his evidence and, to the extent that they rely on his work, the evidence of those who quote him.

II: Other Effects on Human Behaviour

6.60 We have so far considered whether the influence of material of a sexual or violent nature might be manifested in behaviour which is illegal. To consider the possible effects on other forms of behaviour raises problems of deciding what forms of legal behaviour are nevertheless undesirable, bringing to bear certain values. For example, some of our witnesses were clearly concerned at the effect of pornography on sexual behaviour generally. But if sexual arousal results, this is hardly to be condemned in itself; if more frequent sexual intercourse follows, there is no obvious need for concern, while if the result is masturbation, still many will not be alarmed; if a greater repertoire of sexual activity is learned, many people would regard this as a benefit. The prospect of encouraging pre-marital or extra-marital sexual activity raises greater controversy, but the indications from research results are that sexual patterns of behaviour are fixed before reading pornography can exercise any influence. What people do is more affected by their existing habits and values than by exposure to pornography, and the sexual attitudes of groups who have been studied do not appear to have been much affected by seeing this kind of material. It is however true that attitudes towards pornography and its restriction are very much a function of other attitudes towards sex generally (see Appendix 5, paragraph 2).

6.61 Concern is expressed that readers of pornography might be led into deviant sexual practices, particularly through a progressive seeking after novelty. We have already referred in Chapter 4 to the successful publisher's philosophy of "keeping one step ahead", but the context of that progression was straightforward sexual explicitness, and we are sceptical of the extent to which the appeal of novelty, as represented in publications, draws people into sexual deviancy. Indeed, all the evidence points to the fact that material dealing with bizarre or perverted sexual activity appeals only to those with a pre-existing interest established by the experiences of early life, and that such material is of very little interest to others except perhaps as an occasional or once-for-all object of curiosity. The usual reaction of those who are not predisposed to the particular form of deviant behaviour portrayed is disgust and revulsion, and there is no evidence that exposure to such material inculcates a taste for it among such people. Even among adolescents, as Yaffé points out in Appendix 5, the reaction of the individual appears to relate to his previously established sexual identity rather than influencing the development of that identity.

6.62 We received some evidence to the effect that although exposure to deviant pornography might not induce a sexual taste in a person without a pre-existing bias in that direction, it might nevertheless bring to the surface a deviant ingredient in a person's character which he or she did not even know existed, or make it more difficult for people with deviant tastes to deal with that aspect of their personalities. Dr Hyatt Williams was one of those who made this point to us; we also heard from a man who said that he suffered from, and struggled against, sado-masochistic tendencies, and who made a plea for the suppression of the kind of publications which could arouse such feelings. On the other hand, there is the view that people who possess certain interests and tendencies should not be prevented from having material which meets those interests, when the material might in fact provide a cathartic effect, offering some means of relief for tensions that arise from those tendencies. Where the balance lies as regards the control of this material is not easy to judge. We discussed with Dr Hyatt Williams, for example, whether the protection of a small susceptible minority he had identified justified restrictions on the availability of such material more severe than restrictions on other sexually explicit material: he was inclined to think it did not, and the view of other psychiatric witnesses tended in the same direction.

6.63 A particular aspect of behaviour to which some of our evidence was directed was that between partners in marriage and it was put to us that pornography could be influential in damaging human relationships and in leading to marital breakdown. The typical aspect of the argument seemed to be that pornography sometimes implanted in husbands the desire to engage in sexual experimentation which their wives found abhorrent, and which therefore introduced tensions into the marriage. Other ingredients of the argument were that pornography's emphasis on sex divorced from any notion of love, and the wildly exaggerated ideas which it offers of sexual fulfilment and sexual performance create dissatisfaction with existing partners and the desire to look elsewhere. We have to say, however, that we received very little concrete evidence to this effect. The Nationwide Festival of Light expressed the belief that the problem was a very considerable one. Mrs Mary Whitehouse told us that she had received a large number of letters about the deleterious effect of pornography on marital relationships, some of which she quoted in her book *Whatever Happened to Sex?*, but she said that it would not be practicable for her to produce them for us to see. We received one letter of personal testimony of how the writer's interest in pornography had harmed his relationship with his wife; and a Methodist minister told us of two cases from his pastoral experience in which pornography had played a part in marital breakdown. This was, however, the limit of the specific evidence we received. If there was a real problem of this kind arising from pornography we had expected to hear more of it, and we were interested to hear from Mrs Angela Willans, who has had long experience of conducting the problems page of the magazine *Woman's Own*, that she received few letters from wives complaining of the demands of their husbands instilled by a reading of pornography. Many of her readers were upset to find their husbands taking an interest in pornography, but that is a rather different point. Indeed, we also received evidence of how pornography had been of help in enabling married couples to overcome their sexual problems: one correspondent told us how his marriage had been saved when the physical relationship between him and his wife was rekindled in their looking together at sexually explicit magazines. More generally, as paragraph 6 of Appendix 5 makes clear, such material is also used in the clinical treatment of sexual dysfunction, to alleviate the problems of those whose relationship is suffering through impotence or frigidity. In short, the evidence in this area once again tends both ways and we came to the conclusion that the evidence of detrimental effects was too insubstantial to suggest overall that pornography was a significant cause of harm to marriages or other personal relationships.

6.64 We received a number of submissions, not only from women, which stressed the degradation of women which is a feature of much pornography. While it is true that if pornography degrades then it degrades also the men it portrays as well as those who consume it, there is a special sense in which, as pornography seems to be almost exclusively designed for male consumption, it *uses* women as simply the objects of men's sexual needs. Many organisations considered that this was not merely offensive to women but was demeaning in a way that could be regarded as a social harm. Some of these were those with a religious view of human dignity who saw pornography as an assault on women, and we received both Christian and Jewish views of this. But much evidence also had a specifically feminist viewpoint, which tended to see pornography as but one form of sexism, perhaps a particularly blatant and vicious form but essentially reflecting the same view of women commonly encountered in advertising, entertainment and other aspects of our social existence. Much of what we received from Women's Liberation groups was indeed directed as much at the world of advertising and at the general reinforcement of women's subservient role which society was seen as pursuing than at pornography itself, which was seen as only one of the instruments of women's repression; and some radical groups specifically distinguished their views on pornography from those more traditional groups by emphasising that, quite apart from other differences, their approach was based on a different attitude to the nature of women's sexuality. It follows from this view, of course, that pornography (at least on these grounds) should not be singled out for special treatment under the law, since the desire is to alter fundamentally society's attitudes towards the role of women rather than to legislate against one symptom of those attitudes. Many of our women correspondents wanted the law to be invoked against the degradation of women in pornography; but the consensus of those parts of the Women's movement from which we heard tended to attach greater importance to freedom of expression than to the need to suppress pornography.

6.65 The effects of pornography and violent material were widely seen as particularly dangerous to the young, and most of our witnesses wished to see children and young persons protected. We did hear from some of our expert witnesses a certain caution about just how susceptible children were to such influences, for this is not a field where much is known: for obvious reasons children have not been used in experimental work on exposure to pornography, and we heard no evidence of actual harm being caused to children. Some witnesses suspected that children would not take very much notice of pornography and that they might be more robust than was commonly assumed, but there was nevertheless a reluctance to take any risks where the young were concerned. Dr Hanna Segal saw in particular two ways in which such influences might be harmful to children. First, children learn to overcome their own sexual fantasies by looking at behaviour in the real world, but if their view of the adult world confirmed those fantasies, they were likely to become fixated by them; secondly, she felt that an essential element of all pornography was cruelty and that this could establish a link between sexual activity and violence. Dr Gallwey of the Portman Clinic thought that a particular experience of exposure to pornography at a time of stress in the child's process of growing up, particularly when trying to evolve an understanding of aspects of life, could be very confusing to a child and, if in constellation with other disturbing factors, could tip the balance towards psychological damage. Dr Gallwey also offered the comment that it was better to avoid exposing children to the infantile conflicts of adults. The greatest harm, in the view of Dr Hyatt Williams, might be to those on the verge of puberty, but he saw the danger more in terms of pornography being used by an adult with a view, for example, to homosexual seduction than in relation to pornography being passed around among children.

6.66 It was clear from our discussions with witnesses that no very definite answer can be given about the age at which the special protection of children is no longer necessary. Individual sexual maturation is so variable that, as Dr Segal put it to us, some 15 year olds could quite well cope with exposure to pornography while others even in their early twenties could still be susceptible to outside influences of this kind, while Professor Sir Martin Roth also felt that a person's sexual development might sometimes be in the balance until after the age of 20: his concern was primarily with children being subjected to propaganda for homosexuality. Because of this lengthy period of varying maturity, some of our witnesses declined to offer any view as to the age at which special protection should cease; the choice of others tended to hover between the ages of 16 and 18.

6.67 Rather similar considerations applied to the exposure of the young to violent material. Children have to learn what violence is and it is clearly better if they do so, and are introduced to certain potentially disturbing material, within a secure and loving framework. There is of course no shortage of unpleasant and horrific subjects in traditional children's literature, but some of our witnesses thought that there was no reason for parents to be concerned about fairytale violence on the one hand—including that in westerns, for example—or, on the other, the real-life violence of news stories. But there is concern in particular about the effects on those young people who have been deprived of a secure background and the normal socialising influences which enable them to develop their own healthy personality. It was, Dr Gallwey told us, the more disturbed children who were both more frightened and more fascinated by violent material, and also the most vulnerable who were the very people likely to be exposed to violent influences. Brody makes the point from research evidence that it is those who lack firm contact with ordinary life, with severe neurotic problems or of frankly disordered states of mind, who are likely to be most susceptible to adverse effects from films. Ordinarily, although children may be upset or disturbed by watching films, the solid base which they have to fall back on means that the effects are only temporary; but those whose development has already been impaired, and who have to find a substitute for reality in a fantasy world, are the minority likely to be at risk. We found a wide feeling that it was right that those still in the process of emotional development should be shielded from some of the very powerful images of violence, particularly material which appeared to exploit and glorify violent behaviour.

6.68 The protection of children also figured largely in the evidence we received about the harm done to those who were exploited in the production of pornography; in this connection we turn now to the question of harmful effects on participants rather than on the consumers of published material. Even in relation to children, the evidence we received did not all point in the same direction: Professor Trevor Gibbens, for example, told us that he thought that young girls often had the ability to exploit what they saw as a "good racket" and were quite capable of still growing up into well-adjusted women. This did not mean that Professor Gibbens was arguing that the use of children in pornography was anything but undesirable, but he was suggesting that long-term damage to those involved was more doubtful than is widely assumed. Few people would be prepared to take the risk where children are concerned and just as the law recognises that children should be protected against sexual behaviour which they are too young to properly consent to, it is almost universally agreed that this should apply to participation in pornography. Participating in pornography, it ought to be said, will often involve the commission of what are anyway offences, such as unlawful sexual intercourse with girls under sixteen, indecent assault and indecency with children, and there is only a small area of pornographic activity which is not covered by the law on sexual offences; on the evidence we received, this area is even smaller in practice than it may appear on paper. But there are strong arguments that the prevention of this harm also requires the power to suppress the pornographic product as well as the original act, so as not to provide the incentive to pornographers to flout the sexual offence law, or to deal without inhibition in products which are imported from other legal jurisdictions. We should not be parochial about the prevention of harm to children: if English law is to protect children against offences in this country, it is hypocritical to permit the trade in photographs and films of the same activities taken overseas. These considerations reinforce the view that the law on sexual offences is not enough: a law dealing with the published product is required in addition.

6.69 Children are the most obvious example of a group who are capable of exploitation because they do not enjoy a fully developed right to choose. But our evidence on participants went a good deal wider, and it was submitted to us that adults were also exploited and harmed in the production of pornography. The question of consenting adults being exploited raises broader issues and merges with the kind of argument which suggests that much employment is exploitation because people are obliged to do what they have no desire to do in order to earn their living. A more limited view of exploitation would be that people are taken advantage of in ways that are against their best interests, and are forced to suffer harms which they themselves are capable of recognising as harms. If there are people who willingly and even cheerfully or enthusiastically take part in pornographic films or photographic sessions and are able lucidly to square that activity with their own values and consciences and to decide that it is advantageous to them to do it, then it is very difficult for other members of society to impose on them a view that they are demeaning themselves or allowing themselves to be exploited in undesirable ways.

6.70 At the very least, we would suggest that a particular kind of moralism is involved in pressing the charge of exploitation with respect to participation particularly in pornography, when that participation is by ordinary criteria voluntary. It may be that much employment which by those standards is voluntary can justly be seen as exploitation, but there is no particular reason to pick out employment in the production of pornography. Some who do specially pick out pornography in this connection perhaps believe that no-one, knowing what was involved, and not under the direst pressure of economic or other necessity, would want to engage in it. If that is their thought, we can only report that our enquiries do not suggest that it is true.

6.71 We were not able to conclude that participation in these activities was a cause of harm. Allegations to this effect were sometimes made to us, but these were usually in the context of evidence that assumed pornography to be evil and any association with it to be contaminating. We received little evidence of a more objective kind. One of our psychiatric witnesses, Dr Gallwey, suggested to us that there was much misery in the trade and that many of the girls in strip clubs, for example, were disturbed and mentally ill. Mr. Raymond Blackburn suggested that the most dangerous risk to participants was of their being subjected to blackmail. However, the other evidence we received contained no substantiation of these suggestions. Evidence from within the trade denied it. This is hardly surprising; but, for what it is worth, Mr David Sullivan told us that the models used by his magazines were a complete cross-section of society and that, in his view, the work had no effect on them. He saw no reason to believe that to embark on such work was to step on a slippery slope to corruption or prostitution or, for that matter, to step on a stairway to stardom. The vast majority of models in this field undertook the work simply because they regarded it as an acceptable way of making money.

6.72 There have been instances in which the alleged harm to participants has fallen in a very different category. It has been suggested, for example, that there is a *genre* of film—the so-called "snuff" movie—usually said to originate in South America, in which sadistic pornography is taken to the extreme of having an unsuspecting model actually mutilated and murdered in front of the camera. There has been much scepticism about the existence of films of this kind and although rumours about their existence were indeed followed in America by the appearance of a film called *Snuff* ("the film that could only be made in South America . . . where life is cheap!") there appeared to be general agreement that the violence in the film was simulated rather than real; it is possible that the rumours themselves had been engineered for the purposes of advance publicity for this film. Another film, which we saw, which purported to include actual documentary sequences of mutilation and death, was subsequently reported to have been, at least in part, faked. Clearly the danger of physical injury does represent an undeniable harm, even if it is potential rather than actual. As with offences against children, however, this is an area where the criminal law already operates for the protection of the individual and the infliction of physical injury may be punishable in the courts even where the injured person consented to be so treated. Nevertheless, again as with children, we do not think that the authorities in this country will have discharged their responsibility for discouraging such behaviour just by legislating to punish such acts which are committed in this country. There is a strong case for taking measures against the circulation of material which involves real cruelty or physical injury, even when it originates overseas.

6.73 The broadest arguments put to us concerned the social harms flowing from the widespread availability of pornography, in terms of cultural pollution, moral deterioration and the undermining of human compassion, social values and basic institutions. Arguments of this kind were less concerned with the possibility of specific effects on individual behaviour than with the gradual infecting of society with a disregard for decency, a lack of respect for others, a taste for the base, a contempt for restraint and responsibility: in short, with the weakening of our civilisation and the demoralisation of society.

6.74 A leading exponent of the view associating pornography with a cultural sickness is Mr David Holbrook and we discussed his concern with him. Mr Holbrook sees pornography and sadism as having been allowed to increase in our culture in recent years, with the result that a stream of hate—which he sees as an essential element in pornography—and debased sexuality has been thrust into our consciousness through powerful mass media. In consequence, in his view, there is now a widespread mental obsession with sexuality, a considerable degree of commercialisation of sex, a growing egotistical nihilism, a preoccupation with satiation and a corruption of culture. Culture had been debased to the extent that it is now difficult to write about sexual matters in an adult way because the expectations of the audience had been so corrupted. Writers wishing to appear trendy had committed intellectual treachery by praising the latest work of sex and violence, while those who attempted to raise a debate on the serious issues involved in the spread of pornography and its effect on culture were ignored and isolated. Mr Holbrook complained that his books were no longer being reviewed because editors disagreed with the stand he had taken.

6.75 The emphasis given to the nature of the social harms naturally varied from witness to witness. Some witnesses, for example, saw violence in the media as contributing to public attitudes which regard violence as a legitimate means of achieving desired ends or of expressing feelings; or as encouraging a callous disregard of the effects of violence. The particular question of psychological desensitisation to violence was one which we discussed with a number of witnesses, and Dr Guy Cumberbatch sought to reassure us from the results of research on the subject. As he told us, and as Brody has also pointed out, experiments have certainly shown that the viewer may become desensitised by exposure to violent material, but this appears to occur in a specific rather than a general way. For example, volunteers had repeatedly been shown an extract from a violent film, with the effect that their measured response to it declined with each showing; but when they were afterwards shown the complete film, their reaction to other scenes of violence had been normal and it was only the familiar scene to which responses had been dulled. In any case, Dr Cumberbatch argued, responses to fictional and dramatic material were quite different from those of real life, and there were no indications that a person's ability to feel pity and willingness to help the victim of an act of aggression was lessened by watching representations of similar acts of violence.

6.76 However, the arguments range more widely than such delimited psychological effects. As we have said, many of our witnesses claimed that there were more generalised damaging effects of pornography, violent publications, and films, effects which were necessarily of a less identifiable kind. These arguments should not be discounted or ignored simply because they are not based on direct tangible effects. Long-term effects on civilisation and culture are self-evidently important and should be considered as carefully as one can, even if they cannot be quantified and demonstrated. The arguments here do, however, involve the danger, as we have already said and is very obvious, of citing as a cause something that is itself only an effect or part of a cultural and historical process. There is also the danger that the cultural process is itself disliked because it is new, unfamiliar, and perhaps threatening, and things that are indeed extreme and ugly cultural phenomena, but perhaps not deeply significant ones, are seized on in order to attack social and moral developments which are indeed more significant, but less obviously to be rejected. In these reactions, an idealised image of the past often plays a part. In considering the dangers that are sometimes seen as threatening our social fabric in the area of sexual conduct and of pornography, one needs a sense of historical perspective.

6.77 There were almost certainly more child prostitutes in London a hundred years ago than there are today. Pornography, in any case an age-old phenomenon[1], flourished then and is by no means a modern development. Of course, technological innovations have offered new scope to the producer of pornography, but it would be a mistake to minimise the circulation of pornography in earlier years, even in Victorian times. Needless to say, we are no more able to quantify the availability of pornography a hundred years ago than we are to chart its progress in recent years, but the comments which we quote in Appendix 1 from those who were trying to combat pornography in nineteenth century England have a familiar ring today. H Montgomery Hyde has written that the output of purely erotic pornography in England during the nineteenth century was prodigious. This was not merely the production of leather-bound limited editions for a minority of specialist collectors, as can be seen from the results of some of the police activity against such material. In 1874, for example, one raid on a dealer led to the seizure of about 135,000 obscene photographs and slides. A raid in 1895 netted about two tons of obscene literature. The trade must have been considerable.

[1]At least in pictorial forms. Pornographic prose fiction seems, at any rate in Europe, to have first appeared in the middle of the 17th Century. The first original English prose pornography (as opposed to translations), and also the first to take the form of a novel rather than a dialogue, was John Cleland's *Memoirs of a Woman of Pleasure* ("Fanny Hill"), 1748. See David Foxon, "Libertine Literature in England, 1660–1745 (*The Book Collector*, 1964).

6.78 What became clear to us in the course of our discussions about the social harms of pornography and violent material was that many of our witnesses had in mind a class of material which included much that could not remotely be dealt with under the kind of laws we were appointed to review, or were considering the type of harm which certainly could not be ascribed to such material alone or even predominantly to such material. Often, the arguments that were put to us about damage to culture, morality and social values were not primarily directed to the effects of pornography at all. Some of our witnesses recognised this: the Catholic Social Welfare Commission, for example, admitted that pornography and representations of violence may be symptoms of a more general malaise and may be considered effects, or at most partial causes in particular contexts, rather than sufficient explanations; their case rested on the belief, however, that pornography and the representation of violence in certain forms and circumstances is one of the elements which threaten some basic institutions and values. Mrs Mary Whitehouse too is well-known for her passionately held views on the erosion of standards over a wide area. The degradation of sex figures strongly in her thinking. She did express to us very strongly the view that pornography is corrupting our society, and indeed that it is being used by the extreme Left for this purpose, in much the same way as the Nazis used pornography as part of their assault on the cultural life of the Poles or, she alleged, Communists, while clamping down on sex shows and prostitution in Mozambique, have been pouring pornography into South Africa. But Mrs Whitehouse has in general concentrated her attention on television programme content—which in this country is hardly ever pornographic—and this fact illustrates her concern with the far wider aspects of media influences on the quality of life.

6.77 There was a sense, we felt, in which pornography was being used by many of our witnesses as a scapegoat. The tastelessness and depressing awfulness of pornography generally makes it easy for its detractors to attack it without fear of contradiction and to gain a sympathetic hearing for their description of its anti-social effects. Mr David Holbrook was one of our witnesses who made it clear that his attack was directed at a broader target. In deploring the commercialisation of sex, he referred to the use of sexuality in advertising in order to give a wide range of products a greater appeal to a consumer society; in deploring the glamorisation of sexual aggression, he referred to what he regarded as the social evil of the James Bond image, in which, as with Don Juan, he perceived a degree of latent fascism; in deploring an obsession with perversion and hate, he was in fact speaking in the context of the intellectual debate rather than on the effects of pornographic magazines.

6.80 While there are some serious and interesting questions about the character of pornography, what the experience of pornographic work is like, and how that relates, for instance, to the experience of art, little of this, it seems to us, is very directly connected with the causation of social harms. Conversely, Mr Holbrook's diagnosis of a cultural sickness and collapse is not very closely connected, in our view (which we put to him in discussion), with pornography and still less with the laws on obscenity. The point goes more generally. One factor that we have not so far mentioned is that sexual matters in general are more openly discussed now than before, and the fact that pornography is less concealed is one aspect of this development. Our witnesses recognise this development; some seemed to regret it, preferring the subject to remain a private one to be treated in public with more reticence than is often the case, even in serious discussion. Others welcomed it, regarding the denial of an interest in this basic and integral part of the nature of all of us as something that can only obstruct understanding of ourselves and others and impede the development of true maturity. Whichever of these views is taken, we have no doubt that this new openness is among the things that have influenced the availability of pornography, rather than the reverse. Cultural artefacts themselves play a role in not merely reflecting but in influencing social development, but given the multitude of factors, and from everything we know of social attitudes and have learnt in the course of our enquiries, our belief can only be that the role of pornography in influencing the state of society is a minor one. To think anything else, and in particular to regard pornography as having a crucial or even a significant effect on essential social values, is to get the problem of pornography out of proportion with the many other problems that face our society today.

CHAPTER SEVEN

OFFENSIVENESS

7.1 The *deprave and corrupt* test of obscenity, the history of which we have already referred to, defines a concept of obscenity which is of course exactly suited to fit in with the harm condition: it is a causal notion of obscenity, based on the idea that the rationale of suppressing obscenity is the harm that it causes. But, as we noted, the actual use of the test in the past seems often to have had little to do with proving that there had been any harms at all. It has almost been as if people, accepting the harm condition, agreed that pornography should be suppressed only if it did harm; were quite clear that it should be suppressed; and concluded that somehow it must do harm.

7.2 One idea that may confuse the issue here is the assumption, which we touched on in discussing law and morality, that if something does no identifiable harm, then any objection to it must be (merely) a matter of taste. As we have said, some of those who have written to us do regard reactions to pornography as a matter of taste. Others go a little further, in saying that it is a matter of taste not just in the sense that some people have a taste for it and others do not, but that a taste for it is bad taste. This would make it, at any rate, a matter of aesthetic judgement.

7.3 Certainly most pornography is also trash: ugly, shallow, and obvious. (We will consider in Chapter 8 why this is so, and whether it is necessarily so—whether, that is to say, there could be a pornographic, or again obscene, work of art, a question which has constantly recurred to plague the Obscene Publications Act.) But this fact is not enough to explain its offensiveness; we are surrounded by shallow trash of all kinds but few people, however sensitive their taste, find it as upsetting and disagreeable as many people certainly find pornography. For many people, pornography is not only offensive, but deeply offensive.

7.4 Pornography essentially involves making public in words, pictures or theatrical performance, the fulfilment of fantasy images of sex or violence. In some cases the images are of forbidden acts: so it is with images of violence. In other cases, the line that is transgressed is only that between private and public; the acts represented in the images would be all right in private, but the same acts would be objectionable in public. There will of course be disagreement about how many acts are of this second sort rather than the first. Even the most puritanical will agree that there are some, if only straightforward sexual relations between husband and wife. Others may take more liberal views about what is legitimate sexual activity, but retain the view that the proper place for it is in private. People have strong sentiments attached to these notions of public and private, of what it is "unsuitable"—in its original sense, *indecent*—to show.

7.5 Obviously, as with the display of parts of the body, these perceptions vary over time. Some predict, indeed hope, that the time may come when such restrictions will have finally disappeared. One witness whom we saw made it clear that she looked forward to a society in which nothing one saw going on in the park would be more surprising than anything else, except perhaps in the sense of being more improbable. Most of us doubt whether this day will come, or that nothing would have been lost if it did. Still less do we look forward to a world in which sexual activity is not only freely conducted in public and can be viewed, but is offered to be viewed, copulating parties soliciting the interest of the passer-by. But this is, in effect, what publicly displayed pornography does.

7.6 Pornography crosses the line between private and public since it makes available in the form, for instance, of a photograph, some sexual act of a private kind and makes it available for a voyeuristic interest: since it is itself a public thing, a picture book or a film show, it represents already the projection into public of the private world—private, that is to say, to its participants—of sexual activity. The represented activity is in the first instance something offered to be seen, and can have the shock effect of something suddenly revealed. The consumer of the pornography does not of course necessarily, or perhaps typically, remain conscious of himself as an external viewer of what is represented. The material rather is incorporated into his fantasy; it is characteristic, for instance, that photographs, which must inevitably be records of sexual activity with the usual human limitations, will be incorporated in fantasies of the mythical, inexhaustible, limitless sexual activity which is the typical product of the pornographic imagination. The exact relation of pornographic material to the consumer and to his fantasies is a subtle matter. Even when it is taken up into fantasy, pornography often retains an assaulting quality—there is a sense in which it can be found offensive even while it is being enjoyed. In other cases, the sense of offensiveness evaporates for the consumer who involves himself in the images offered by photographs or films, or develops his own fantasy from the written word.

7.7 The basic point that pornography involves by its nature some violation of lines between public and private is compounded when the pornography not only exists for private consumption, but is publicly displayed. The original violation is then forced on the attention of those who have not even volunteered to be voyeurs. They are thus forced or importuned to see things which they do not think should be seen, and images are thrust into their mind which they reject. Whatever may be true of the willing consumer, pornography is straightforwardly offensive to those who do not want to take it in. There are some differences here between the visual and the written. Visual material displays its content to anyone within line of sight; when, moreover, it is photographic, real people and actual events are on display. Written material is further removed from any particular reality, and an activity is in any case needed in order to take in the content. These points help to explain the fact, to which everyone agrees, that written material, casually encountered, is less offensive than visual, and in particular photographic, material. It is probably a result of this that, as we have already explained, almost any printed book now seems likely to secure acquittal; it is worth recalling, too, that magazines with rather less explicit pictures, such as the DPP classifies as "Grade 2" and which are widely accepted at present, are sometimes prepared to carry written material which is straightforwardly hard-core pornography.

7.8 For those who are not disposed, as willing consumers are, to make the scenes of pornography into objects of their own fantasy, those scenes have a special and saddening ugliness. In people who are particularly resistant to such fantasy, either in general, or as involving objects such as these, anger, disturbance and oppression will be the reactions. It is tempting to speculate—it cannot be more than speculation—that it is such reactions which are understood by some who experience them as a perception that pornography is intrinsically harmful and destructive. This perception, taken as a social judgement, we believe may well be incorrect. But this does not mean that the reactions themselves, or the less violent reactions of others who find the display of such material in various degrees offensive, are incorrect. It seems to us that they can be entirely appropriate, and that the world would not necessarily be a better place if people ceased to have them.

7.9 When the material is violent, these reactions are typically intensified. Here the scenes are such as no person who is not disturbed could want to happen in reality. The scenes are offered in pornography as objects of sado-masochistic fantasy (we should repeat that there is no reason to believe that this usually expresses itself in sadistic behaviour in reality). For those resistant to that sort of fantasy in general, or on this occasion, or who reject fantasy on material as crude and explicit as this, these scenes will be totally revolting. Similar reactions may be felt to fictional or pictorial violence which, while it is not pornographic, in the sense of involving or invoking sexual arousal, nevertheless is offered directly as an object of aggressive fantasy. It is no doubt because aggressive impulses have to be contained and denied expression in actual life to an even greater extent than is the case with sexual impulses, that the reactions to sadistic and other violent material are typically stronger and more alarming than to sexual material—except in so far as an aggressive presentation of the sexual material, very characteristic of pictorial pornography, is itself expressive of sadism. "I don't mind the sex ,it's the violence"[1], as many people said to us.

7.10 In this discussion, we have inevitably been drawn a short distance into the psychology of the experience of pornography, a subject in which we would not feel confident in claiming that there existed any very definite knowledge, let alone that we possessed it. But even if this account is not quite right, something like it must be true. Such an account will explain how it is that the reactions that many people experience to publicly displayed pornography are not just a matter of arbitrary taste, but are deep reactions; and how it is that the offensiveness it displays to them is, in both a psychological and an ethical sense, a deep offensiveness.

7.11 The fact that one is being forced or importuned to see some unwanted scene can be signalled without the scene itself being shown to one. If the context is one in which such scenes are threatened (or, to the willing, promised) then associated material can take on an appropriate appearance, and produce a milder version of the same reactions. This helps to explain the fact which has always caused difficulty for legislation on these subjects, that it is not an intrinsic degree of undress, for instance, nor even particular postures of the body (with some obvious unambiguous exceptions) which are found objectionable. It is

[1] A phrase which has also been used by Mrs. Enid Wistrich as the title of her book about her experiences as Chairman of the Film Viewing Board of the GLC.

notable for instance that a picture of a girl in underwear is perceived differently if it is on the cover of a woman's fashion magazine from the way it is seen if it is on the cover of a "man's magazine". This has an important consequence for any recommendation about the control of such material: it is not solely what is to be seen on the outside of a publication that governs the reaction appropriate to it. One and the same photograph in different contexts can mean something quite different, and become, in experience, effectively two different things. This means that a control simply on *indecent displays,* which has been proposed on various occasions, does not meet the case. Such proposals are based on a superficial view of what the offensive element is in publicly offered pornography.

7.12 Public sexual activity, except of the milder kinds, is prohibited, and this provides a clear and well-known example of legislation which is directed against the performance in public of acts which (with regard to many of them, at least) are legitimate in private. (Indeed, if the publicity is intentional, the acts are not, strictly speaking, the same as sexual acts done in private—they have a different motive). Laws against public sex would generally be thought to be consistent with the harm condition, in the sense that if members of the public are upset, distressed, disgusted, outraged or put out by witnessing some class of acts, then that constitutes a respect in which the public performance of those acts harms their interests and gives them a reason to object.

7.13 If there is an element of soliciting, that is all the more a nuisance to which citizens can reasonably object. It was in this spirit that the Wolfenden Committee recommended curbs on the public activities of prostitutes, recommendations which became law in the Street Offences Act 1959. In their report they wrote "... we feel that the right of the normal, decent, citizen to go about the streets without affront to his or her sense of decency should be the prime consideration and should take precedence over the interests of the prostitute and her customers ..."[1], and they made the point that these restrictions should properly apply both to loitering and to soliciting. The offensiveness of publicly displayed pornography seems to us to fall clearly within the sorts of considerations advanced by the Wolfenden Committee, and to be in line with traditionally accepted rules protecting the interest in public decency. Restrictions on the open sale of these publications, and analogous arrangements for films, thus seem to us to be justified.

7.14 Naturally, any system of restriction must involve some phenomena which themselves could, indirectly, offend someone. Thus pornography might be legitimately sold (as we shall propose) in shops which announced their nature but did not allow their contents to be seen from the outside. The presence of such shops is something which itself could be found offensive by someone; we have indeed received complaints about shops of some such kind (though we cannot be sure how reticent the particular examples may have been). If there were no such shops, but only mail-order distributors, then the advertisements for these, even if they displayed no material, would certainly be found offensive. If one goes all the way down this line, however, one arrives

---

[1] Cmnd. 247, paragraph 249.

at the situation in which people objected to even knowing that pornography was being read in private; and if one accepted as a basis for coercing one person's actions, the fact that others would be upset even by the thought of his performing those actions, one would be denying any substantive individual liberty at all[1]. Any offence caused by such shops would clearly be much less vivid, direct and serious than that caused by the display of the publications, and we do not accept that it could outweigh the rights of those who do wish to see this material, or more generally the arguments in favour of restricting, without suppressing, pornography.

7.15 We have suggested that proposals for restricting pornography would be clearly in line with existing provisions to deal with other kinds of offensiveness. We have also tried to explain why the offensiveness of pornography is found a serious matter, and reactions to it represent more than a mere divergence of taste. However, it seemed to us also that we should carry the argument further than this, and examine with rather greater precision what principle might justify legislation of this kind. For, as several witnesses said to us, to restrict publications "because they upset people" could be a dangerous precedent. There can be various public manifestations, publications or other forms of utterance which may upset people, even deeply upset people, without those people thereby having a right to have those public manifestations suppressed. We think therefore that we should try to set out some considerations which would distinguish the kind of matter for which we propose restrictions from other cases in which restriction would be unjustifiable.

7.16 We suggest that there are two important characteristics of the case of restrictions on pornographic materials and of restrictions on them which help to distinguish that case from others where restriction would not be justifiable. An extended treatment of the subject of free expression would no doubt give an account of how far these considerations go, how they relate to one another, how they apply to difficult cases, and so on, but we do not think it either necessary or appropriate to pursue those further questions here.

(1) *The restriction is not directed against the advocacy of any opinion.*

7.17 Clearly some publications could have the effect of outraging or deeply upsetting many people because of the opinions or view of the world they advocated, which those who were outraged found deeply offensive to their own beliefs and outlook. However, many people would think that it would be contrary to basic principles of free expression even to restrict, let alone suppress, publications *on this ground alone* (as opposed, for instance, to controlling them on the ground that they incited to riot). So it is important to the rationale for restricting pornographic publications that it is not for advocating any opinion that the restriction is proposed, and that the upset that they cause to the public is not a reaction to opinions which are found unacceptable. For the most part, this will be because the publications do not advocate any opinions at all. But some may do so; thus some pornographic magazines contain letterpress which advocates a "swinging" life-style, while there could also be a piece of pornography which as a whole was designed to advocate some opinion. But, in the first case,

[1] This point is very clearly shown by Hart: *Law, Liberty and Morality*, pp 45 following.

it would not be on the grounds of that part of the content that the magazine would be a candidate for restriction, and in the second example, it would not be because it had that character, but rather because the form of its advocacy was offensive, apart from what was being advocated.

7.18 Because we attach some weight to this principle, we do not entirely accept the emphasis given in their evidence by the Catholic Social Welfare Commission, among other witnesses, who particularly associated the harms of pornography with its encouraging a view of sex as trivial amusement or gratification. Whether or not that view is as distorted and damaging as the witnesses believe, the view that sex should not be taken seriously is at least an opinion, and if the bad character of pornography lay principally in its advocating such an opinion, then there would be, in our view, a difficulty of principle about one's right to restrict it.

(2) *Restricting the publication to a volunteer audience does not defeat its aims.*

7.19 If someone burns an IRA symbol or a photograph of the Ayatollah Khomeini, or sings an offensive political song, it *could* be that his purpose will be carried out if he is demonstrating or singing only to the converted. But it is much more likely that some part of his intention will be to make his point to people who would not originally have volunteered to see or hear him make it. This consideration obviously overlaps with the point about advocating opinions, but it goes further, since it applies also to activities which are not themselves the advocacy of opinions.

7.20 With pornographic publications, the restriction to a volunteer audience constitutes in general no hardship or defeat of the publications' intentions. The pornographer is offering a product, to be consumed by those who want to consume it. We say that there is no defeat of his *publication's* intentions. The pornographer himself may have some aims which would be impeded by restriction—thus it may be that he will make less money if his pornography is restricted and if his purpose in publishing it is to make money, that purpose will be impeded by restriction. But that is not the kind of purpose or intention that is in question.

7.21 There are exceptions among pornographic publications to this general point. There are some of a proselytising tendency, no doubt, and there are also pornographic works of a serious artistic intention, the writers of which might not necessarily be equally content with an audience who would volunteer under conditions of restriction. Moreover, the present point, that if the audience is restricted to volunteers this does not defeat the aim of the publication, is anyway not so directly related to a general principle about the restriction of publications as is the point that restriction is not directed against any opinions which are being advanced. It is plausible to claim that no publication should ever be restricted solely on the grounds of the opinions it advocates, but it is quite implausible that publications should be restricted only if those who produce them would be content with a volunteer audience. But it is nevertheless a relevant consideration that the nature of most pornography is such that there can be no complaint if its audience is confined to volunteers.

7.22 We have already remarked that works which consist only of written text are in fact found less offensive than pictorial matter, and that there are basic psychological reasons for this fact. If, as we have suggested, it makes a difference whether a proposed restriction is directed against opinions or not, this introduces a further point about the written word as contrasted with pictorial matter. Besides actual speech, it is the written word that is the principal medium for the advocacy of opinions, and which is accordingly likely to give rise to the most serious borderline cases in this connection. The written word, moreover, is the medium which, together with the film (for which we shall propose separate methods of control), has chiefly given rise to the traditional problem of serious artistic intent in supposedly obscene material. While written works can no doubt be found to some extent offensive, we believe that these various considerations provide a very strong case for withholding the possibility of restriction (let alone of suppression) from the written word, and we shall propose that, with respect to the area of the law we have been appointed to review, no publication shall be liable to either suppression or restriction in virtue of matter that it contains which consists solely of the written word.

7.23 We shall explain the details of our proposals for restriction in Chapter 9. The operative term that we have chosen for the characteristic which merits restriction is "offensive". "Indecent" seems to us too narrow in some respects (there is grossly offensive material, suitable for restriction, which would not naturally be called "indecent"), too wide in others (some material conventionally called "indecent" is not really offensive), and it suffers above all from having too long and disputed a legal history. The Defence of Literature and the Arts Society, whose carefully argued and constructive evidence we found helpful, offered us the term "outrage" in this connection, but we rejected this on the grounds that it seemed stronger than was appropriate. We also suspect that it may carry a misleading implication. "Outrage" is something chiefly felt towards actions, of an unjust or appalling character, but when it is applied to publications it seems usually to be on grounds of the opinions they express, which, as we have just explained, is something that we seek to exclude. "Offensiveness" is the term that seems to represent most clearly what is in question. To make clear, however, what kinds of offensiveness are at issue, we have thought it right to specify the kinds of respect in which material has to be offensive if it is to be restricted. Since, further, some people will be offended by almost anything, and others by nothing at all, it is also necessary to specify whose reactions in finding something offensive are to count, and we have decided in favour of the requirement that matter to be restricted should be "offensive to reasonable people". This seems to us to catch as well as any phrase can the central idea that at any given time there can be material which sensible people of mature tastes will quite properly demand, for the kinds of reasons we have discussed, not to have forced on their attention. We shall return in more detail to the terms of our formula in paragraph 9.29 and following.

CHAPTER EIGHT

PORNOGRAPHY, OBSCENITY AND ART

8.1 In the course of Chapter 7, we have referred almost all our discussion to *pornography,* rather than to *obscenity*. This emphasis was deliberate. "Obscene", we shall suggest in this chapter, is a term which itself expresses the kinds of reactions we were discussing in Chapter 7, rather than telling one what kind of thing actually arouses those reactions. "Pornography", on the other hand, we take to be a rather more objective expression referring to a certain kind of writing, picture etc. We have suggested that pornography does tend by its nature to be found offensive; and most of the publications and pictures which people find offensive are indeed pornographic. But we shall need to consider a little more precisely what pornography and obscenity are, in order to discuss an important question, the relations of pornography and obscenity to art. There is more than one reason why we thought that we should discuss this question. It has repeatedly surfaced in the history of this subject; it has constantly recurred, not surprisingly, in our own discussions; and it has been raised in various forms by many witnesses, some of whom were as certain that there could not possibly be an obscene work of art as others were that there could. The issues here are, moreover, deeply involved in both the theory and the practical use of the "public good defence" under section 4 of the Obscene Publications Act 1959. The discussion in this chapter directly bears on our recommendations and has, we believe important consequences for legislation on these subjects. We have not been convinced that it is impossible for any pornographic or obscene work to have artistic merit, and we shall try to explain why we have not. At the same time, we are convinced, for reasons that we shall give, that a public good defence with respect to artistic merit is inevitably unworkable. Any proposals for legislation must, we believe, accommodate both these conclusions.

Pornography

8.2 The term "pornography" always refers to a book, verse, painting, photograph, film, or some such thing—what in general may be called a *representation.* Even if it is associated with sex or cruelty, an object which is not a representation—exotic underwear, for example—cannot sensibly be said to be pornographic (though it could possibly be said to be obscene). We take it that, as almost everyone understands the term, a pornographic representation is one that combines two features: it has a certain function or intention, to arouse its audience sexually, and also a certain content, explicit representations of sexual material (organs, postures, activity, etc.). A work has to have both this function and this content to be a piece of pornography.

8.3 It is useful to distinguish works that extend over time (novels, films) from those that do not (paintings, photographs: series of pictures are obviously an intermediate case). The former offer the possibility that they may have some sections that are pornographic and others that are not, leaving room for borderline questions about whether the work as a whole is pornographic. Some such questions are unanswerable. However, it has proved to be the case up to now that there has been a demand for works which maximise pornographic content, so there is, in both the novel and the film, a definite *genre* of the pornographic work, which consists almost exclusively of pornographic representations of sexual activity, often complex. There is virtually no plot, no characters, no motivation except relating to sexual activity, and only a shadowy background, which may involve a standard apparatus of a remote and luxurious *château,* numerous silent servants, and so forth. This is the "ideal type" of a pornographic work evoked by Steven Marcus[1].

"*Obscene*" *and* "*Erotic*"

8.4 We suspect that the word "obscene" may now be worn out, and past any useful employment at all. It is certainly too exhausted to do any more work in the courts. However, leaving aside the peculiar legal *deprave and corrupt* definition we have considered in earlier chapters, it seems to us that, insofar as it is not just used as a term of abuse, it principally expresses an intense or extreme version of what we have called "offensiveness". It may be that it particularly emphasises the most strongly aversive element in that notion, the idea of an object's being repulsive or disgusting: that certainly seems to be the point when a person or animal is said to be, for instance, "obscenely" ugly or fat.

8.5 The term "erotic" sometimes seems to be used just as an alternative to "pornographic", being milder with regard to both the content and the intention: the content is by this interpretation more allusive and less explicit, and what is intended is not strong sexual arousal but some lighter degree of sexual interest. There is another interpretation[2] of the term, however, perhaps more accurate and certainly more interesting, under which the erotic is what *expresses* sexual excitement, rather than causes it—in the same way as a painting or a piece of music may express sadness without necessarily making its audience sad. Theorists have not found the notion of expression at all easy to explain, but a work which expresses a given feeling can at least be said to 'fit' the feeling or to 'match' it, and, in virtue of doing that, to put one in mind of the feeling. In this sense an erotic work will suggest or bring to mind feelings of sexual attraction or excitement. It may cause some such feelings as well, and put the audience actually into that state, but if so that is a further effect. This difference comes out rather clearly in the case of romantic love. Many erotic works—and of course many works that are not erotic—express the feelings of romantic love, and invoke images of them in their audience, but the state they bring about in their audience is very rarely that of being in love. On this kind of account of the erotic, it will follow that what is represented in an erotic work of art need not be a mild version of the pornographic at all. There are countless erotic works of art, many of which have no explicit sexual content of any kind.

8.6 As we understand these various notions, pornography, obscenity and eroticism will be related in the following ways. Pornography will have some

---

[1] "Pornotopia": *Encounter* 1966. The concept of an "ideal type" is applied to Marcus's account by Morse Peckham: *Art and Pornography* (New York 1969).

[2] Suggested in a paper by Antonia Phillips, commissioned by us, to which the present chapter is indebted.

tendency to be obscene, but will not necessarily be so. We claimed in Chapter 7 that a tendency to be offensive is built into it, but it is not universally even offensive—it may have some other merit which cancels that effect. Still less must it inevitably be very strongly offensive or obscene. On the other hand, there will be obscene things which are not pornographic (e.g. it would be obscene to exhibit deformed people at a funfair, but that would not be a pornographic exhibition). Some pornography is erotic, but it is not altogether easy for it to be so: the explicit content and the intention of arousal tend to work against the expressive effect of eroticism rather than with it. Many things, certainly, will be erotic without being pornographic. The most unlikely combination, on the present account, is that of the erotic and the obscene. Since the erotic is intended to attract and hold the attention by being, in the sexual dimension, pleasant or delightful, it is hard to see how this could be combined with the object being found at the same time disgusting and repulsive. The idea is so difficult, that this combination might be said to be impossible, except that human reactions in these areas are so complex that we hesitate to say that anything is impossible.

8.7 Some people may find it paradoxical to say that it is hard, if not impossible, for something to be both erotic and obscene. Several of our witnesses have certainly found it natural to say of many publications or films that they were both. We do not deny that these words, and the word "pornography", are often used with meanings which are more general and overlapping than those that we have just proposed. We claim only that there are significant and useful distinctions to be made here, and these words can helpfully be used, in the ways we suggest, to mark those distinctions. One body which submitted evidence to us, the Board for Social Responsibility of the Church of England, made some careful suggestions for distinguishing between these terms, and we found these helpful, even though the account we have given of the matter is not exactly the same as theirs.

Art

8.8 We have already assumed that there can be an *erotic* work of art, and we take it that few would disagree with this. The questions now are: Can there be a work of art which is pornographic? Can there be one which is obscene? As we have already explained, these are for us two different questions. We take first the question about pornography.

8.9 As we said in an earlier chapter, it is incontestable that almost all the pornography sold across (or under) the counter, or seen in the cinema, is from any artistic point of view totally worthless. However, there is more than one possible explanation of that fact. The interesting question, which we shall be concerned with, is whether it just follows from the nature of pornography that it is bound to be worthless. If it does not just follow, then other and more circumstantial explanations may be considered (though we shall not consider them here): as that it is simply not worth anyone's while, at least in the modern world, to make pornography more artistically interesting than it is.

8.10 Several arguments have been put to us, or have been implicit in evidence we have received, to the effect that pornography cannot possibly have any artistic value. The most general argument to this effect is probably that which has been expressed by Steven Marcus in saying "literature possesses a multitude of intentions, but pornography possesses only one."[1] A related consideration is that the "one intention" of pornography—sexual arousal—is achieved through a blankly explicit, unmediated, content. Marcus' point is made with respect to literature, but if it is valid it can be applied just as well to the visual arts. It will be claimed that pornography is by its nature purely instrumental, a crude device for achieving a particular effect, and has nothing to do with the complex concerns and intentions which properly belong to a work of art.

8.11 However, it is not clear why it should be impossible to combine other aims with the "one intention" of pornography. In the case of the visual arts, there do exist some works which are indisputably pornographic in content and intention, but which are thought to succeed in realising other, artistic, concerns. There are many pornographic Japanese prints of the 18th century, works of the admired master Utamaro and others, which are regarded by critics as brilliant achievements. It can be reasonably claimed, moreover, that they are not merely of artistic interest despite being pornographic, but that their sexual intention is integrally bound up with their merits as expressive designs. Many great Western artists have of course produced pornographic works "on the side", to make money or for diversion, and some of these works no doubt have merit; the peculiarity of the Japanese case is that there was a tradition of very considerable artists applying their talents to this *genre*. Of course—to repeat ourselves—there is no suggestion that the existence of these exotic works somehow sheds artistic respectability on the vast range of current pornographic material. What they do prove, however, if their merits are agreed, is that it is not the simple fact that it is pornographic that makes all that material artistically worthless.

8.12 In the case of works which are extended in time, such as the novel and the film, more specific arguments are advanced to suggest that if they are pornographic, they must be no good. Their participants are not characters, but mere locations of sexual possibilities; there is no plot, no development, no beginning, middle or end (a point made by the critic Adorno). Moreover, since there are no characters or genuine human presence, the whole effect is dehumanizing—destructive of any sense of personal individuality or life. These descriptions are obviously correct. It is perhaps worth adding that we do not entirely agree with those who in evidence to us or elsewhere have expressed this sort of idea by saying that the effect of pornography is to reduce everything to the *physical*. Among the various kinds of human presence which are lacking from literary pornography is, usually, any real sense of the human body. Because pornography ministers to fantasies of boundless sexual satisfaction, everything is weightless, untiring, effortlessly restored. The attempt to accommodate the same fantasies with photographs of actual people with actual bodies is partly what makes so many pornographic photographs and films grotesque.

8.13 These descriptions apply more strongly, of course, the closer the fiction in question gets to the schema of the unrelievedly pornographic work. But obviously they would not apply unqualifiedly to a work which had only some

---

[1] "Pornotopia": *Encounter* 1966. A similar point is made by Norman St. John-Stevas, *Obscenity and the Law* (London 1957), page 137.

pornographic sections along with other matter, even if those sections were integral to the work. Moreover, even works which are totally pornographic can occasionally break away from the "ideal type"; and one or two writers have experimented with introducing psychological elements into the *genre*. Claims have been made by serious critics for the artistic merits of certain pornographic literary works (we have heard of none, as yet, with respect to thoroughly pornographic films). The arguments from the character of pornography do seem to suggest that concentratedly pornographic novels are going to be interesting pieces of literature only in rare cases, and then on a minor scale; but it does not seem to be impossible, even in the extreme case, and it would certainly be rash to claim on general grounds that any use of pornographic elements even in the context of other material must make a work worthless.

8.14 The arguments of the last four paragraphs have been concerned with questions of the intention and the structure of pornographic works. What has not yet been mentioned in this connection is their tendency to be offensive or obscene—in our present sense, that is to say, intensely or repellently offensive. This tendency raises a question about artistic value: can a work have any artistic interest and in that way command the attention of a reader or spectator, if it is at the same time found offensive? The question gets more pressing, the more insistent the offensiveness of the work. There may indeed be some pornographic works of artistic merit which do not even raise the question; these will be works in which the sexual content should not reasonably be regarded as offensive at all, and the merits of the work themselves contribute to cancelling the aspects of intrusion or violation that make other pornographic works offensive. The Japanese works already mentioned, and some Indian erotic sculptures, might be examples. Artistic merit can itself, in a case of this kind, contribute to the judgement whether a work is even offensive. There is another kind of work which may be experienced as offensive, and also be experienced as having aesthetic interest, but in the case of which these two experiences do not occur at the same time. These will be works which are found offensive at first, or by a spectator who remains distanced from them, but which lose that character for someone who is involved in them. The question of how one can combine at the same time aesthetic interest in the work and a sense that it is offensive will not then arise, though these works will still be "offensive works", in the sense of works which could prove offensive to a casual viewer or to someone who came across them and was unwilling or unable to involve himself in them.

8.15 Thus there can be pornographic works of merit which are not reasonably regarded as offensive; and there can be initially offensive works which can, once the offensiveness is past, display their merits. But it would be unwise to deny that, beyond all this, there could be works which were, and remained, offensive, indeed intensely offensive or obscene, and yet possessed real merits. Experience of those merits, in such a case, would surely have to involve the fact of their obscenity, and not just co-exist with it; the repulsiveness would have to be an integral part of what was being displayed by the artist. Where the work is itself pornographic, the repulsiveness will not just be forgotten in sexual arousal, but will be part of it. Some critics have claimed that certain pieces of French literary pornography, notably by Georges Bataille, are significant works of this extreme kind.

8.16 An extraordinary work which illustrates, in a unique way, some of the complexities involved here is Pasolini's last film *Salò*. This film came repeatedly into our discussions, both because of its nature, and also because it was, during our enquiries, the subject of legal action. Having been refused a certificate by the British Board of Film Censors, it was shown in a London club but was quickly seized by the police, and those who had shown it indicted. While they were awaiting trial, the Criminal Law Act 1977 came into force, which changed the law applying to the cinema from the test of indecency to the *deprave and corrupt* test. Because of this, the Director of Public Prosecutions withdrew the proceedings, but took the unusual step of announcing that anyone who subsequently showed the film would be prosecuted. It has however recently been shown, though in a cut version. It has appeared in most other European countries.

8.17 The film displays scenes of extraordinary cruelty and repulsiveness, supposedly happening under the short-lived Fascist republic set up at Salò in 1944. It has the ritual form of a pornographic work—indeed, it is specifically modelled on Sade's *120 Days of Sodom.* All of us agreed that it is obscene, in the sense that it is ruthlessly and almost unwatchably repellent. On its other qualities, and its merits, we found ourselves in great disagreement. Most of us felt that it was manifestly not designed to produce sexual excitement, and that it took great care not to do so, even incidentally; on this view of it, the work, though obscene, is not pornographic, despite its form. Some of us, however, were more suspicious of its intentions. Those who were most impressed by it thought that it presented an extraordinary metaphor of political power and was a remarkable work, perhaps a masterpiece. For anyone with that opinion of it, it is a work that combines artistic control and seriousness with a deep and sustained obscenity.

8.18 Our conclusion is that there is no intrinsic reason why pornography or even obscene works should not be capable of having artistic merit, though there are undoubtedly reasons in the nature of such works, and even more in the general conditions of their production, to make that an unlikely and marginal occurrence, and the works, even when successful, generally of minor stature.

The public good defence

8.19 The conclusion that a work can be pornographic or even obscene and still be of artistic merit is one that of course agrees verbally with the assumptions of the Obscene Publications Acts which, as we have explained in Chapter 2, allow for the possibility that a work might be obscene and yet it be for the public good that it be published on account of its literary or artistic merit. But the agreement is only verbal, since the Obscene Publications Acts of course adopt the definition of obscenity in terms of the tendency to deprave and corrupt, rather than a notion of extreme offensiveness. Moreover, the merits of the work which would allow it to be acquitted of an offence, even though obscene, are themselves implicitly expressed in causal terms, to match the causal nature of the *deprave and corrupt* test. The work's tendency, as obscene, to produce bad effects has to be weighed against its tendency, as having artistic merit, to produce good effects, and the jury is expected to weigh one of these causal properties against the other. But if there is a difficulty, on the side of "obscenity", in ascribing harmful effects to a specific book (we shall take for the present discussion just the case of books), there is at least as much difficulty in ascribing good effects with respect to literary merit, and the task of showing why it was "for the public good" that some particular book, with its particular literary merits, should be published, is one that might understandably have baffled the expert witnesses who were called under this section.

8.20 We emphatically reject a view which a few witnesses put to us, that books have no good or bad effects at all. Quite certainly books have all sorts of effects, and in particular it is a reasonable assumption of much education that good books—for instance, masterpieces of imaginative literature—tend to have a certain kind of good effect, such as deepening a reader's understanding of human life: though one should not suppose that they are the only effects those books can have, nor that their merit is just to be calculated in terms of such effects. It has been said to us as an argument for the suppression of pornography: "If good books have good effects, then bad books must have bad effects". First, it must be said, this does not even follow: if good books have good effects it may be that all that bad books do is fail to have good effects. This is not a purely formal or verbal point. In the sense in which great works can draw the reader to new possibilities and extend his grasp, bad works may merely do nothing—they are inert, acquiescent, leave the reader as he was. Apart from this point, however, and indeed granting that bad books can have bad effects, the relevant contrast with good books does not of course lie in "bad books" in the sense of pornographic or obscene books—it lies rather in books which are "bad" because they fail to be works of creative literature, for instance because they are unoriginal and shallow and possibly, one may add, complacent or evasive as well, projecting some delusive image of life. There is room for much disagreement about the kinds of harms that might be ascribed to different kinds of bad literature, but if harm is done by bad fiction, there is certainly no reason to think that it is peculiarly done by obscene fiction, rather than by books that are bad because they are deceitfully sentimental, or even (some purist critics would suggest) just because they are badly written.

8.21 Critics, writers and other expert witnesses called by the defence under section 4 have been required to speak of the merits of the work in question in terms of these causal concepts, supposedly relating some good effect specifically to the work, of such a kind as to outweigh any tendency to deprave or corrupt which the work might also possess. The supposed causal character of these considerations, and the supposed weighing of them, constitute the first intractable feature of the public good defence. Moreover—and this point would apply to any such provision, even in less directly causal terms—the exercise has to be conducted in a court of law, the witnesses faced by cross-examination—circumstances which cannot make for the most sensible discussions of literary merit. It is not surprising that many absurd things have been said in the course of such proceedings, as by several expert witnesses for *Lady Chatterley's Lover,* or by the distinguished authority who was trapped into trying to think of otherwise unknown facts about 18th century London which one might learn from *Fanny Hill.* We have considerable sympathy for those who have gallantly

---

[1] For details of the history of the interpretation of section 4 of the Obscene Publications Act 1959, see paragraph 2.19 and following.

gone to bat for works of art under these rules, but we can only regard the rules as absurd, as many of them must also have done.

8.22 Besides the causal nature of the concepts of section 4, and besides the drastic limitations of any court procedure, there is quite another reason of principle against any such exercise. The procedure involves weighing merit, but the merit will be possessed only by works which are, to some appropriate degree, *successful* works of art. The defence therefore has to take the form of claiming that the work in question is a good work; but this cannot be an appropriate requirement. If the law on obscenity is to protect artistic activity, it has to protect experimentation and the rights of new writers in particular, to try something out. It follows that it must protect the right to try and fail, and the experiment which issues in a bad book. The public good defence in terms of actual merit cannot do this, and it is entirely to be expected that its most famous victory was in defence of a work by a writer, D H Lawrence, who was absolutely outstanding, long dead, and already highly respectable. By contrast, the defence, using section 4, of *Last Exit to Brooklyn,* an indifferent book by an unknown writer, failed before a jury, though an appeal later was successful; in that case, the expert witnesses tended to exaggerate the book's merits, and they could scarcely have done anything else, granted the underlying idea of section 4.

8.23 Not only the requirement of merit, but the mere idea of the evidence being given by experts, tends in this same direction. It is as though informed persons, literary and artistic experts, are supposed to appear from the world of culture and inform the jury of how things stand there with the work under trial. Granted this, and the other features of the Act, it is not surprising that it has been criticised as elitist in conception, and as saying in effect that corrupting books are to be permitted so long as they are admired by professors. This criticism is largely unjust, but it hits at a basic fault in the Act, its absurd model of the role of expert opinion with regard to artistic or literary merit. The model is not so much elitist, as scholastic: it implies an informed consensus about merit which, for each work, already exists. In the real world, new works have to find their own way, and see whether they elicit any appreciation or not. No one may know, for some time, what to think about them. It is not just a matter of the *avant-garde:* works in some despised medium or style may subsequently turn out to have had more meaning than most experts would have originally supposed. (The recent history of critical taste with respect to Hollywood movies of the thirties and forties, compared to "art" films of that period, is an object lesson in this.) The critical reputation of a work can continue to vary. Expert consensus, if it comes at all, and if it stays the same, must come after the event, and to assume that expert opinion is available at the event, that is to say at the time of publication, is merely to make the deathly assumption that all forms of artistic significance have already been recognised.

8.24 For all these reasons, we conclude that the idea of a public good defence, relating to artistic or literary merit, is basically misconceived, not merely in the form presented by section 4 of the Obscene Publications Act, but quite generally. We have argued earlier in this chapter that it is not to be excluded in advance that pornographic or even obscene works can, to some degree, possess serious artistic interest. If our argument is correct, the law will have to accommodate that possibility, but without resting on the illusory hope of calling in experts to tell it when the possibility has come about.

PART 3—PROPOSALS

CHAPTER NINE

THE RESTRICTION OF PUBLICATIONS

The balance of our evidence

9.1 The evidence put to us showed a remarkable balance of opinion in favour of the idea that the principal way of controlling pornography should be to restrict its availability. A large proportion of the people who wrote to us emphasised that there is a public nuisance as things are, and they asked for controls which would ensure that those who did not want to see pornography were not forced to do so. Many of the organisations who submitted memoranda to us took the same view, and proposals of this kind constantly came up in our discussions with witnesses.

9.2 In a sense, there was virtual unanimity among our witnesses that something should be done about what was seen as a public nuisance. However, the attitude of witnesses varied enormously, from extreme libertarians like the National Campaign for the Reform of the Obscene Publications Acts who were only reluctantly prepared to accept that there should be restrictions on public displays, to groups who wanted the strongest possible measures to suppress pornography but who, like the Nationwide Festival of Light, wanted these supplemented by a rigorous control of offensive displays in public places. What we found remarkable was that between these strongly opposed groups there was a very broad consensus that the main objective of the law should be to protect members of the public from the nuisance of offensive material in places to which normal life happens to take them. In many of our discussions with witnesses, from the Law Society to the Catholic Social Welfare Commission and from the Greater London Council to the Free Church Federal Council, we were struck by their readiness to agree with one another that the right way to deal with a lot of explicit sexual material at least, was to confine it to those who wanted it and prevent its offending everyone else.

9.3 The then Secretary of State for Education and Science expressed to us her view that what is allowed on open display should be clearly distinguished from other material available to adults who want it. Sir Geoffrey Howe MP commended to us the idea that if the law were effectively to meet three areas of legitimate concern, corruption of the young, affront to public decency and invasion of privacy, then society's grievances would be so well satisfied that more general restraints on obscene publications might no longer be needed. Mr Norman St John-Stevas MP made a similar proposal in an article in *The Observer* in February 1976, suggesting that the law should be shifted on to a basis of public nuisance, being confined to protecting people from being impinged on or annoyed by pornography as they go about their ordinary business, and to protecting children. Lord Justice Lawton expressed the opinion to us that the right approach was to regard pornography as a public nuisance and that the law should therefore concentrate on containing it rather than prohibiting it.

9.4 It was to be expected that bodies to whom the idea of freedom of expression is paramount, such as the Society of Authors, the Writers' Guild and the Defence of Literature and the Arts Society, should regard a law against public nuisances as more acceptable than one aimed at total suppression. To emphasise the broad support which we found for this approach, however, we quote other examples of the evidence we received from various bodies, often from those not committed in advance to any particular attitude on such questions. For example, the National Federation of Women's Institutes told us that there was a general feeling among their members that it was impossible to suppress pornography and that this, coupled with views about individual freedom, meant there should instead be strict supervision over its sale so that it would be less easily accessible to children and less likely to offend ordinary people. The Penal Affairs Committee of the Society of Friends considered that the control of pornographic material, particularly ensuring that people are not unwillingly exposed to it, was preferable to attempting to prohibit it. The Liberal Party believed that the law should be confined to protecting non-consenting adults and children, with adults otherwise having the right to see what they wished. That this should be the only form of control was not generally conceded, but there were other bodies who considered that there should be some range of material available only under restricted conditions: the Mothers' Union, the Magistrates' Association and the Police Superintendents' Association of England and Wales, for example, all put forward the view that there might be special closely-regulated or licensed shops to which the sale of certain material should be confined.

9.5 The idea of protecting the public from a nuisance was also accepted by those with a commercial interest in the material likely to be so restricted. The British Adult Publications Association emphasised that their members had no wish to offend reasonable people and accepted that society is justified in regulating public display more severely than private sale; they wanted to keep within the law and would adapt to whatever new restrictions might be imposed. The Association for Cinema Club Standards agreed that considerations of public nuisance were important and told us that their members had agreed on restrictions on advertising and front of house displays. We were told by the National Federation of Retail Newsagents that many ordinary retailers would welcome the establishment of special shops for the sale of material of this kind if the result was to make it easier for the newsagent to determine what he could and could not legally sell. We also found some sympathy among wholesalers for the idea that this particular aspect of the trade should be segregated in some way.

9.6 The idea of permitting some kind of restricted trade in a certain class of material was nevertheless opposed by some witnesses. The Nationwide Festival of Light saw it as condoning the traffic in pornography, and a similar argument came from others with strong views about the evils of pornography, such as Mrs. Mary Whitehouse and Mr. James Anderton, Chief Constable of Greater Manchester. Mrs. Whitehouse stressed the problem of "leakage", that is, that publications of this kind are widely circulated after their initial sale and that a control on the retail trade cannot stop them becoming available to children, and obvious to people who find them offensive. Mr. Anderton thought that those who advocated restrictions on the trade just because they believed that suppression could not be satisfactorily and strictly enforced by law were being defeatist. There were also arguments of a different kind; that there would be physical problems in finding separate rooms in which the material could be segregated, for example; and that shops concentrating on such material would not be viable or, on the other hand, that they would be excessively profitable and attract the attention of crime syndicates. There was also an argument from the British Humanist Association and some others that to separate the trade in this way would increase the burden of guilt and repression on those who wanted access to pornography. There was some conflict of psychiatric opinion on this question; the Portman Clinic thought that there was now a well-established need for certain material and that to put it into a ghetto carried the danger of making it the prerogative of psychopathic and criminal groups; but at the same time value was seen in there being some kind of social barrier which would help a disturbed patient to tell the difference between what was and what was not acceptable.

9.7 Despite these reservations about the notion of imposing a control rather than a prohibition, we were convinced by the evidence we received that an approach directed primarily at curbing a public nuisance would command very wide support. The arguments that we have explored in Part 2 of this Report have convinced us that such an approach would be appropriate and acceptable in principle, and also that it is neither necessary nor desirable to give the law the task of trying to suppress all pornography. We conclude, therefore, that the law should primarily aim to restrict pornography so that it will not be offensive to the public, and to satisfy the widespread feeling that young people should not be exposed to material of this kind.

The means of preventing offensiveness

9.8 The proposition that the public should be protected against unwilling exposure to offensive material is not of course new. It is embodied in the existing and long-standing law against indecent public displays and has found recent expression in the various attempts to introduce fresh legislation to modernise that law. This inevitably gives rise to certain questions. If we already have such a law, why is there so much dissatisfaction with the lack of protection it gives? If the situation is such that people are so frequently offended, why is the law so rarely invoked? If the present law is inadequate to prevent public offensiveness, why is a new statute enacting broadly the same provisions considered to be the solution? Our answer goes back to a point that we have already made in paragraph 7.11. So far as pornographic materials are concerned, it is not usually the degree of undress or the nature of the scenes actually visible to the casual public that are very special: often, considered entirely in themselves, they need not differ greatly from much material that is accepted elsewhere. It is the fact that they are obviously associated with pornography that makes them specially offensive. Magazine covers, for instance, are usually comparatively inoffensive compared with what is between the covers. But if legal control is in terms of indecent displays, it is the cover alone which is at issue, since the contents are not on display. It seemed to us, however, that public concern was less about what people actually saw as it was about what they knew it to be. Attempts to stop indecent displays, aimed as they must be just at the intrinsic character of what is shown, are necessarily misdirected, and doomed to disappoint those who put their hopes in them. The problem lies not with indecent displays, but with displays of the indecent, and to control these, one needs to go beyond the content of the mere display itself to the character of the item being displayed.

9.9 Of course, to an extraordinary degree, nudity, titillation, eroticism and sexual imagery are generally deployed in present capitalist societies, above all for purposes of advertisement, and having nothing to do with pornography or obscene publications at all. These motifs appear on hoardings, on the sides of buses, on posters in Underground stations, in magazines and newspapers, outside cinemas and theatres and in entertainments generally. People differ in their reactions to these displays, and in the degree to which they notice them. Many people, as is clear from submissions to us, dislike them. But three things seem to us quite clear. One is that the reactions to such displays (for instance, the kind of gigantic advertisement for stockings or underwear which can confront one from the other side of the Underground line), even when the reactions are hostile, are very rarely anything like the sense of offensiveness many experience with pornography. Second, it is highly unlikely that our society is going to take the view that the law should step in to suppress such displays; and many even of those who dislike them would say that this should not be a proper task for the law. Third, no law could be effective unless it were either so oppressive as to require radical changes in many features of life (publications, advertising, television, films and other entertainment) which are now regarded as generally acceptable, or else gave dictatorial powers to some person or body to enforce good taste. But if a law against indecent displays is insufficient to banish these advertisements for rum or tyres, it will touch very little of what is presently seen on the outside of pornography, either.

How to achieve restriction

9.10 We thus arrived at the conclusion that positive steps should be taken to restrict the availability of a certain class of material, so that children and young people, and adults who had no interest in it, were less likely to come into contact with it. We considered whether measures to restrict such material within shrink-wrapping or to high shelves or to plain wrappers or to sale from under the counter would meet this desire, but we decided that such restrictions would be less than satisfactory in removing this material from the consciousness of people making routine transactions in their local shop, and in some ways it could just make the situation worse. We also considered whether the idea of a separate part of the premises, such as a back room in a newsagent's—as would have been permitted under the proposals of the Vagrancy Working Party—would represent an adequate segregation. Here again, we thought that the object of the control would not adequately be answered by such a scheme. We had to bear in mind that the Vagrancy Working Party's proposals represented in effect a secondary control on offensive material: their recommendations for protecting the public from indecent material assumed that the existing law against obscene material would operate to ensure that a large range of offensive material would not be sold even in the back room. Our proposals, on the other hand, are to make restriction the primary control (though not the only control) on pornography and if the aim is to avoid knowledge of the presence of objectionable material offending the day-to-day customers of ordinary shops, we considered that a stricter demarcation was called for.

9.11 We therefore decided that material of this kind should not be available at all in ordinary shops. We realise that even a separate shop will not avoid public consciousness of the existence of pornography, but we have already argued in Chapter 7 (paragraph 7.14) that there must be some point along the line where the balance has to be found between public upset and individual liberty. If this material is available only to those who choose to look for it and if children are automatically excluded, this seems substantially to satisfy the objective. What is achieved is that members of the public who go to ordinary retailers in order to buy publications of general interest, newspapers, sweets and tobacco etc, will be freed from the offensive presence of pornography, and generally they will not run into it as they go about their ordinary business.

9.12 As we have made clear already, some of our witnesses wanted the sale of material of this kind to be specially regulated or even specially taxed, and suggested licensed premises to sell it, on the model of off-licences or betting shops. We considered these arguments, but in the end saw no grounds on which we needed to make a recommendation to this effect. The main objective, in our view, is merely to restrict the availability of pornography. We see no reason to dignify pornography with the trappings of a licensing system or to make provision for those carrying on businesses in such material to be subject to vetting or for their premises to be subject to inspection. We do not think that the analogy with gambling or alcohol has any validity, since in those fields there are considerations of protecting the consumer from dishonesty and sharp practice and of reducing the chances of public disorder, and these have no relevance to the sale of pornography. The need for a licensing system to ensure that a service is carried out properly scarcely applies to this kind of business, which in any case is of interest to a relatively small part of the population and therefore lacks a place in national life that would justify the establishment of a formal system of control.

9.13 We also received proposals that there should be additional planning controls on shops selling pornography and similar establishments. This would involve the amendment of the use classes designated under the Town and Country Planning Acts, since the present use classes do not, subject to certain exceptions, distinguish between one shop and another. A butcher's shop may become a boutique, and a cycle shop be transformed into a sex shop, without any form of approval being required from the local planning authority. If, however, an exception to the use class covering shops were made in respect of shops selling pornography, the planning authority would be able to control the numbers and location of such shops. It was emphasised to us, on the other hand, that this change would not secure the object which our witnesses had in mind, since the planning authority, in giving permission for a particular use, is not able to have regard to every factor it believes to affect the public interest, but only to those strictly related to planning considerations. The potential effect on local amenities which attaches to the existing exceptions concerning shops for the sale of such things as hot food, tripe and pets, is, it was said, of a different and more objective nature than that attaching to sex shops. There was therefore real doubt as to the extent to which the planning authority could properly take into account the nature of the goods which such a shop was to sell. It seemed to us that the pressures which would be placed on planning authorities when they were considering an application to open a pornography shop were unlikely to be based strictly on planning and amenity grounds and that it would be undesirable, by requiring special permission for such shops, to arouse expectations that other kinds of objection would be relevant. It is clear in any case that market forces are likely to restrict the number of such shops. We do recognise the concern felt by some communities about the way particular localities appear to attract businesses of this kind, and we noted the steps that many cities in the United States have taken to secure the zoning of this trade, either by confining it to a particular locality and preventing it from spreading elsewhere, or, conversely, by ensuring its dispersal and avoiding an overconcentration in certain areas. However, we found it hard to see sufficient reason why pornography shops out of so many other kinds of retail outlet should be singled out for special planning control. We concluded that the balance of the argument was against seeking to amend the Town and Country Planning Regulations to impose such a control.[1]

9.14 We are satisfied that the restriction of pornography should be in negative terms only; that is, that it should aim only to place it behind certain obstacles, so as to protect the public at large, and young people in particular, from exposure to it. We do not advocate the setting up of pornography shops nor do we suggest any other positive measures for regulating the way in which pornography is made available. We sympathise with those who told us that we ought to avoid according to pornography any legal or bureaucratic recognition, and we see no need to do so.

The nature of restriction

9.15 The nature of the conditions to be placed on the lawful sale of offensive material flows fairly naturally from what we have so far said about the aims of restricting it. We think it should be unlawful to sell or display this material other than in separate premises, or at least a part of premises having a separate access from the street, to which no person under the age of eighteen should be admitted. (The choice of the age of eighteen will be argued later, in paragraphs 9.39-40.) We consider in addition that the aim of avoiding public offensiveness arising from the public presence of this material demands not only that it should not be displayed publicly but that shops selling it should be required to maintain a discreet existence and not display in their windows similar but slightly less offensive material: the best course, we believe, is for any such shop not to be allowed any window displays at all but to present a blank exterior, subject only to the display of its name and the nature of its business. Exterior signs, in our view, need not be subject to any particular control other than that provided by the existing law on the control of advertisements. To protect the unwary member of the public, we think it right that any shop wishing to sell restricted publications should exhibit a warning notice at its entrance in such a way that an unsuspecting customer could not see any of the goods offered for sale until he had seen the sign; the sign would state that what was displayed could be offensive and that persons under eighteen were not admitted. There might be advantage in the text of such a notice being prescribed by legislation.

[1] For a further consideration about planning control, see paragraph 9.41.

9.16 We considered whether the restrictions should go further than this. One suggestion we looked at, for example, was that a shop wishing to meet these conditions in order to be able to sell restricted material should be further restricted in the goods it was able to sell, so that, for example, a shop selling pornography would be precluded from selling goods of a wider appeal, perhaps as loss leaders, in order to entice customers into the shop. We were conscious that this would involve problems of definition, particularly as we consider it unnecessary and undesirable to insist that these special shops should sell only restricted material. Nothing came to our notice to suggest that this was a problem which has arisen in relation to those existing shops specialising in pornography. We decided that it would be consistent with our approach of applying only a negative control to the sale of pornography that a shop which accepted the conditions that we have so far recommended should not be faced with any further constraints on what it could and could not sell. We concluded that the obstacles we have already proposed were sufficient. No ordinary shop would be prepared to exclude persons under eighteen, to operate behind blank windows and to exhibit warning notices to those contemplating entering. If a shop is prepared to go to those lengths, we think that the protection of the young and of the unwilling adult from offence are sufficiently secured.

Mail order trading

9.17 There are other methods of trading besides shops. There already exists, though in most cases strictly against the law, a mail-order trade in pornography. From the point of view of avoiding public offensiveness, this trade has much to be said for it; if a customer wants material which others would find offensive, his ordering it to be sent to him by a dealer does not impinge at all on the public at large. We were therefore satisfied that any scheme intended to avoid public offence should permit the supply of restricted material by post. However, this mode of trading involves two kinds of difficulty. First, a shop can fairly easily keep out people who look as if they are under 18, whereas a mail-order trader does not know much about those who send in orders. Secondly, only a customer who chooses to enter will find himself inside a pornography shop, whereas it is much easier for the unsuspecting to find himself in receipt of material through the post, even where the dealer conscientiously avoids indiscriminate mailing, because there will always be hoaxers who arrange for matter (usually free brochures rather than an article which has to be paid for) to be sent to others.

9.18 We must make the point that neither of these difficulties was mentioned to us as significant in the way the trade has so far been carried on, and we do not think that they tell against allowing mail-order trading altogether. Clearly, however, some safeguards are necessary, particularly to protect the individual from invasion of privacy. We think it right that it should be an offence for a dealer to send restricted material to persons under eighteen or to other persons who have not ordered it. In framing a criminal offence along these lines, one will have to require some degree of guilty knowledge on the part of the dealer, though he will be expected to take reasonable steps to ensure that the law is not broken.

9.19 Where we are considering matter addressed to an individual in his or her home, there are good reasons for insisting that individual privacy needs protection against a class of material wider than that which would be restricted in a more generalised public setting. We noted in this context that section 4 of the Unsolicited Goods and Services Act 1971 had penalised the unsolicited circulation not only of material of a prohibited class but of advertisements for such material, and satisfaction was expressed to us that the Act had effectively stopped many unsolicited circulars which had caused offence to their recipients. We think this approach is reasonable and we propose that the unsolicited circulation of advertisements for restricted material should be prohibited. This has, after all, some parallel with our proposal that shops selling restricted material should not be allowed to display publicly even material which falls short of being restricted, and we think it will make a positive contribution to avoiding unnecessary offence being caused to members of the public.

The definition of restricted material

9.20 We have so far left on one side what is perhaps the most crucial problem, that of defining the material which is to be the subject of restriction. The question of definition occupied a central position in our review: as we have emphasised earlier, it is the definitions of the existing law which contribute very largely to dissatisfaction with it and it is the problem of drawing lines for the future with which a good deal of our evidence was concerned. It was the aspect of our review which preoccupied us more than any other: it became clear to us that the success of any new system would depend very heavily on the effectiveness of any legal definition we proposed and also that there were very considerable difficulties in formulating a test of the right kind.

9.21 One of the first decisions we took was to escape from the words which have been a part of the law for so long. The "tendency to deprave and corrupt" and the words "obscene" and "indecent" were, we concluded, now useless. The charges of vagueness and confusion were so widespread that it was clear to us that we should break with the past completely. But how should a new law tackle the problem? The alternative formulations we received were almost as numerous as the people who offered them. We considered three fundamentally different approaches to the problem, each resting on a different basis. One was to find some catch-all word or phrase or general formula, such as the law had used hitherto, but a new and more useful one. The second was to be totally specific, by listing or describing in detail what it was that could not be shown. The third was to abandon formulae or lists in favour of personal judgement, and to recommend that a tribunal should be established which would determine exactly where the line should be drawn in particular cases.

9.22 Some witnesses who were chiefly concerned for certainty in the operation of the law favoured the idea of a tribunal. They argued that it was in effect applying to publications what was already well-accepted in the case of films, and that models for such a system were to be found in New Zealand and Australia. It would mean that those involved in the trade in publications would know exactly where they stood in relation to what they could or could not handle, because the tribunal would tell them in advance. Such a system avoids the need for a sophisticated legal definition because the tribunal itself can contribute all the finer tuning in the course of its own determinations on particular publications. There are various ways in which a tribunal system could work and those in the Australian states and in New Zealand are not identical. However, we concluded that despite those precedents a system of precensoring publications would be quite unacceptable in this country and should be ruled out without detailed consideration of the practicalities. It seemed to us that there were strong objections to the idea that publications should be subject to vetting before being put on sale, even if the vetting were confined to a certain class liable to be at risk of restriction and even granted that the aim was not to ban publications entirely but only to confine their sale to certain outlets. We also found it hard to imagine how such a tribunal would be recruited, what suitable people would be willing to serve on it, or by what means it could hope to gain public acceptance. We turned away from the tribunal back to some legal formula or list to be used in the courts.

9.23 Some of our witnesses considered that certainty in the law would be best served by an explicit statement of what was not allowed. Words like "obscene" and "indecent", it was argued, would always be interpreted in different ways by different people, but if the law said that photographs should not show *x*, *y* or *z*, there could be no dispute. Faced as we were with so much criticism of the vagueness and uncertainty of the existing law, we could see the attractions in making the law explicit and we therefore gave this proposal detailed consideration. We did not go far with our consideration, however, before seeing some difficulties and pitfalls.

9.24 One problem with this approach is that immediately an explicit statement of what is disallowed is written into the law, the law becomes ossified. If we imagine that twenty years ago the legislators had enacted the Obscene Publications Act on the basis of an explicit description of what was to be regarded as obscene, how curious their list would now seem. How many times in the meantime would the list have needed amendment to keep in step with changing public attitudes? More to the point, perhaps, how many times, given Parliamentary pressures, would the list have actually been amended? Where, as we propose, the object of the law is to prevent offence, it must necessarily apply to what is generally found offensive and it is therefore essential in our view that the law should be responsive to flux in public opinion. To specify exactly what we regard as representing the level of offensiveness against which the law should act involves fixing a standard relative to our conception of current reactions. But that standard may no longer be valid even when legislation comes to be enacted; and once it is enacted it will become an extremely inflexible standard which will tend to attract even more ridicule and odium to the law.

9.25 Another problem with the explicit statement is that it needs to draw fine distinctions about precisely where the line is drawn, as opposed to enabling a judgement to be made as to whether the overall effect is offensive or not. This misdirects attention from the main concern, and can produce absurd results. An illustration can be taken from the guidelines of the British Adult Publications Association, to which we referred earlier. Publications intended to conform with the Association's guidelines must not contain photographs showing "actual sexual contact", and to draw the line at that point implies that a photograph is permissible so long as actual contact is avoided; a centimetre of daylight satisfies the guidelines, though it may not in fact alter the offensiveness of the picture in the slightest. The Association goes on to muddy the water by explaining that illustrations showing near contact may also be prohibited "if considered to be over-explicit"; uncertainties about what is "over-explicit" then begin to detract from the value of trying to be specific.

9.26 To take another example from the opposite end of the spectrum, possibly the most repressive proposals submitted to us were from a group of people who wanted the meaning of obscenity made explicit through a list which included "photographic portrayal of the adult female breast". Leaving aside the question of whether it could be realistic to set the law against this target, it was far from clear to us just how the courts would interpret this test in relation to many of the photographs frequently seen, for example, in advertisements, taking account of the degree of *décolletage*, the transparency of covering, the discreetness of the angle and similar factors. And even the most repressive would no doubt recognise that this could not be an absolute prohibition and that some kind of allowance must be made for legitimate use of such photographs. To be specific, it seemed to us, involved being arbitrary and ignoring the contribution which the context or the manner of presentation would inevitably make: material on the illegal side of the line might be in fact inoffensive, and material which managed to fall on the permitted side might nevertheless be quite offensive.

9.27 Another problem is that to base a law on an explicit statement of what is prohibited requires that the statement should also be exhaustive. We found, however, that it was far from easy to be satisfied that any definition covered all the ground that it should. There is always the danger that the enterprising pornographer will be able to develop from any explicit list a blueprint of what he can get away with; using it as a basis he can employ his ingenuity in identifying forms of activity which had never occurred to the wholesome minds of Committee members and legislators. We found that it was not difficult to pick holes in the various lists presented to us by our witnesses, and concluded that loopholes were inevitable in any list that it was practicable to produce. But it also seemed to us that it was peculiarly unattractive to attempt to set out an exhaustive list of what was forbidden: in trying to forestall the fertile imagination of pornographers, the list would become ridiculous, embarrassing and itself potentially offensive.

9.28 Having considered the list approach in the light of the difficulties we have described, we reached the conclusion that it would not satisfactorily form the basis of a legal scheme of restriction. We did not abandon the hope that a more specific test would be possible than was to be found under the existing law, but we decided that it was impractical for the law simply to embody a description of those types of pictorial matter which at any particular time Parliament happened to think were those that caused offence and were therefore to be restricted. We considered that it would be preferable for the law to be explicit about its objectives rather than about what the result of pursuing those objectives at one particular time was thought to be.

The formula we propose

9.29 We accordingly considered with some care what formula might be appropriate to the aims that the law legitimately should pursue. We have already explained in Chapter 7 (paragraph 7.23) our reasons for preferring, among general terms, the word "offensive". As we also mentioned there, we were conscious that people do differ in the extent to which they find things offensive, and that therefore something should be incorporated to refer to what is, at any given time, the norm. After a great deal of consideration, we decided in favour of the definition's referring to what is offensive to *reasonable people*. The notion of a reasonable person (usually in the unduly restricted form of "the reasonable man") is already known to the law, in connection with judgements of responsibility, negligence, and reasonable foresight. While that is a rather different kind of matter, we thought it was appropriate to apply the term to the notion required here, which is that of a person who takes a balanced view of the material in question, and is neither excessively upset by each item nor totally indifferent to everything. Such judgements will manifestly be affected by contemporary taste and expectations, but that is part of the point—as we have already said, in this kind of field any formula must permit its effect to shift with time. Conclusions that something is "offensive to reasonable people" are bound to be rather loose or rough, in the sense that it is not a matter of simple verifiable fact, and a magistrate will have to use his or her judgement. But in any question of this kind, this is inevitable, whatever the formula—that is the kind of question it is. Our proposed formula does not try to conceal that fact; moreover, unlike the existing formulae, it does make it clear what the rough judgement is a judgement about.

9.30 Our discussions up to this point about what should be restricted have been in terms of there being a certain kind of material which reasonable people at a given time would find offensive material. This is the basic case, and in a sense the root of the whole question. This naturally suggests that the definition of what is to be restricted should be expressed in terms of material *which is offensive to reasonable people*. However, the problem is not as simple as this makes it seem.

9.31 First of all, the notion of offensiveness needs further qualification. There are various kinds of matter which might prove in various ways offensive to reasonable people but which would not properly be caught by a law aimed at pornography and similar material. We need a provision to make it clear what kind of offensiveness is in question. To meet this point we propose that matter should be restricted only in virtue of offensiveness which arises by reason of the manner in which it portrays, deals with or relates to violence, cruelty or horror, or sexual, faecal or urinary functions, or genital organs. The introduction of this specification does not mean a reversion to the list approach; it does not offer any ground of restriction independent of the notion of offensiveness. It merely makes clear what kind or dimension of offensiveness is in question. This clarification of the notion of offensiveness should, we propose, be spelled out in the law governing restriction. In the rest of this Report, when we use the term "offensive" unqualifiedly, it should be taken to mean offensiveness of the kind specified in this paragraph.

9.32 Granted that this is what is meant by "offensive", is it in fact satisfactory to define the material to be restricted simply in terms of the offensiveness of that material, as suggested at the end of paragraph 9.30? As we have said, that is a very natural proposal, but after extensive discussion we have come to the conclusion that that provision would not actually effect what is required. In Chapter 7, we claimed that there are two different boundaries crossed by publicly displayed pornography. Its nature involves a violation of lines between private and public, and this is often in itself found offensive; but, further, its public display forces this violation on to unwilling spectators, and this is also something offensive. The formula suggested in paragraph 9.30 relates essentially to the first consideration, the offensive character of the material itself. But this will cover only material which a reasonable person would find offensive wherever he encountered it—even if, for instance, he were privately given it by a friend. This leaves out the possibility that there could be pornographic or similar material which a reasonable person would not find offensive under those circumstances, but would find offensive if it were publicly displayed. Granted the two separate boundaries which, we have claimed, are crossed by publicly displayed pornography, it seems to us entirely possible that there should be material, presumably of a milder kind, which a reasonable person could scarcely find offensive if privately encountered, but which he or she would not want to see openly displayed and available next to the sweets in the local newsagent's. It seems to us that the definition of restricted material should explicitly involve the notion of public availability, and we propose that restriction should apply to matter *whose unrestricted availability is offensive to reasonable people.* It is to be understood all the time that the offensiveness in question is the kind already specified in paragraph 9.31.

9.33 We must emphasise that, so far as adult persons are concerned, it is not any paternalist interest that recommends this form of restriction test. The reason that we have introduced the notion of the public availability of the material being offensive is not that we are concerned with the case in which a reasonable person, not finding the material in itself offensive, thinks that other people, presumably less reasonable than himself, would find it in itself offensive. We are concerned with the case of material which in itself a reasonable person does not find offensive (in the sense of being upset or put off by it wherever he might find it), but the public display and availability of which that same person finds offensive. Paternalistic protection of other adults is thus not the motivation of the test. However, paternalistic protection in the literal sense, the protection of children and young people, is a proper and very important aim of the law in this area, one which has been put to us by many witnesses, and this provides another reason for adopting the kind of restriction formula we propose. There may well be material which reasonable people would not find offensive in itself, but which responsible parents would not want to be available to children and young people, and this is properly something to be restricted.

9.34 We considered very carefully the idea that a separate restriction test should be introduced to cover this area of concern, but we have finally decided that this not necessary. Moreover, we believe that to associate the protection of the young with the same provision as has already been introduced for other reasons serves to bring out an important point, that the concern for the young is focused on just the same features of the material as makes its display offensive to adults. What moves people to feel that pornographic and similar material should not be available to the young is just the same sort of thing that makes them find its display offensive. Someone may of course think that there are other, quite different, sorts of reasons why certain publications which are suitable for adults, and which, granted that there are no young people around, are even suitable for display to adults, should not be available to young people. To this we would say that if there are such publications, they will have to be controlled by methods other than our restriction test, and this seems to us the correct result. We would not think it right that law designed to control the availability of pornography and similar material should be capable of being extended to control the availability of other matter to the young. If someone thinks, *for the kinds of reasons that are our concern,* that a publication should not fall into the hands of the young, then he will find its public availability, not merely undesirable in some general sense, but indeed offensive. We conclude, therefore, that the interest in protecting the young is appropriately met by the restriction formula we propose.

9.35 We have suggested that our restriction formula is to be preferred to a simpler test, in terms merely of offensive material, because it desirably goes rather wider. The question then arises, whether it catches everything that the simpler test would catch. Could there be material which was offensive to reasonable people but whose public availability would not be offensive? So far as pornography and similar material is concerned, we think that the answer is obviously "no". If anything of that sort is offensive in itself, so is its availability, and it will be caught by our formula. However, there might be another kind of material for which this was not so: for instance, certain kinds of news or historical material. There could be news photographs of some atrocity which were very shocking, and could properly be described as offensive by reason of the way they related to violence and cruelty. Reasonable people would be upset or repelled by them, and indeed, in that sense, find them offensive. However, if the photographs are circulated or made available genuinely in order to inform, instruct, warn, and so forth, and not in any exploitative spirit, then, it seems to us, a reasonable person would not find their public availability offensive.

9.36 We have already argued (paragraph 7.22) that no publication should be liable to restriction in virtue of matter that it contains which consists solely of the written word. What we propose as a restriction test, then, fully spelled out, is that matter should be restricted

> which, not consisting of the written word, is such that its unrestricted availability is offensive to reasonable people by reason of the manner in which it portrays, deals with or relates to violence, cruelty or horror, or sexual, faecal or urinary functions, or genital organs.

9.37 It seems to us that this definition would clearly apply to the pictorial sex magazines which have come into circulation in Britain in recent years. It would also, in our view, apply to horror comics of the kind that the Children and Young Persons (Harmful Publications) Act 1955 was aimed against, though it will mean that the test of the "tendency to corrupt a child" will be superseded by what we believe to be the more realistic and straightforward test of what is, in the respects mentioned in the last paragraph, offensive to reasonable people. The effect of our proposals is that nothing to which this definition applies will be able to be displayed in public places or be sold in shops to which children and young people have access. Restriction will not be imposed on naturist magazines or on pin-up magazines of a more old-fashioned variety, since we do not propose that simple nudity should bring a publication within the prescribed class. Restriction will apply not only to publications, but to 8 mm films etc; also, the kind of sex hardware to be found in many sexshops would we think be equally covered by the definition. It is certainly not our intention that contraceptives should be restricted in the same way, and we think it desirable that the law should make it clear that contraceptive materials are not included under the definition.

9.38 It is appropriate at this point that we refer to the subject of blasphemy. The offence of blasphemy does not fall within our terms of reference and indeed it is the subject of separate review, along with other offences against religion, by the Law Commission. We do not, therefore, have to deal with it. However, we think that it would be artificial for us to leave it out, since the only recent instances in which the offence of blasphemy has been used (in the case of the publication by *Gay News* of a poem by James Kirkup) or the possibility of its being used has been in issue (principally as regards the projected film of the purported sex life of Christ) have been in a connection which falls plainly within the field we have been considering. We therefore express the view that the principles we have set out relating to harm and offensiveness apply equally to matter of this kind and that the appropriate way for the law to deal with such matter is through the scheme we have outlined here. We do not believe that the law should seek to restrain material of this kind if it does not offend against the test we have recommended and consequently we consider that in these connections there is no need for a separate offence of blasphemy. Whether there are other reasons for keeping an offence of blasphemy is not for us to decide.

The age limit for special protection

9.39 There is no obvious choice for the age below which young people should be specially protected against exposure to restricted material. Sixteen is the age of consent in relation to heterosexual activity and the age at which young people, with their parents' consent, may marry. Some witnesses thought that it would be odd—and was already odd in relation to the present film censorship system—that married couples free to engage in sexual activity should be considered too young to view the portrayal of sexual activity by others, and this was an argument put to us strongly by the British Youth Council as reflecting the views expressed in the course of their consultations among young people themselves. This argument did not prevent the minimum age for admission to 'X' films being raised from sixteen to eighteen in 1970, and we noted that eighteen is the age customarily adopted by the owners of existing pornography shops as the minimum for entry to such shops. Eighteen is of course the age of majority and the age at which young people may marry without their parents' consent. It seemed to us that the real choice lay between these two ages rather than between either of them and some other age, higher, lower or in between.

9.40 We thought that the argument that those who could lawfully engage in sexual activity should be allowed free access to pornography took an over-simple view of pornography. Much of what we have seen does not merely portray straightforward sexual activity of the kind that those who propose such arguments seem to have in mind. Those responsible for the censorship of films firmly believe that there is much film material that is totally unsuitable for adolescents, and the modification of the censorship categories in 1970 reflected the concern of those then responsible that an age limit of sixteen did not sufficiently protect those likely to be at risk from seeing films of this nature. Arguably, many publications fall into the same category. We have already reported in Chapter 6 that there was no consensus among our expert witnesses about the age at which young people cease to need special protection, given the varying ages at which a certain level of maturity is reached. But the evidence we received gave some grounds for thinking that many young people of sixteen might still be vulnerable. Moreover, we felt bound to take into account, as the film censors sometimes do, that there is often a "slippage" problem in applying age restrictions, and that, for example, the adoption of eighteen as the age below which protection is given will in practice mean that far fewer fifteen-year-olds will be put at risk than if the prescribed age were sixteen. Given these doubts, and the recognition that the present practice in relation both to the showing of films and the sale of pornography adopts eighteen as the appropriate age to which to continue restrictions, our conclusion is that it would be wrong for us to recommend that the age be lowered.

A public good defence?

9.41 We had to consider one other issue relating to the scope of the definition. This was whether there were grounds on which some matter might need to be exempted from restriction. Exemption might be on the kind of basis which allows the present exemption under the Obscene Publications Acts—artistic, literary or scientific merit, for example—or on the kind of basis urged on us by the Defence of Literature and the Arts Society that it might be for the public good to display frank posters illustrating the dangers of venereal disease. So far as artistic merit is concerned, we have already argued that a public good defence is anyway unworkable; and since the restrictions are not to apply to the written word, the question, for literary works, cannot arise (this is indeed one, but only one, of the reasons for not applying restrictions to the written word). Bearing in mind the terms that we propose for the definition, we doubt that there is a need for any exemptions at all. Medical textbooks deal with and depict sexual organs, etc but we do not think that reasonable people are likely to find their availability offensive. There are visual works of art which, despite the fact that their content falls within the area described in the specification, would also not be reasonably found offensive. However, there could be others, as we have argued in Chapter 8, which are such that they or their display would reasonably be found offensive; in that case, there is no objection to their being on restricted display. Restricted display, after all, does not necessarily mean display in a sex shop; an art shop or gallery could satisfy the law by making no display outside the premises, restricting admission to adults, and putting up a warning notice, for the duration of that particular exhibition. (That one should be able to provide for this possibility is another argument against making restricted premises a special use-class under the planning regulations: see paragraph 9.13 above).

9.42 We also think it highly unlikely that reasonable adults would find that the display of straightforward posters about venereal disease or about road safety—even if their intention is to horrify and shock the viewer out of a state of complacency—were offensive, but we think it right that such posters should even so be subject to the law. Posters need not be offensive to be effective and we see no reason why posters of that particular kind should not be subject to restrictions designed to protect the general public from offensiveness with respect to sex and violence.

Enforcing restriction

9.43 It remains for us to deal with the arrangements for enforcing the restriction of publications and displays. First, we envisage that the sale or displays of restricted material other than in the circumstances we have described above should constitute an offence. This would clearly not be an offence calling for the heaviest penalties: restricted material is not to be regarded as inherently objectionable to the law and the mischief lies only in its being sold in the wrong place. Accordingly, it does not seem to us that either the nature of the offence or the need for an effective deterrent against non-compliance requires that it should be triable other than in a magistrates' court, though we think that magistrates should be given their normal maximum sentencing powers, including the ability to send offenders to prison, so that they can effectively deal with a person who might otherwise consider it worth while to break the law in a persistent way. The same should apply to offences of sending restricted material through the post to persons under eighteen and to people who had not solicited it. It seemed to us that in all these proceedings what was offensive to reasonable people should be a simple matter of judgement for the court: it is not an issue on which evidence ought to be admissible.

9.44 In considering the creation of offences, the question arises whether there should be a legal deterrent against a person under eighteen who tries to gain entry to restricted premises or solicits restricted material to be sent through mail order. This is similar to the arguments put to us strongly by cinema interests that there should be a sanction on the young customer as well as on the cinema licensee in relation to the restriction of entry to films with "X" certificates, an issue which we shall discuss at greater length in Chapter 12. We do not think that the pressures will in any case be the same, because the evidence we received was that young people were far less interested in pornography shops than in seeing the latest film given an "X" certificate. We are not proposing that it should be an offence for a shopkeeper simply to admit a person who is in fact under eighteen—as opposed to failing to take reasonable steps to enforce the restriction—and we simply record our view that it is not necessary for a person under eighteen to be liable to criminal charges if he or she attempts to gain entry to a shop closed to persons of that age or orders material by post.

9.45 Although it may often be the case that a restriction offence will be a blatant one, in the sense that a shopkeeper will be openly selling from his shelves material which should be restricted, there could well be other cases where restricted material is being sold more discreetly, from under the counter for example, and where evidence may be harder to obtain. For this reason in particular, we propose that the police should have power, with the authority of a magistrate's warrant, to enter premises to search for restricted material being traded in contravention of the restrictions, and to seize such material as may be necessary for purposes of evidence. We heard some complaints that the present seizure powers are exercised in a way that denies the occupier of the premises a receipt or at least some form of record of what has been taken by the police. We think that this is wrong and although we consider it preferable, in the light of the practical difficulties which undoubtedly exist in some circumstances, not to lay down a formal requirement for a receipt to be given at the time of seizure, we express the view that a person from whom goods are seized should be given at the earliest practicable opportunity a detailed record of what has been taken from him. We also heard complaints that the police sometimes seize irrelevant items along with the publications believed to be obscene; there is already a civil remedy available in such cases and we do not think it necessary to make any proposal to deal with the possibility of abuse of seizure powers. We believe, however, that our proposals will mean that in future there will be less scope for the seizure of irrelevant material.

9.46 It does not seem to us appropriate, however, that the police should have a power of arrest for this offence, nor that there should be a procedure similar to that under the Obscene Publications Acts, by which a court can be invited simply to order the forefeiture of material as an alternative to considering criminal charges against the person from whom it was seized. As we have already made clear, it is not the material itself which offends against the law but only its mode of sale, and we therefore consider that the proper way of proceeding is to take action against the person who is dealing in it illegally. We propose, however, that the court considering such a charge should have power to order the forfeiture of seized material if it considers that course to be justified.

The right to prosecute

9.47 One enforcement matter which created controversy in the evidence we received, as we have mentioned in Chapter 2, was the right to institute proceedings in the courts. The arguments in favour of the right of private prosecution are that it is an important constitutional safeguard that the citizen should have the power to challenge the refusal of the prosecuting authorities to enforce the law; that without that safeguard the prosecuting authorities may feel obliged, to avoid allegations of inactivity or worse, to undertake more prosecutions than they judge are really justified; that to channel all cases of a particular nature through a central authority will place a burden on that authority which will hinder the effective operation of the law; that central control involves turning whoever exercises that control into a censor or an arbiter of taste; and that where an offence depends on judgement rather than fact, that judgement should properly be exercised by the courts rather than by a person with the power to decide what should be put before the courts.

9.48 As Appendix 1 explains, the present law contains no consistency of approach and existing provisions are of various kinds. The arguments set out in the preceding paragraph are of varying relevance to the different solutions.

Basically, three choices faced us: allowing offences to be prosecuted by any individual; imposing a centralised control on prosecutions; or, a middle way, restricting the institution of proceedings to the normal police prosecuting machinery, without central control but also without allowing private prosecutions. An argument for central control in this field has been the desirability of consistency in the operation of an imprecise law, particularly where the national circulation of a particular book, magazine or film may in theory give rise to offences which could lead to a multitude of prosecutions in different places. However, bearing in mind also the arguments against a central control we have already referred to, we took the view that it was hardly appropriate to impose centralised control with regard to violation of the restriction requirements, especially as we have proposed that it should be an offence triable only by magistrates.

9.49 There are also, however, arguments against allowing individuals to invoke the law. Where a law embodies a concept of offensiveness, there will inevitably be varying views of what is offensive. We do not think it difficult for the law to apply a general standard of what is offensive to reasonable people but we know from the evidence we received that there will be a number of individuals who will be much more liable to be offended than the generality of their fellows. We doubt if it is in the public interest for people of this kind to be able to use the courts for the purposes of pursuing their own unrepresentative view of offensiveness, particularly as the offence of which they are complaining will not be against them in particular (contrast it, for example, with the case of the individual being able to ensure that his or her assailant is charged with assault) and they will have only a self-appointed status to institute proceedings.

9.50 We therefore take the view that restriction offences should normally be prosecuted by the police and that private individuals should not have the right to institute proceedings. This does not mean, in our view, that no safeguards exist against lax or improper exercise of police discretion. An individual who believed that the law was not being enforced could act in several ways, for example, by generally making a fuss and writing letters to the Chief Constable or the newspapers or the local MP, or by bringing a formal complaint if the circumstances made that appropriate, or by instituting proceedings by prerogative order of *mandamus*, as is not unknown in relation to the enforcement of the obscenity laws. Given these alternative avenues, we do not believe that the case for the private prosecutor in this field can be sustained.

CHAPTER TEN

THE PROHIBITION OF PUBLICATIONS

The need for prohibition

10.1 In the previous chapter we explained our decision that the principal objective of the law should be to prevent offence to the public at large and to protect young people from exposure to unsuitable material. We described how some witnesses thought that measures of that kind were the limit of the law's concern, how others felt they were no more than a starting point and how others considered that the appropriate course was to supplement them by more rigorous measures against certain types of material. We shall consider in this chapter what the law needs to do once it has secured its prime object of curbing public offensiveness. Is there anything that one should prohibit totally, even for adults who want to have it?

10.2 Under the general principles discussed in Chapter 5, any such proposal has to be related to harms. Our proposals in this chapter therefore have to take account of the detailed study we made of allegations of harm in Chapter 6. Leaving aside offensiveness, which is dealt with by restriction, some of our witnesses thought that there were no harms involved in pornography which were not already outlawed by other penal provisions; we could either leave protection from those harms to be dealt with by the schemes of law concerned, or simply provide a prohibition on material depicting acts which contravened the law. At the very least, this would have to be a prohibition on pictures which not only depicted an illegal act but were also offensive; otherwise it would be illegal for there to be a photograph of someone driving across a double white line. But even with material within our terms of reference, great anomalies would be involved.

The depiction of sexual offences

10.3 A basic problem is that the present law on sexual offences itself contains anomalies, so that to use these laws as the basis of prohibitions on pornography would produce very odd results. What two consenting male adults do in private is not by and large the concern of the law. Heterosexual buggery, on the other hand, even between a married couple, constitutes an offence. It did not seem to us defensible to produce a law which had the effect of banning photographs of such acts between a man and a woman but allowing them if the activity involved two men. In fact, we could not see why it should be necessary to prohibit photographs of acts of buggery at all and we derived support for this conclusion from various of our witnesses. The Catholic Social Welfare Commission, for example, considered that the right treatment of representations of the act of buggery was what we have called restriction rather than prohibition, and that there was no reason why such pictures should not be available to those who chose to have them.

10.4 Another difference in the law relating to sexual offences concerns the treatment of group sex. Heterosexual or lesbian behaviour is subject to no sanction dependent upon the number of people involved. Homosexual activity between men, on the other hand, is legal only if it happens between two adults in private, and the presence of a third person creates the presumption that the activity was not in private. It seemed to us that the implied presence of a photographer might serve to make any photograph of a homosexual act arguably one of an illegal act; but it would certainly show an illegal act if it depicted more than two persons. Again, this was a distinction between heterosexual pornography and homosexual pornography which we thought the law should not introduce. We make no comment on the law on sexual offences which produces this situation, noting that it is itself the subject of review by the Criminal Law Revision Committee. For reasons of which we have given these examples, we considered that it would be unsatisfactory to introduce any prohibition on pornography which depended just on whether or not the act depicted was against the law.

Identifying harmful material

10.5 One class of potential harms which seems to us very clear and definite, and to call for a prohibition on certain publications, is that of harms to those involved in the production of pornography. We have already expressed in paragraphs 6.68 and 6.72 our conclusion that there were such harms involved in the exploitation of children and also of others where the infliction of physical harm was involved. We suggested that this harm lay not only in the original act, which might already be caught by the existing law on sexual offences or on personal violence, but in the circulation of depictions of that act, because they both exploited that act and provided the motive for it. Moreover, we thought that point applied as strongly, or more so, when the original offences were committed outside British jurisdiction. We think it right, therefore, that the law should prohibit both the acts concerned and the circulation of material depicting them. (In this connection, a 'depiction' must be something the existence of which implies that the event represented happened in actual fact—that is to say, in effect, a photograph). In considering how the law should achieve this, we decided, following the line that we found most useful in defining material to be restricted, that the law should be specific about its objectives, making clear what the particular harms were at which it was aimed.

10.6 The formula we devised in the light of this decision and of the nature of the harms we wished to prevent, is in the following terms:

> Material whose production appears to the court to have involved the exploitation for sexual purposes of any person, where either
>
> (a) that person appears from the evidence as a whole to have been at the relevant time under the age of sixteen years; or
>
> (b) the material gives reason to believe that actual physical harm was inflicted on that person.

In our discussions about exploitation, we recognised arguments that exploitation might lie in a person's being used for some purpose without his or her consent. However, we do not think that consent should constitute any defence in the context of the material we have described. We consider that the law should explicitly state that consent by a person under the age of sixteen years is to be regarded as irrelevant; in relation to adults, such a provision would not be appropriate but we note that there is already law on the subject of consent to injury. Although the position is not entirely clear, consent to the infliction of serious injury does not necessarily make the infliction of that injury lawful. It may therefore be appropriate to leave the courts to determine in the context of the formula we propose above what should be the precise scope of the effect of consent in such cases. We would not rule out the possibility of specific legislative provision, but since it would raise questions of general principle extending beyond our terms of reference we offer no view on the nature of such a provision.

10.7 Where material comes to light which seems to contravene the description we have set out, there will clearly be doubts as to the circumstances in which it was produced, and it may well be impossible to resolve them, particularly if the material comes from abroad. These doubts are most likely to relate either to the age of a young person who appears in a photograph, or to the question whether what seems to be physical harm is actual or simulated. To require the prosecution to prove that a person was under sixteen, or that someone was actually harmed, seems to us to be a quite unrealistic burden to impose, and it would probably result in the prosecuting authorities being unable to act, particularly against child pornography (as we made clear in Chapter 6, we regard the case of actual physical harm being inflicted as more hypothetical). The only possible course, in our view, is to leave these issues to be decided by the court by way of the best assessment it can make of what the material depicts, coupled with any evidence which can be adduced by either prosecution or defence. It may be that an appropriate way of securing this result is to provide that in any case in which it appears to the court that material is *prima facie* prohibited, the burden of proof should shift to the defence to show that it is not. It may be that the effect of such a provision would be to discourage pornographers from dealing in material which shows young people who look as if they might be under sixteen even though they are in fact older, or which displays realistic-looking sado-masochistic violence which the dealer cannot prove is simulated. If that happens, it would not disturb us.

10.8 We carefully considered whether there were any other forms of publication that should be prohibited, rather than merely restricted. We have provided for the protection of those participants that we think the law should cover. Is it necessary, further, to invoke prohibition in order to protect consumers of pornographic and violent material, or society from those consumers? We have stressed in Chapter 5 the weight of proof that rests on anyone who proposes this, and have mentioned (in paragraphs 5.30–5.33) two principles, that the alleged harms should be shown to exist beyond reasonable doubt, and should be traceable specifically to the kind of material in question. We believe that Chapter 6 shows fairly clearly that these requirements have not been met with regard to any kind of material other than the sort we have specified in paragraph 10.6 above, and accordingly we do not think that there is need for a law to prohibit any other kind of material that falls within our terms of reference.

10.9 There are two areas which perhaps require rather more comment: pornography depicting bestiality and material of an extremely violent nature. We found that many of our witnesses thought that pornography depicting bestiality should belong to a nucleus of material which was banned, and we noticed that some foreign countries which retain a tightly drawn prohibition regard it as properly applying to bestial pornography. Having spent some time examining the question and discussing it with witnesses, we are satisfied that the feelings we encountered about the treatment of bestiality are based simply on its ability to arouse extreme distaste and disgust among most members of the population. The arguments for prohibiting pornography which depicts bestiality reduce to the proposition that it is too revolting for any civilised society to tolerate. But this kind of consideration clearly places such material within the class to be restricted, not in that to be prohibited. Such material seems to be of appeal and interest only to those with a pre-existing disposition towards it; the reaction of others is of disgust and aversion, and the idea that pornography of this kind has a corrupting effect on those who see it appears to have no basis in fact. We felt unable on any rational judgement, therefore, to say that publications depicting bestiality should be prohibited to those who want them. Some people may be concerned about this material on the rather different ground of the ill-treatment of animals in its production. It did not seem to us that the production of this material often caused harm to animals and we considered it sufficient that recourse could be had in appropriate circumstances to the law protecting animals from cruelty.

10.10 The subject of extreme violence gave rise to very serious concern; but we found that there applied very particularly to this area a consideration which has repeatedly impressed us in this enquiry, and which we have already mentioned more than once, that the various media have a different impact and demand different treatment. Violence has its strongest impact on the screen, above all in the cinema; it is of course also a matter of constant discussion with regard to television. To freeze violent activity on to the page greatly reduces its impact, and in fact we do not think that the issue of violence is very relevant to publications. To some extent, the protection of children from unsuitable violent publications has been a matter of concern, but this is met by our proposals for restriction. Otherwise, there is simply no form of publication which gives rise to the problems raised by violent material. The sorts of films, usually 8mm, which are sold in sex shops, do not raise a serious problem in this connection; while the cinema, we decided, could be dealt with separately, in the ways which we shall discuss in Chapter 12. Given that that is so, it did not seem to us that in the field of violence our prohibition law needed to cover anything other than the protection of participants from actual physical harm, as we have already proposed.

Transactions to be prohibited

10.11 We propose that any form of trade in the material we have described in paragraph 10.6 should be prohibited. We propose that the importation of this material and its transmission through the post should also be prohibited. But we think the law must go further. The taking of photographs or the making of films of that description should be made unlawful whether the motive was commercial or not, and the private circulation of the results, whether or not for gain, should be equally prohibited. This would be consistent with the existing law relating to child pornography, enacted in the Protection of Children Act 1978, and indeed with the present law on obscene publications generally. If we are to narrow the law to the area where positive harms are plainly to be seen, we believe that it is right for the most rigorous steps to be taken to ensure that those harms are effectively prevented. When imposing control through the criminal law, however, we think it valid to recognise some limits: we consider it neither practicable nor desirable for the law to penalise the private possession of this material, any more than mere possession is subject to the law as it now stands.

A public good defence?

10.12 We considered in relation to our proposed scheme of restriction whether there was material which ought to be allowed to escape control on the ground that it possessed some quality which overrode the need for it to be controlled. We must now consider the same question in relation to our prohibition proposals, bearing in mind that it is a more serious step to suppress material entirely than merely to restrict its availability. However, the object of the prohibition we have proposed is to avoid harms of a highly specific kind and it seems to us, first, that the chance of meritorious material falling within the categories we have specified is fairly remote and, secondly, that the harms we are guarding against are not easily outweighed by merits of some other kind. We do not think that artistic merit, for example, will be capable of justifying the sexual exploitation of a child or the infliction of physical injury on anyone. We therefore conclude that the terms of the prohibition are such that no material should be able to secure exemption on the grounds of any other merits it may be held to possess.

Enforcing prohibition

10.13 We propose that it should be an offence to produce or distribute prohibited material, whether or not for gain. So far as the importation of prohibited material is concerned, however, we think it sufficient that material within our prohibition class should be added to the list of prohibited imports, so that it will be dealt with by the normal Customs procedures which apply to all goods prohibited from import including, hitherto, indecent and obscene articles. This course will be an alternative to creating a new offence of importing prohibited material and providing fresh powers to deal with material discovered in the course of importation. The effect will be to apply the provisions of the Customs Acts, which will enable any such imports to be seized at the port of entry and will make it an offence to import such material with intent to evade the prohibition.

10.14 The same material should be prohibited from being sent through the post. This would largely meet our international obligations under the Universal Postal Convention, which are described in Appendix 1. However, Article 33 of the Convention forbids the posting to other countries of articles of which the importation and circulation is prohibited in the country of destination and we noted that Denmark at least, despite its lack of domestic restriction on pornography, embodied in its law a provision giving effect to this requirement of the Convention. We do not envisage that the inclusion of a similar provision in our law would be of much practical effect but we recommend it as a means of securing conformity with the Universal Postal Convention.

10.15 As for the new offence we propose, we consider it should be triable either in the Crown Court or in a magistrates' court. The offence is more serious than the offence we have proposed in relation to restriction, and we think that the issue of a publication's being totally suppressed should be capable of being determined by a jury rather than by a stipendiary or a bench of magistrates. We do not rest the case for trial by jury on the basis, often urged on us, that questions of public morality should more appropriately be decided by the jury as representatives of society as a whole. On our proposals, general issues of morality or what is publicly acceptable no longer play a part in what should be prohibited; the test we propose is now to be determined much more objectively. Nonetheless, the arguments for jury trial are still compelling. It seems to us that when the offence is tried at the Crown Court the maximum penalties should be three years' imprisonment and an unlimited fine or both, and that on conviction in a magistrates' court the normal maximum powers should be available to magistrates.

10.16 When the law imposes a total prohibition, such as we propose here, allowance must be made for the quite proper use of the material concerned. This obviously arises where it is being handled by the police and the courts in the course of the prosecution of a person in relation to the material, but other cases might also arise. The Protection of Children Act 1978 dealt with the need to exclude such use from the sanctions of the law by providing a defence of legitimate reason for distributing or showing prohibited photographs, though the defence was not extended to the offence of taking the photographs in the first place. Although some misgivings were expressed at the time that it might be possible for this defence to be exploited in undesirable ways, no problem of this kind has come to our notice and we think that a similar defence might appropriately be provided for the equivalent offences we are now proposing.

10.17 The police will clearly need powers to enter and search premises and to seize material they believe to be prohibited. These powers should be similar to those they already possess and to those we have proposed in relation to restriction offences, to be exercised with the authority of a warrant issued by a magistrate. In addition, however, we believe that it is appropriate in these circumstances for the police to be given a power of arrest. This is not a power they possess at present under the Obscene Publications Acts and our police witnesses emphasised to us the difficulties they often meet because of this in dealing with the shadowy figures they found to be in charge of premises selling pornography, who frequently gave false names and addresses and subsequently disappeared. The Metropolitan Police told us, for example, that in 1973 they searched 332 premises under the Obscene Publications Acts and questioned the managers but that in 93 cases the men concerned could not subsequently be traced. In other cases those responsible simply carried on trading normally until the case came to court, whereas if they had been arrested and bailed, the prospect of bail being revoked might have been a more effective deterrent against their continuing the offence. We have not suggested that a power of this kind is necessary in relation to offences concerned with the restriction of publications, but the more serious offences connected with prohibition seem to us to justify giving the police powers to take more effective action.

10.18 We considered whether there was any scope for requiring a person found in possession of prohibited material to give information about where he got it from, so as to make it easier for the police to trace sources of supply. We recognised, however, that it was very likely that the answers would be useless and that, given the penalties for trading in prohibited material any additional sanctions on refusal to give information of this kind were probably futile. In relation to material printed in this country, the Newspapers, Printers and Reading Rooms Repeal Act 1869, as amended by the Printers Imprint Act 1961, already requires the printer to put his imprint on publications; clearly, however, a person prepared to print material prohibited by law is unlikely to be worried about the additional penalties attached to breach of such requirements.

10.19 We have also considered the question of allowing separate proceedings for the forfeiture and destruction of seized publications. We rejected this idea in relation to restriction offences because it was the circumstances of sale, not the publications themselves, which offended against the law. In the case of prohibition, the objection of the law is to the publications themselves irrespective of the way they are sold, but all the same we still see good reason for avoiding separate forfeiture proceedings. As we have already emphasised, we regard prohibition offences as serious; in effect, we regard them as too serious not to be prosecuted. It seems to us that if the police seize from a dealer a quantity of child pornography, the appropriate course is to institute criminal charges against the dealer. To let him get away with his offence by merely asking a court to order the seized material to be forfeited is, in our view, to minimise the seriousness of the offence in a way that is wholly undesirable. We therefore propose no separate procedure for forfeiture as an alternative to instituting a prosecution. We propose, however, that the court convicting a person of these offences should be under an obligation to order the forfeiture of prohibited material to which the conviction related.

10.20 We do not think that there will be as much room for varying opinions as to what material contravenes the prohibition as there may be about material that violates our proposed test of offensiveness for restriction offences. Nevertheless, we still see ground for restricting the right to institute prosecutions and, in view of the greater seriousness of prohibition offences and the fact that they involve the effective suppression of certain published works, we think it appropriate that any prosecutions should require the consent of the Director of Public Prosecutions.

10.21 We have discussed in this chapter material containing representations of a certain kind. We envisage that the controls we have proposed should apply to all kinds of published material, most notably of course to pictorial magazines and the sorts of films that are sold to private customers. In the next two chapters we shall discuss what we believe to be considerations which call for additional controls on live entertainment and the cinema.

CHAPTER ELEVEN

LIVE ENTERTAINMENT

How live entertainment differs

11.1 We have made clear earlier in our Report that little of the controversy surrounding our subject and only a small part of the evidence we received has touched on the field of live entertainment. For Lord Longford's Committee in 1972, the production of *Oh! Calcutta!* in 1971 represented a new level of pornographic activity, and some of those who gave evidence to us referred to that and to certain other theatrical presentations and regretted the failure, or refusal, of the prosecuting authorities to take action against them. But for most of our witnesses this area of our review gave rise to no interest or concern at all. As we submit our Report, *Oh! Calcutta!* is, perhaps surprisingly, still running in London but the point which deserves comment is not so much that such a show should have lasted so long as that it has been running for a number of years with virtually no controversy.

11.2 The reason for the low level of public concern about live entertainment no doubt has much to do with its not being a mass medium. A pornographic magazine can be printed in quantity and distributed throughout the country, to come to the notice of innumerable people when displayed in local shops. A film can be made with immense skill and utilising specialised techniques for producing startling effects and an extremely powerful impact, and prints of it can be distributed throughout the world and shown to audiences in most of the principal towns in Britain. Live entertainment, on the other hand, affects few people. It has to be created anew for each performance, which is seen only by the people actually attending at the time. No performance will impinge on more than a tiny fraction of the population, and even the places where performances can be given are more rarely encountered than shops or cinemas. Live entertainment, too, is predominantly an adult interest and the fact that it does not attract children in the way that the cinema does has meant that people are less concerned about children being exposed to shows that might be thought unsuitable for them.

11.3 The lack of public concern also has something to do with the real difference between what is now commonly seen in publications and films and what is presented in live entertainment. By and large, we believe, there is less to be concerned about. The law has something to do with this: despite the institution of only one prosecution under the Theatres Act (which applies only to plays and ballet) there have been instances where proceedings for common law offences, such as that of keeping a disorderly house, have been brought in relation to live entertainment. The prospect of proceedings probably represents a more substantial deterrent to the person presenting a sexy show than it does to the publisher whose financial return from selling a hundred thousand magazines provides a greater incentive to take the risk. But we think that there is another reason for the lower threshold which is in practice applied to live entertainment; this partly comes out in the way the law is likely to be interpreted and partly in the perceptions of those who present live shows of what is likely to be acceptable. In quantitative terms, the impact of any given pornographic live show is less, but qualitatively it has a different effect on its audience, just because it is live.

11.4 Pornographic publications and films standardly depict sexual activity but we believe that the situation is changed completely when the spectator is confronted with, where that involves *being in the same space as,* people actually engaged in sexual activity. This is the ground of a relation between performer and audience which is not present with, for example, a film of the same activity. There, the performer's relations are to a camera, and the audience's to an image; in the live show, it is a relation between people. The film is a historical record of past acts which the audience can merely observe and which remains unchanged irrespective of their reaction; the live show is a contemporary happening with an unknown future end, which the audience may be capable of influencing or in which they might participate. It is no longer, as it is with all other pornography, a matter of fantasy. It is also from this relationship between actual people that arises the peculiar objectionableness that many find in the idea of the live sex show, and the sense that the kind of voyeurism involved is especially degrading to both audience and performers.

11.5 We believe that the different quality of the live show justifies its being treated by law in a way that is different from what we have proposed for publications. It seems right, however, that the principle of 'two level' control, which involves separate standards for restriction and for prohibition, should apply to live entertainment.

Restricting live entertainment

11.6 Leaving aside the question of performances which are "live shows" in the more or less technical sense of sexual intercourse on stage, there clearly can be other shows which are potentially offensive in the sorts of ways that make it appropriate to restrict them to adults who want to see them. A theatre performance is already to some extent restricted in that people have to make a conscious decision to go to see it; and the fact that we received few complaints no doubt shows that the performances there do not force themselves on public attention. Nevertheless, we think it right that a show which infringes the restriction test we have outlined in Chapter 9 should be closed to persons under eighteen and should be required not to offend the general public by the manner in which it advertises itself outside.

11.7 We noted that some theatres already restricted entry to certain shows to persons over eighteen, presumably to protect themselves against charges under the present law that the presentation concerned was likely to deprave and corrupt children. Further, the Greater London Council (at least) in licensing establishments providing public music and dancing (such as strip clubs in Soho) makes a point of imposing a condition prohibiting the entry of persons under eighteen to premises presenting the kind of show it believes to be unsuitable for children and young people. There is therefore nothing new in the idea of age restrictions on live entertainment. The restrictions on exterior displays on premises presenting this type of entertainment will in our view help to avoid offensiveness in public places; we do not envisage that these controls will in practice hamper the legitimate theatre.

11.8 It seems to us that the general formula we set out in paragraph 9.36 in relation to the restriction of publications will apply equally well to the live entertainment that we think should be restricted. We propose that broadly the same scheme of restriction should apply to both.

Live entertainment to be prohibited

11.9 It is in relation to prohibition that we think live shows should be dealt with differently from publications. We have suggested that the need in relation to published material is to protect only certain participants from what is clearly harm. In the light of what we have already said about the different quality of live entertainment, we do not think the same approach is adequate here. It would permit, for example, a wide range of real sexual activity to be presented to an audience in a way that now happens extremely rarely, compared with the availability of representations of similar activity on film or on the printed page. We have mentioned the possibility that the live sex show may invite or precipitate audience participation and this carries some dangers of public order problems. We were interested to hear from the Danish authorities that they encountered such problems in relation to the live sex shows which burgeoned after restrictions on pornography were lifted in the late nineteen-sixties. The Danes have had no second thoughts at all in relation to the total freedom allowed to published pornography, but they found it necessary to take measures to curb live sex shows. When we visited Copenhagen in 1978, there were no such shows openly available, despite some lingering advertisements which suggested that some such shows might still exist. The Danish experience reinforced our own view that we should avoid changing the law in a way that allowed such shows to proliferate.

11.10 The peculiarity of the live show that attracts these objections is that it involves actual sex. The theatre involves the representation of human activity of various kinds and sexual activity may sometimes figure among the things represented. We have already proposed that any such representation which is offensive should be restricted. What artistic or dramatic requirements do not involve is the performance of real sexual activity; it seems to us, in fact, that the presentation of actual sex on the stage immediately introduces a presumption that the motives no longer have any artistic pretension.

11.11 Differences between reality and representation are at the centre of the issue. We therefore think it appropriate that in determining what is to be prohibited we should take as our starting point whether sexual activity is real rather than merely represented. But "sexual activity" needs qualifying: kissing is a sexual activity. We have discussed at some length in Chapter 9 the possibility of providing an explicit statement of what is disallowed by the law and have explained why we reject that approach. We regard the same objections as applying to any attempt at being totally specific as to the meaning of "sexual activity", though we think there is value in suggesting in general terms what the scope of the prohibition should be. But the work of qualifying the term "sexual activity" should be done by some general term, and we concluded that it was appropriate, once again, to use the concept of offensiveness.

11.12 The idea is that insofar as simulated or represented sexual activity is in question, its offensiveness will justify its merely being restricted; but as soon as it is a matter of real sexual activity, offensiveness will justify prohibition. The logic is simple. Under the general laws of public decency, the law prohibits thorough-going sexual activity in public, and, so far as our proposals are concerned, will continue to do so. Photographic representations of such activity will be permitted under our proposals, but, if offensive, will be restricted. The analogy to these two provisions, in the case of live entertainment, lies in the distinction between the actual and the simulated: the actual, if offensive, is prohibited, and the simulated, if offensive, is restricted. Thus for any given activity that occurs in the course of live entertainment there will be two questions: is it real or simulated? Is it offensive or not? What is real and offensive, is prohibited; what is simulated and offensive, is restricted; what is real but inoffensive, such as kissing, gets off. It would be foolish to deny that the business of applying such distinctions to actual cases could raise problems; we just do not believe that difficult cases would arise very often.

11.13 The scheme still leaves open the question of "offensive to whom, and with regard to what circumstances?" It would be silly to suppose that reasonable people would regard as offensive in a theatre anything that they would regard as offensive in the park. On the other hand, if one made into the canon of judgement for these purposes the reactions of an *habitué* of live shows, one would have gone too far in the other direction, and the test would have no effect. The appropriate test, it seems to us, is what a reasonable person would find offensive to see performed in the circumstances of a performance, and this is what we propose.

11.14 We started off by saying that our prohibition test for publications was inadequate for live entertainment. But it is still relevant, and it needs to be combined with the kind of prohibition we have been discussing in the preceding paragraphs. The protection of children from exploitation for sexual purposes would not necessarily be adequately covered by a prohibition on actual sexual activity, and it needs a specific provision. The question of protection from physical harm raises slightly different considerations. As we made clear earlier, the infliction of physical harm would constitute an offence anyway and our point in adding the reference to it in the prohibition test for publications was to enable the law to deal with the subsidiary harm of the circulation of published material exploiting the original acts. In the case of live entertainment, however, it is the acts themselves which are in point and not any photographic depiction of them, and we think it sufficient to rely on the law relating to personal violence.

11.15 The considerations we have discussed in the last few paragraphs bring us to the point of being able to set down a description of what it is we wish to prohibit. We propose that a performance should be prohibited if

(a) it involves actual sexual activity of a kind which, in the circumstances in which it is given, would be offensive to reasonable adults; and for the avoidance of doubt sexual activity should include the act of masturbation and forms of genital, anal or oral connection between humans and animals as well as between humans; or

(b) it involves the sexual exploitation of any person under the age of sixteen.

Enforcing controls on live entertainment

11.16 We propose that restriction and prohibition should be enforced by criminal offences similar to those applying to publications. The restriction offence will be committed by the person who presents a restricted performance other than in the conditions which constitute restriction. We consider that the prohibition offence should be cast slightly more widely, so as to penalise those who present, organise or take part in a performance which contravenes the prohibition. The mode of trial, penalties and provisions about the institution of proceedings should be the same as for the offences we have proposed in relation to publications.

11.17 Since we are proposing more stringent controls on live performances than we consider necessary in relation to published material, it will follow that a performance should not be defined in such a way that the production of permitted published material will be prevented. The Theatres Act 1968 contained a provision of this kind in relation to plays performed for the purpose of being filmed or televised and an exemption along similar lines would be appropriate in the context of our proposals. There should also be another exemption based on the Theatres Act, for performances given on a domestic occasion in a private dwelling; but in accordance with the proposals of the Law Commission in its Report on Conspiracy and Criminal Law Reform we consider that this should apply only when no person under eighteen is present and when no charge is made.

11.18 Before we turn to the control of the showing of films, we add the comment that we have not thought it appropriate to suggest that any form of pre-censorship should apply to live entertainment in the way it now applies to films. Even in the context of restriction, where the spectre of the Lord Chamberlain would not loom so large, it seems to us that the old arguments against pre-censorship could be employed against the idea of there being a body which is charged with deciding whether or not a theatrical presentation should be restricted; the arguments relate particularly to the point that it is impossible to categorise a live production in advance, when by its nature it will not remain constant, and also cannot be adequately imagined on the basis of an advance script or scenario. It could be, of course, that theatre interests might see advantage in having such a board in order to provide the kind of certainty which cinemas enjoy as to what they can properly show to what kinds of audiences; if so, we see no reason why they should not argue for it.

CHAPTER TWELVE

FILMS

The need for censorship

12.1 In turning to the control of films, we come to the only area covered by our review which is subject to a sophisticated system of pre-censorship. We have already described how the system works and its rather haphazard origins. The effect of the system is broadly that what is regarded as objectionable, for reasons only partly concerned with what the law prohibits, is never allowed to gain a showing in a public cinema, so that those who are responsible for enforcing the laws on obscenity and indecency on a "subsequent punishment" basis scarcely have to concern themselves with investigating whether the law is being broken. The system therefore combines prior restraint with extra-legal control. The first and fundamental question we had to consider was whether a system of this kind was necessary or desirable.

12.2 Despite the system's haphazard origins and despite the fact that this style of control is in this country peculiar to the cinema, it has many friends and few enemies. It has operated for a long time with a remarkable degree of public acceptance. Objections of principle to any idea of pre-censorship have to a large extent been suspended in favour of film censorship. It has undoubtedly been an effective system, both making it fairly certain what cinemas can legally show and under what conditions, and providing fairly watertight procedures to ensure that the rules are kept. It is not surprising that such a system should hold an appeal, as we mentioned in Chapter 9, for those struggling with the uncertainties of the law on obscenity in other areas.

12.3 The acceptance of special controls on the cinema is not confined to Britain. Almost everywhere in the world there is a system for the prior vetting of films. Sometimes this is only to categorise films with regard to their suitability for children, such as in the United States of America, where the principles of the "free speech" amendment to the Constitution are regarded as paramount. Often, however, the system works to prevent certain material from being shown to adults. France, Germany, Italy, Sweden, Norway, Australia, New Zealand and Canada all, like us, have film censorship systems which control films intended even for adult viewing. Belgium, the Netherlands and Denmark concentrate on protecting children only and take the view that there should be no prior controls on what adults are able to see. It is also notable that most of these foreign systems are officially instituted by statute and exert formal powers. No other country, unsurprisingly, has a system with anything like the basis of ours. Nor has any other country a system quite as relaxed as that of the United States, which is purely voluntary and aims solely at classifying films in order to provide advance information to help parents to judge whether their children should be allowed to see particular films. It has been estimated, we were told, that only 80–85 per cent of American cinemas adhere to the classifications issued by the Classification and Rating Administration of the Motion Picture Association of America.

12.4 While public acceptance of film censorship in this country is widespread, it is not universal. We referred in Chapter 4 to growing doubts about the future of censorship, and a significant proportion of the evidence we received suggested that there should be no censorship of films for adults. Mrs Enid Wistrich, in a paper submitted to us by the Fabian Society, placed this proposal in a political context. Modern democratic society, she argued, is based on the belief that individuals are competent to take decisions on matters concerning their own lives and on the best course for the society in which they live: if such a society is to function properly, barriers to the free communication of both facts and ideas, from which the arts and entertainment were in her view inseparable, needed to be removed. Some other witnesses placed greatest emphasis on the importance of artistic freedom; others simply stressed the right of adults to freedom of choice and the unacceptability of the notion that certain people were qualified to judge what it was right and wrong for everyone else to see. Views of this kind came from the Defence of Literature and the Arts Society, the Films Committee of the Writers Guild, the British Federation of Film Societies, the Independent Film Distributors Association and the British Humanist Association.

12.5 In addition, as we mentioned in Chapter 4, the attitude of the mainstream of the British film industry towards film censorship has changed. The case urged on us by the Cinematograph Exhibitors' Association, who told us that they were speaking for the film industry as a whole, was that the cinema should have parallel treatment to the theatre: there should, in other words, be no prior restraint and films which were challenged should be able to fight for their rights before a jury in open court. However, enthusiasm for this freedom was not universal in the industry. The major film distributors, as represented by the Kinematograph Renters' Society (since renamed the Society of Film Distributors) thought it important that there should be centralised film censorship, not only because of its commercial advantages but because they recognised the different quality attaching to film and to the experience of watching it. The commercial advantages were related to the enormous capital tied up in the production of a film and to the industry's need for some assurance that a film would not be vulnerable at law: once a film was completed, it could not readily be varied, whereas a play was capable of modification to meet objections made to it. The sense of certainty that a certificated film could be shown throughout the country without any legal interference was a real commercial benefit. But prior censorship was also necessary because the experience of seeing a film was quite different from that of reading published material, and the cinema, unlike the theatre, catered for a mass audience, penetrating far deeper into society than the theatre. Witnesses from the Society made it clear that they would have no sympathy with changes which would allow material to be shown which would not pass the present censorship controls.

12.6 The exhibition side of the industry recognised and also attached importance to the commercial arguments for prior censorship, and it was for this reason that the Cinematograph Exhibitors' Association proposed to us that the British Board of Film Censors should continue in existence not only to assess the suitability of films for children but also to certify films as suitable for adults; but, under their proposals, the absence of a certificate would not prevent the showing of a film. The Association rejected the argument that pre-censorship of films was necessary because they were different from books and plays. Instead, they argued that the possibility that a film would have a greater impact on the viewer was already capable of being taken into account by the criminal law: if the effect on the viewer was more powerful in the case of a film than a book or play, it followed, they claimed, that a film was more likely to be found to be depraving and corrupting. We understand this argument but, as we suggested to the Association's witnesses, it presupposes the continuing existence of the Obscene Publications Acts or legislation having a similar basis.

12.7 We claimed in Chapter 11 that there is a difference between the live show on one hand and publications and films on the other, which justifies the law treating them in a different way. We have mentioned in Chapter 10 differences between publications and films which led us to the conclusion that extreme violence did not constitute the same problem with publications as it might with the cinema. We think that the aim of treating all the media uniformly is misconceived; there is no reason why one solution should be expected to apply equally to a series of different problems. That the problems are different we have no doubt at all. No one can dispute that reading a magazine, watching a live show and watching a film are three very different experiences. We suggest that it is sensible and reasonable to apply three different standards of control, and not to hope, unrealistically, that the same control can be stretched to cover all three.

12.8 This conclusion, in rejecting the argument for parity of treatment, removes one type of objection to accepting the pre-censorship of films. We are taken further towards accepting it by the facts that the major part of our evidence supported the continuation of film censorship, that the present system has, in the main, worked effectively and well and that most other countries appear to regard film censorship as acceptable and desirable. What clinched the argument for some of us at least was the sight of some of the films with which the censorship presently interferes. We feel it necessary to say to many people who express liberal sentiments about the principle of adult freedom to choose that we were totally unprepared for the sadistic material that some film makers are prepared to produce. We are not here referring to the explicit portrayal of sexual activity or to anything which simply attracts charges of offensiveness. Films that exploit a taste for torture and sadistic violence do raise further, and disturbing, questions.

12.9 We made clear in Chapter 6 that research had not demonstrated any convincing link between media violence and violence in society. That, however, is due in part at least to the weakness of experimental research as a means of determining human motivations and we expressed the view that in this area, where the activity portrayed was, unlike sex, itself harmful, it was right to exercise caution. Caution was indeed urged even by those who told us that there was no evidence of harm: Dr Guy Cumberbatch, for example, whose assessment of the research literature on media violence we quoted in Chapter 6, told us that his own view was that there should be restrictions on the portrayal of violence.

12.10 Concern is always being expressed about the violence shown on television. This concern is understandable because of the size of the audiences likely to see television programmes compared with those likely to see some of the films we have alluded to; the lack of control over who may be in the audience; and the element of intrusion into the home, to which the Annan Committee referred[1]. But we should make the point that the violence we have seen on film (from films refused a certificate, or cut before the film could be certified) far exceeds in nastiness anything likely to be seen on television. It is not simply the extremity of the violence which concerns us: we found it extremely disturbing that highly explicit depictions of mutilation, savagery, menace and humiliation should be presented for the entertainment of an audience in a way that appeared to emphasise the pleasures of sadism. Indeed, some of the film sequences we saw seemed to have no purpose or justification other than to reinforce or sell the idea that it can be highly pleasurable to inflict injury, pain or humiliation (often in a sexual context) on others. Film, in our view, is a uniquely powerful instrument: the close-up, fast cutting, the sophistication of modern makeup and special effects techniques, the heightening effect of sound effects and music, all combine on the large screen to produce an impact which no other medium can create. It *may* be that this very graphically presented sadistic material serves only as a vivid object of fantasy, and does no harm at all. There is certainly no conclusive evidence to the contrary. But there is no conclusive evidence in favour of that belief, either, and in this connection it seems entirely sensible to be cautious. If displacement or abreaction theories could be shown to be true, which hold that the arousal of aggressive or sadistic reactions by fantasy material tends to displace those motivations from the real world and to discharge them, then there would be an argument for showing these films (indeed, for encouraging them). But we have not been convinced by any such theory, and in fact no expert witness has put such a theory to us, except in the most qualified form. This being so, we are more impressed by the consideration that the extreme vividness and immediacy of film may make it harder rather than easier for some who are attracted to sadistic material to tell the difference between fantasy and reality.

12.11 Some people told us that if there is material which we were satisfied should not be made available to the public, the proper way to suppress it is by way of making it the subject of determination by the courts, rather than by prior restraint. Prior restraint, it is commonly recognised, is a more effective means for suppressing material than is offered by the subsequent punishment approach. Its advantages are that it provides certainty, consistency and speed of decision and the possibility of continuous review by the same group of people; it avoids the delays of criminal trials and decisions by courts who know nothing of films and are not representative of the film-going public; it provides a more refined control, capable of identifying which elements of a film are objectionable and therefore allowing the distributor the opportunity of reacting; and it prevents objectionable material from becoming available at all rather than trying to retrieve it after publication and thereby giving it more publicity. We freely admit, and have already made clear, that we are in part encouraged to favour pre-censorship by the fact

[1]Cmnd 6753, paragraph 16.3.

that it is what already exists. What we have to consider is, realistically, not whether we would institute a system of censorship if it were a novelty but whether we should abandon a functioning system; or rather, to put it more exactly, whether we should continue to use the system for the protection of young audiences (as almost all our witnesses considered necessary), but at the same time refuse to use the system to control films for adult viewing. We were very much impressed, moreover, by a different kind of argument. The impact of a film can depend on very subtle factors, which will not at all be caught by simple statements of what is being shown on the screen, and because of this the law is too inflexible an instrument through which to impose a control. An *ad hoc* judgement, grounded on certain guidelines, is a more efficient and sensitive way of controlling this medium. All these considerations together led us to the conclusion that films, even those shown to adults only, should continue to be censored.

Local authority control

12.12 We have so far concerned ourselves only with the question whether films should be subject to censorship, and not in any way with the structure of the system or, more particularly, whether the present form of censorship should continue. In turning to this further question we must discuss first the present legal basis of censorship and the role of local authorities.

12.13 As Chapter 3 explains, the only legal powers of film censorship rest with cinema licensing authorities, and the fact that most licensing authorities are content to leave the censorship of films to the British Board of Film Censors does not alter the fact that if it were not for the requirements imposed on cinemas by licensing authorities, there would be no legal obligation for films to be censored at all. So far as we are aware, every licensing authority in the country enforces the censorship of films; some of them, as we have explained, impose their own control to supplement that of the British Board of Film Censors.

12.14 We have already reported that the local control of films was overwhelmingly repudiated by our witnesses. It is not surprising that the film industry, from producers to distributors and exhibitors, should be unanimously against a local system of control: it is commercially inconvenient, in a national film distribution system, that local authorities should be able to stop particular films being shown in their areas. Many other bodies, however, covering a wide variety of different outlooks, also rejected local censorship, including the Free Church Federal Council, the Catholic Social Welfare Commission, the Nationwide Festival of Light, the Progressive League, the Police Federation, the National Council of Women, the British Youth Council and the Law Society.

12.15 Not all of these bodies addressed themselves to the arguments for and against allowing local authorities, rather than someone else, to exercise powers of censorship, but the most frequent arguments were that in an age of mass media and easy mobility, disparities of taste between geographical areas were plainly diminishing and were likely to be over-emphasised; that in a country as small as ours, when the nearest cinema subject to a different authority's control was often no more than a few minutes' drive away, the idea of a local authority censorship was futile and nonsensical; and that local councillors were far from being the best people to perform a censorship role since, granted the realities of local politics and the very minor role enjoyed by film censorship, they were not in any real sense answerable to local electors for the way in which films were censored and, being often middle-aged and not cinema-goers, they were liable to be out of touch with the contemporary cinema and the tastes of its predominantly young audiences. In addition, as the Association of District Secretaries pointed out to us, reinforcing from a different viewpoint the problems put before us by the Cinematograph Exhibitors' Association, any local authority which wishes to vet films shown in its area faces severe practical difficulties in obtaining advance warning of films it might wish to challenge, in being able to arrange to see films sufficiently far in advance of a prospective local exhibition etc. District Secretaries, on the whole, did not favour the retention of local discretion.

12.16 The representatives of local authorities themselves were divided on the issue. The Association of Metropolitan Authorities told us that the mainstream view of their members was that local authorities' responsibilities for assessing films should be brought to an end. They did not regard this as a proper function of local government and considered that the ridicule which the exercise of the power had brought on some authorities was better avoided. But the Association was reluctant to see local influence abandoned entirely and considered that there should be local authority representation on the new statutory body which they proposed should be set up, and that appeals should be decided by a panel with majority local authority membership, though the decisions themselves should apply on a national basis. The Association of District Councils and some individual authorities belonging to the Association of Metropolitan Authorities preferred to retain greater power in the hands of local authorities, by continuing the present system or at least by allowing local authorities the right, even if limited to specified circumstances, to overrule the decisions of a national censorship body. The Cities of Bradford, Coventry, Leeds, Liverpool and Newcastle upon Tyne were Metropolitan authorities who joined the Association of District Councils in stressing to us the importance of the local option.

12.17 The British Board of Film Censors also strongly supported the local option, arguing that it represented the assertion of the judgement of elected representatives of a local community about the standards they wished to see maintained in that community. The existence of the local option, they said, enabled the Board to keep in touch with grass-roots feeling in the country and, so long as variations in local tastes and attitudes continued to exist, it was right that central control should not be imposed from London. The Board recognised that difficulties sometimes arose because of the local option, but considered from their point of view that the advantages of local discretion outweighed the disadvantages.

12.18 We easily understood how the Board's rather peculiar position is helped by the existence of the powers which local licensing authorities can exercise: that the possibility of losing local authority confidence strengthens the Board's hand in dealing with film distributors; that the prospect of review by a local authority takes some weight off the Board's decisions; that the Board can be relieved of pressure by being able to recommend that an approach on a controversial film should be made direct to a licensing authority. We also accept that attitudes do vary in different parts of the country and that some films may be more acceptable in some localities than in others. In our view, however, these arguments fall a long way short of being conclusive.

12.19 The way in which the local option is actually exercised seems to us to provide very weak support for the argument in favour of local variation. The British Board of Film Censors, in urging on us the value of the local option, appended to their written submission full details of censorship exercised in Leeds and Manchester and its effect in either banning films granted a certificate by the Board or forbidding a local showing until a film has been seen by the authority, or in some cases (in Manchester at least) allowing a local showing to a film refused a certificate by the Board. This information seemed to us to provide arguments against the local option rather than for it. Coupled with information given to us by the Cinematograph Exhibitors' Association about the activities of other authorities energetic in this field, such as Sefton, it suggests that the exercise of the local option is not as well grounded in varying local opinion as its proponents would suggest. We cannot believe that local attitudes and *mores* vary to the extent that these differing decisions imply; dissenting decisions are often confined to the area of one particular local authority, are not consistent throughout a given region of the country, and are not shared by neighbouring authorities. We believe that a situation in which local censorship means that people wishing to see a particular film have to travel a few extra miles to the next town, simply brings ridicule on the system with no compensating advantages. The majority of our witnesses seemed to be of the same view and we conclude that the possession by local authorities of the power to control the films shown locally cannot be justified by any local variation in taste and opinion.

12.20 It seems to us that the other arguments which influence the British Board of Film Censors in favour of the local option are peculiar to the present system; they arise, for example, from there not being any avenue of appeal from the Board's decisions other than to local authorities. These points could be dealt with by a modified system, and do not on their own justify the local option. We therefore have no hesitation in concluding that the disadvantages of a locally based system of film censorship outweigh any advantages it may have, and we propose that powers to censor films should no longer rest with local authorities.

A statutory system of control?

12.21 Some of our witnesses who rejected the idea of local censorship did so because they were against censorship generally, an approach we do not accept. Others rejected local censorship because they saw a need for a stronger central control and advocated a statutory body to exercise this control. Indeed, a number of our witnesses who were in favour of the retention of some measure of local control wanted to link it to central control exercised by a new statutory body. We must now consider the arguments for a body of this kind.

12.22 Support for a statutory film censorship board came from many of our witnesses. Among them were the Association of Metropolitan Authorities, the Greater London Council, the Cities of Bradford and Coventry, the Cornwall County Branch of the Association of District Councils, the Women's National Commission, the National Council of Women, the Mothers' Union, the Free Church Federal Council, the Catholic Social Welfare Commission, the Nationwide Festival of Light, the British Youth Council, the Association of District Secretaries, the Cornwall Community Standards Association and the Metropolitan Police. Some others who accepted film classification rather than censorship, such as the Law Society and the National Campaign for the Reform of the Obscene Publications Acts, thought that this should be the responsibility of a statutory body rather than an unofficial one. Yet others, like the Association of District Councils, made it clear to us that although they favoured the existing system they would have no strong objection to the establishment of a statutory body.

12.23 Those who called for the replacement of the British Board of Film Censors were not necessarily dissatisfied with its operation. Many witnesses made it clear that they were concerned with the position of the Board rather than with its actions: in particular with its origin as a creature of the film industry, the implication that it continued in that position, and its lack of statutory authority and power. Some went out of their way to stress that they would be happy for the existing personnel to continue in post with a new official body. Other witnesses, however, were dissatisfied with the Board and wanted a statutory body because they hoped that it would act more responsibly. The Nationwide Festival of Light, for example, blamed the present Board for a breakdown in the control of films, suggesting that in the last ten years extreme violence and pornography in the cinema had reached "almost inconceivable depths".

12.24 No body exercising the kind of control undertaken by the Board will find that what it does is acceptable to all the people all the time. We do not pretend that after studying in some detail how the Board censors films we agree with all their decisions. But we do not support the criticisms of the Nationwide Festival of Light. Rather, we found a slight air of unreality in the Board's tendency to try to limit, by requiring minute cuts, the quantity of the potentially disturbing or offensive, as if the third glimpse of a bloodied face or the third twitch of the buttocks changed the quality of what had already been allowed twice. We also wondered whether they might not have spent too much time and energy on such questions as whether a given swear word should be allowed under a 'A' certificate or only under an 'AA'. But we do not think there is any point in our discussing in detail where our judgement might have differed from that exercised by the Board; no two groups of people are likely to reach complete unanimity about all the decisions which the Board is obliged to take week after week, and our task was not to decide which films might have been cut more and which less. It is enough for us to say at this stage that we do not consider that the way the Board has exercised its functions gives any ground at all for suggesting that it is unfit to continue the practice of film censorship.

12.25 We think however that there are more solid reasons for a change. We agree with those who find the position of the Board anomalous. The public esteem of the Board undoubtedly suffers to some extent because it was originally set up by the film industry and because it is still often thought to be linked with the industry in some way—though we have already said (paragraph 3.31) that there are no grounds on which the public need be concerned that the Board is not truly independent. But even so the Board is an entirely unofficial body without any authority given by law and without the power to ensure that its decisions are recognised and implemented.

12.26 This point assumes crucial importance granted our conclusion that local authorities should no longer have powers to censor films, for at the moment the authority possessed by the Board derives from the delegation of the powers which Parliament has given to local authorities. The Board effectively rules because local authorities use the powers they have to require cinemas to follow the Board's certificates. If local authorities lost those powers, the Board has none of its own with which to replace them. But if there is to be film censorship, as we propose there should be, it will need to be legally enforceable. How?

12.27 Two possible solutions can be disposed of fairly briefly. One is that local authorities should continue to have the legal power but should be prevented from exercising it in any way other than by following the Board. This seems to us to be a highly artificial solution. The courts have held under the present law that it is improper for a local authority to exercise its powers by simply deciding that the Board should exercise them on its behalf, with the authority reserving no power to itself. Similar objections would attach to the legislative expedient of giving local authorities powers which they were not permitted to exercise themselves, solely in order to give legal power to the British Board of Film Censors.

12.28 The second solution is the more direct one of attaching enforcement measures to the Board's certificates themselves instead of their having effect at one remove via local authorities. This would give legal recognition to a body which has so far not had a legal existence, and in fact the Board itself suggested to us that it might be given legal recognition. But this solution would involve rather more than recognition, because it would be necessary to give the Board's decisions the force of law, in the sense that a cinema failing to adhere to the restrictions attaching to a certain certificate would commit an offence. To go this far seems to incur grave objections, for what after all is the Board? Instituted by the film industry, now a tiny self-perpetuating private body, answerable to no one for the way it conducts its affairs: can a body of this nature properly have legal powers bestowed on it by Parliament? Our view is that the Board in its present form cannot possibly be given the powers needed to ensure the enforcement of the film censorship system.

12.29 We believe this leaves only one realistic course. This is, as proposed by the bodies we have already mentioned, that Parliament should institute a new statutory body which will have the necessary powers to replace those now wielded by local authorities. There will be some people who have misgivings about giving censorship powers to any arm of central government and who will advance the kind of arguments we have ourselves used in turning down suggestions for any pre-censorship of publications. But film censorship is not the radical departure that censorship of publications would be in this country; and we have already argued that it is appropriate to the medium. If it is to continue, as the broad consensus appears to wish, and if the anomalies associated with local discretion are to be removed, again as seems to attract broad support, an officially-instituted national censorship is in our view the only practical solution. As we have made clear earlier, Britain almost went over to such a system in 1916; it is the kind of system that most of the other countries of the world already have; and it is a system that many of our witnesses wished to see. We think it would be appropriate, defensible and desirable.

The nature of a new body

12.30 We think that this new statutory body should be called the Film Examining Board. We envisage that it would be a broadly-based body of perhaps a dozen men and women chosen to reassure the public that censorship was to be operated with sense, independence and understanding of relevant expertise and of public feelings. We think that the film industry should be represented on the Board, by perhaps three members, and that another three members might be nominated by local authorities. Other members would include persons versed in such disciplines as the law, child psychology, education etc.

12.31 We do not think a body of this kind is best equipped to undertake the actual work of examining films. Rather, we think it should have the responsibility for laying down the policy for the censorship of films and for ensuring that the policy is followed by a small staff of professional examiners which it would employ. We think that the Board itself would be the appropriate body to hear appeals from the decisions of the examiners. We think it essential that the censorship system should make provision for appeals and rather than institute a separate appellate body, it makes sense in our view for the professional examiners working under the Board's policy directives to make the initial decision on a film and for the Board itself to review that decision if an appeal is made. We think it right that anyone should be able to appeal against the examiners' decision: in this way we believe that public confidence in the Board and in its ability to take account of public views will be strengthened. This will mean that the film distributor will be able to appeal against a refusal of a certificate, against a requirement for cuts or against allocation to a particular category, as he can do at the moment, though only by taking his film to individual local authorities; but in addition any member of the public would be able to appeal against, for example, the grant of a certificate at all or the grant of a particular certificate. We think that the Board should be required to view the film if appealed to by the applicant for a certificate; but we feel that in relation to an appeal by anyone else, the Board should have discretion whether or not to view the film before reaching a decision.

12.32 We envisage that the Board, like the present British Board of Film Censors, should get its income by charging fees for the examination of films, but there may be a need for it to have an additional subvention from public funds. The fixing of fees and the determination of appropriate cases in which fees might be reduced or waived would be additional responsibilities of the Board.

The application of "restriction" to films

12.33 We concluded earlier in our report that the prime object of the law with regard to publications should be to prevent pornography and violent material causing offence to members of the public and that if this were done there was comparatively little published material which should be not allowed to those people who wanted it. We think the same principle should be applied to the showing of films. At present, the film censorship system denies a public showing to a large amount of material which is judged not unlawful or harmful but merely less than acceptable to local licensing authorities and the public at large. One result is that a number of films of artistic merit and importance have been prevented from being seen publicly in this country, even by the minority audiences who would be interested in them (Pasolini's *Salò* and Oshima's *Empire of the Senses* are obvious examples). At the same time, the certification system does not entirely control what is seen, since a thriving trade exists in uncensored material shown to club members; but the notion of a club, as we have already said (paragraph 3.13) is an absurd fiction, since in many cases the films can be seen by any member of the public who turns up at the door and enrolls as a member of the club. This system does to some extent achieve the sensible aim of allowing a restricted showing of potentially offensive material to people who want to see it; but it is a totally unsatisfactory way of doing this and should not be allowed to continue.

12.34 Many film clubs merely show the kind of explicit sex films which we have made clear are unlikely to involve any recognisable social harms, and which we would not wish to be prohibited to those who want to see them. But since, in order to be able to show these films, the clubs concerned have to place themselves beyond the reach of the censorship system and this means in turn avoiding the cinema licensing system, they evade at the same time what is the main object of cinema licensing, which is public safety. In our view, this represents a social harm of a different kind: it is obviously desirable that this area of film exhibition should be subject to the same safeguards to secure the safety of the public as apply to cinemas generally.

12.35 Moreover, the club system means that, leaving aside the present criminal law, there is a total lack of control on the nature of the films shown and the audiences admitted to see them. Although many clubs show films which we would regard as acceptable for restricted viewing, this is not always the case. We were told that one sadistic sex film which we saw might have been shown in clubs in this country; our view was that the film would be turned down by any censorship system, however liberal, and we noted in our talks with the French film censor that the same and similar films are banned entirely in France despite the existence of a special category there for films which are pornographic or, indeed, incite to violence. There are a number of film clubs which specialise in oriental martial arts films which can be extremely violent and which are often required to be cut by the British Board of Film Censors even before being given an "X" certificate. The admission of children to these clubs means that uncensored films containing the kind of material which would not be passed even for adult viewing in a public cinema, is being shown without any restriction at all on who may see it. We consider it desirable that the scope of the censorship system should be extended so as to impose some control on what at present is subject to none. There is a need both to draw the line at what is acceptable even for restricted audiences and to ensure that restrictions are properly observed.

12.36 These considerations lead us to the view that there should be an additional category of certificate which would permit restricted exhibition to a class of films which the censorship would not presently approve. This would provide an outlet both for films of quality which we consider ought to be allowed to be shown in this country and for films of no merit which we consider adults should be able to see if they so choose. Most of the films concerned would contain explicit sex of a straightforward character, of the kind now seen in many cinema clubs and, for example, in the special "pornographic" cinemas instituted in France in 1975. The French system for allowing pornographic films in restricted conditions seems to have worked well and with a substantial degree of public acceptance. Experience from European countries suggests that if films of this kind are made legitimate, the films may be rather less squalid than they are at present.

12.37 We turn now to the restrictions which should attach to the showing of these films. Some analogy is appropriate to the kind of restrictions which we have proposed should apply to the sale of offensive publications. First, it is clear to us that these films should be for adults only and that no one under the age of eighteen[1] should be admitted to see them. But we also consider that restrictions over and above those applying to the existing "X" certificate are needed. We think that it is undesirable that every cinema should be capable of showing such films: if these films are not to intrude on public consciousness in a way that will be found offensive by many, we think that some further restriction is needed of the premises in which they can be shown (and, whatever the arguments may be about "X" films being televised, we are sure that it would not be appropriate for films of this kind to be shown on television).

12.38 We think that local authorities might have a legitimate role to play here. We propose that films of the new category we have suggested should not lawfully be publicly shown other than in a cinema designated for the showing of such films; and we think it reasonable to allow locally elected representatives to decide whether they wish to have a cinema of that kind in their area, and to control the numbers of such cinemas. One particular

---

[1]See paragraphs 9.39-40.

question is whether one auditorium out of several in a multi-screen cinema complex should be eligible for designation in this way; on balance we think that it should, in particular because so many cinemas now take this form that if this were forbidden it might be impossible in many areas to designate any cinema at all. Designation should be the responsibility of the local cinema licensing authority on the application of the licensee, and whether or not to agree to designation should be at the authority's complete discretion. At the same time, however, approval or rejection of designated status should be the limit of the local authority's power in relation to the films shown in such a cinema; we are not proposing any fresh right to censor films or to impose conditions as to the films that may be shown. The local authority should be empowered to charge a fee for designation in order to recoup the administrative costs it incurs.

12.39 Designation would give the cinema the right to show films of the proposed new category. We see no advantage, however, in requiring that a designated cinema should have to specialise in such films, as is the case in France. We see some objection to actually requiring a cinema to show pornographic films when it proposes to show something else, and no merit in preventing a designated cinema from showing *Bambi* in the school holidays if it wishes to do so. A designated cinema should therefore be free to show any films passed by the Film Examining Board, including those in the new restricted category; at times when it is showing films in that category it should be permitted no pictorial displays outside the cinema and should be required to display in the foyer a notice in terms decided by the Board giving sufficient information about the film to be an adequate warning to unsuspecting cinemagoers about the nature of what they will see if they enter. We believe that if the system we propose is adopted, it will probably result, in practice, in there being two sorts of designated cinema. One will be a blue movie house, which rarely if ever shows anything else. The other will be, to some degree, an 'art' house, which shows a variety of films with various certificates, usually of minority appeal. If this happened, it would avoid a difficulty which we felt was presented by the French system: no-one in France would dream of consigning a film with any serious intention, or by a well-known director, to the *salles pornographiques,* so that such a film will always end up in an ordinary cinema, however offensive or pornographic it may be.

12.40 The legitimisation of sex films which are more explicit than those presently permitted in a public cinema will, we hope, discourage the expedient of setting up a club in order to get round the censorship requirements. But, for the reasons we have already given, we think it desirable actively to discourage clubs of this kind—though we would not wish to do anything to interfere with the genuine film society—and we therefore propose that steps should be taken to ensure that the new censorship requirements (and probably cinema licensing as well) should apply to such clubs. This will mean that certified films only will be allowed to be shown not only by ordinary cinemas but also by any other commercially-run establishment, and this will apply to the kind of club which has hitherto specialised in uncensored sex films. But there are various film exhibitions of a non-commercial nature which are at present outside the scope of the censorship system and in our view should remain so; we propose, therefore, that there should be an exemption for any exhibition not promoted for private gain. We think that there might be value in the law's stating explicitly that film shows promoted by religious, educational and charitable bodies should be deemed not to be promoted for private gain. The exemption we propose here is, of course, an exemption only from the requirements of certification; the prohibition on certain films being distributed or shown which arises from our proposals on prohibited publications (see paragraph 10.11) will apply to any film exhibition whatsoever.

Categories of certificate

12.41 We think that certain modifications to the existing certificates should be made, and that the general criteria for determining the appropriate certificate should be laid down by statute. Parliament would therefore give general guidelines to the Board within which the Board would determine the policy to be adopted in censoring films. The new category we have proposed, for example, is based like the restriction test we have set out in Chapter 9 on the prevention of offence to reasonable people, and it would be appropriate, therefore, that guidelines for the issue of that certificate should be in terms similar to the statutory test for restricting publications. We consider that it would be generally helpful if the names and symbols assigned to the certificates revealed more of their effect, and we propose that this category should be designated **18R,** which combines the minimum age with an indication of restriction. We propose that the symbol for each category should contain the descriptive reference within a circle, represented in the following paragraphs by brackets.

12.42 The experience of the British Board of Film Censors has suggested to them an alteration of the present "A" and "AA" certificates, with which we sympathise. Fourteen, the Board explained to us, is too young an age for the sort of film which they would happily pass for persons over 16: it is possibly the age of maximum sexual confusion and embarrassment and also, they claimed, the age when some boys might be most open to influence by the depiction of certain kinds of violence. Since "AA" admits those of 14, the Board often tends to give an "X" certificate to films which it considers would be quite acceptable for viewing by 16 and 17 year olds. If the age limit for the present "AA" certificate were raised to 16, these films could be given that certificate. We agree with this assessment, and propose that there should be a new category designated **(16).** This would inevitably have some implications for the "A" certificate. There is at present no actual age restriction below the age of 14—the "A" certificate merely suggests parental guidance. If the "AA" limit were raised to 16, that would mean that a very wide range of material would fall into categories (presently "U" and "A") which allow any child to be in the cinema. Some material which is quite suitable for young teenagers might well be disturbing to young children, and we think it right to follow a further suggestion made to us by the British Board of Film Censors and bring back the requirement that young children at least should be accompanied by a parent or responsible adult to see films in what has so far been the "A" category. We think the right age below which children should have to be accompanied is 11, and we accordingly propose that this category should be designated **(11A)** to indicate not that children under that age are not admitted, but that they must be accompanied.

12.43 We see no need to propose any change in the "U" category, which is well understood, or in the "X" category, apart from proposing that the latter should be designated **(18)**. It may be appropriate for us to make the point, however, that we do not envisage that our proposals for an **(18R)** category should significantly alter the character of films assigned to the **(18)** category, at present "X". It may certainly be appropriate for some films now shown in a cut version with an "X" certificate to appear uncut in future as **(18R)** films but we would not otherwise expect that what is now given an "X" certificate would in future be classified **(18R)**.

12.44 One set of guidelines could properly cover all the certificates which are concerned with suitability for children, that is, the **(U)**, **(11A)**, **(16)** and **(18)** categories. These guidelines would require the Board to have regard to the protection of the young from harmful or disturbing influences, or from the kind of material which, having regard to the restriction test for publications, is such that its unrestricted availability to persons under 18 would be unacceptable to responsible parents.

12.45 In addition to the categories we have so far discussed, there is the case of films which are refused a certificate. We propose that the guidelines should simply require refusal if a film is considered unfit for public exhibition, being one that contains material prohibited by law or one that is unacceptable because of the manner in which it depicts violence, sexual activity or crime. But the Board would not be able to refuse a certificate to a film not containing unlawful material without having regard to the importance of allowing the development of artistic expression and of not suppressing truth or reality. Material prohibited by law would include that covered by our proposed prohibition test or by other provisions of law such as incitement to crime, incitement to racial hatred or those of the Cinematograph Films (Animals) Act 1937.

12.46 We considered arguments to the effect that no film which in its production had involved the commission of offences should be permitted to be cut to obtain a certificate, since to require offending sequences simply to be excised, or to acquiesce in that being done, would condone the original offence. We concluded that there are overwhelming practical difficulties in enforcing a ban on cutting unlawful films, particularly in relation to films which had already been cut before submission to the censors, and we also had to bear in mind that the requirements of British censorship, controlling only a very small part of the world film market, would be unlikely to represent a real deterrent to film makers elsewhere in the world. It will be open to the Board to draw the attention of the prosecuting authorities to any film which appears to give grounds for believing that offences have been committed in this country, but we consider it unnecessary to lay down a rule about the Board's treatment of apparently unlawful scenes in films submitted to it.

12.47 Where the Board grants a certificate, we believe that this should carry a presumption that the film does not contain any material prohibited by law and we think it right that the exhibitor should be under no liability for showing it in conditions appropriate to the certificate. In other words, the grant of a certificate should convey a guarantee of immunity from prosecution so long as any restrictions implicit in the certificate are observed.

12.48 Since we propose in these ways that the Board should be the principal arbiter of whether or not a film can be shown in this country, we also think it important that the customs authorities should not decide that a film is a prohibited import without referring it to the Board. The Board should have the power to advise the customs authorities whether or not the import of a film should be allowed and it may be that the Board would be able to find the film acceptable subject to certain cuts being made, a flexibility which would not normally be available under customs procedures.

The enforcement of film censorship

12.49 We have proposed the ending of the powers of cinema licensing authorities to impose censorship; they would consequently lose their power to enforce censorship by instituting proceedings in magistrates' courts for the offence of contravening the conditions attached to a cinema licence. There therefore has to be a new statute, creating specific offences in order to ensure compliance with the proposed system. It should be an offence to exhibit publicly any film which has not received a certificate from the Board (and in this context "publicly" is to be taken as including, in accordance with our proposals, any showing in a club promoted for private gain). It should also be an offence to exhibit publicly any film other than in accordance with the requirements of the certificate issued to it. This offence would cover the admission of children to films designated as unsuitable to them, the showing of **(18R)** films other than in designated cinemas and the showing of an **(18R)** film by a designated cinema other than in accordance with the restrictions laid down. Another offence, continuing the standard provision now made by local authorities, would require that the category of the film should be shown in all advertising matter, at the entrance to the cinema and on the screen immediately before the showing of the film. We think that the most serious of these offences—that of showing uncertificated films—should be prosecuted, tried and punished in the way that we have already proposed for restriction offences (paragraphs 9.43 and 50). The other offences arising from breaches of the censorship controls might be punishable only by a maximum fine of £500.

12.50 An issue raised strongly with us by cinema interests concerned the enforcement of the age limits attaching to films, in particular to "X" films. At present, the cinema licensee is under an obligation not to admit persons under eighteen to performances in which a film with an "X" certificate is exhibited, and if young people gain admission the licensee may be prosecuted for failing to comply with the conditions of the licence. The Cinematograph Exhibitors' Association, supported by cinema managers, represented to us that it was quite unfair for the onus to be placed entirely on cinema staff, who frequently find it hard to assess just how old their customers may be, while the young people themselves, who are the only ones actually to know whether they are of the permitted age, have nothing to lose by trying to pass themselves off as over eighteen. The Association urged us to recommend that it should be an offence for a person under eighteen to seek to gain admittance to a film exhibition designated as unsuitable for them. In support of their case they drew attention to the offence already provided by the Licensing Act 1964 which penalises a person under eighteen who buys or attempts to buy intoxicating liquor in licensed premises.

12.51 We had some sympathy for the cinema manager trying to enforce the minimum age limits, particularly in view of the pressures which we know exist among young people to see "X" films before they are eighteen. Certainly, a large part of the population must have seen an "X" film before they were properly old enough. Nevertheless, it must ultimately be the responsibility of the cinema licensee to enforce this control, just as it is the responsibility of the public house licensee not to serve liquor to those under age. The only question is whether the young person should also bear some responsibility in the matter. Some observers might make the comment that the existence of a sanction on under-age drinkers has not taken the pressure off publicans in the way cinema interests appear to hope. But we are not in any case very sympathetic to the general idea of turning young people into criminals more than is necessary, and we cannot agree to the creation of a new criminal offence capable of being committed only by people under the age of eighteen, especially when the activity concerned is so widespread and so hallowed a teenage tradition. We affirm that we think it desirable that films in the **(18)** category should not be seen by those under eighteen and we think it important that genuine efforts should be devoted to stopping the practice. But we think that it would be going too far to criminalise the attempt by young people to see such films. The responsibility, in our view, should continue to rest on those who accept the payments their patrons make.

Conclusion

12.52 The present system for the censorship of films has by and large served us well. We are sure that most people wish a system to continue on broadly similar lines. But we found a widespread feeling that the time had come to remove the anomalies inherent in the system and to establish censorship on a more rational and deliberate footing. This is what our proposals seek to do. We believe that the system we propose will not only meet this public demand for reform in the system but will provide the basis for the efficient, effective and sensitive practice of censorship in the future in a way that will secure broad public support. We are confident that a system on these lines will be capable of serving society well in the decades to come.

CHAPTER THIRTEEN

SUMMARY OF OUR PROPOSALS

13.1 Since our specific proposals have been scattered through the discussion contained in the last four chapters, it may be helpful if, finally, we summarise in more compact form the reforms that we propose. We take the opportunity to be slightly more specific about some aspects of our proposals, and to fill in details which it seemed unnecessary to spell out in the course of describing what decisions we had reached.

13.2 We have been conscious that the problems associated with our subject are such that it is not enough for us simply to describe how we think they should be dealt with, even if that description is fairly detailed. What is crucial is that one's proposals should be capable of being translated into legislation which will be rational and workable. It is much harder to settle the concrete form of a law than to say in general terms what it ought to do. This is evident in the existing law, which is unsatisfactory because of the vagueness and uncertainty of its definitions; it must be said that it was also apparent in the evidence of our witnesses, many of whom found it easier to make general statements about pornography or about the scope of the law than to suggest to us how a new law might be framed.

13.3 We therefore felt a need to assure ourselves that our proposals could make effective legislation. We have devoted some time to translating our proposals into the form of a draft Bill, a process which has required us to consider the practical problems that always arise when broad policy is turned into legislation, and to look again at certain aspects of our proposals. The content of Part 3 of our Report takes account of this task we have undertaken, and has in some respects been modified as a consequence of our consideration of the requirements of legislation. As a result, we feel able to offer our recommendations with greater confidence in their practicality. We have not, however, thought it appropriate to publish our draft Bill with our Report. It was not our aim in drafting legislative provisions to produce a measure which in all technical respects would be suitable for enactment in the form in which it stood, and we wished to avoid giving the impression, by publishing it, that it might be.

13.4 We propose that:

General

1. The existing variety of laws in this field should be scrapped and a comprehensive new statute should start afresh (see paragraph 2.29).

2. Terms such as "obscene", "indecent" and "deprave and corrupt" should be abandoned as having outlived their usefulness (paragraph 9.21).

3. The law should rest partly on the basis of harms caused by or involved in the existence of the material: these alone can justify prohibitions; and partly on the basis of the public's legitimate interest

in not being offended by the display and availability of the material: this can justify no more than the imposition of restrictions designed to protect the ordinary citizen from unreasonable offence (paragraphs 9.7 and 10.2).

4. The principal object of the law should be to prevent certain kinds of material causing offence to reasonable people or being made available to young people (paragraph 9.7).

5. Only a small class of material should be forbidden to those who want it, because an objective assessment of likely harm does not support a wider prohibition (paragraph 10.8).

6. The printed word should be neither restricted nor prohibited since its nature makes it neither immediately offensive nor capable of involving the harms we identify, and because of its importance in conveying ideas (paragraph 7.22).

Restriction

7. Restrictions should apply to matter (other than the printed word) and to a performance whose unrestricted availability is offensive to reasonable people by reason of the manner in which it portrays, deals with or relates to violence, cruelty or horror, or sexual, faecal or urinary functions or genital organs (paragraphs 9.36 and 11.8).

8. Restriction is to consist in a ban

(i) on the display, sale, hire etc. of restricted material other than by way of postal or other delivery and

(ii) on the presentation of any restricted performance

other than in premises (or a part of premises having a separate access from the street)

(a) to which persons under the age of eighteen are not admitted, and

(b) to which access is possible only by passing a prominent warning notice in specified terms, and

(c) which make no display visible to persons not passing beyond the warning notice, other than the name of the business and an indication of its nature (paragraphs 9.15 and 11.8).

9. No material or performance should be exempt from these restrictions on the ground of any intrinsic merit it might possess (paragraph 9.41).

10. It should be an offence to display, sell, hire etc. any restricted matter or to present a restricted performance in contravention of the restrictions laid down (paragraphs 9.43 and 11.16).

11. This offence should not apply to the showing of films, for which we propose separate controls.

12. It should be an offence to send or deliver restricted material, or advertisements for such material, to

(a) a person who the sender knew or ought reasonably to have known was under the age of eighteen, or
(b) a person who the sender knew or ought reasonably to have known had not solicited the material (paragraphs 9.18–19).

13. It should not be an offence for a person under the age of eighteen to seek to gain entry to premises in which restricted material is being displayed, sold or hired or in which a restricted performance is being presented, or to order restricted material to be sent to him or her (paragraph 9.44).

14. It should not be freely open to any individual to institute proceedings for the criminal offences proposed above; prosecutions should be brought by the police or by or with the consent of the Director of Public Prosecutions (paragraphs 9.50 and 11.16).

15. Restriction offences should be triable only by magistrates and punishable by fines of up to £1,000 and imprisonment of up to six months (paragraphs 9.43 and 11.16).

16. The police should have power to obtain a magistrate's warrant to enter and search premises for material which they believe is being displayed, sold or hired in contravention of the restrictions, and to seize such material as may be needed for the purposes of evidence (paragraph 9.45).

17. A magistrates' court convicting an offender for a restriction offence should have power to order, if it thinks fit, that seized material should be forfeited (paragraph 9.46).

18. There should be no separate procedure aimed at the forfeiture of restricted material divorced from criminal proceedings against an alleged offender (paragraph 9.46).

Prohibition

19. Prohibited material should consist of photographs and films whose production appears to the court to have involved the exploitation for sexual purposes of any person where either

(a) that person appears from the evidence as a whole to have been at the relevant time under the age of sixteen, or
(b) the material gives reason to believe that actual physical harm was inflicted on that person (paragraph 10.6).

20. It should be an offence to take any prohibited photograph or film, to distribute or show it, to have it with a view to its being distributed or shown, or to advertise it as being available for distribution or showing (paragraph 10.13).

21. No proceedings in respect of this offence should lie in relation to any film exhibited under the authority of a film censorship certificate (paragraph 12.47).

22. Prohibited material should be included in the list of goods prohibited from importation, and imports contravening the prohibition should be dealt with according to the normal customs procedures for prohibited imports, save for certain exceptions relating to films (paragraphs 10.13 and 12.48).

23. Prohibited material should be included among articles prohibited from transmission through the post but there should be an additional prohibition as regards overseas mail on articles of which the importation and circulation is prohibited in the country of destination (paragraph 10.14).

24. A live performance should be prohibited if

(a) it involves actual sexual activity of a kind which, in the circumstances in which it was given, would be offensive to reasonable people (sexual activity including the act of masturbation and forms of genital, anal or oral connection between humans and animals as well as between humans), or

(b) it involves the sexual exploitation of any person under the age of sixteen (paragraph 11.15).

25. It should be an offence to present, organise or take part in a performance which contravenes the prohibition (paragraph 11.16).

26. The law should not be so framed as to apply to what is performed in a private house so long as no person under eighteen is present and no charge is made (paragraph 11.17).

27. The law on live performances should not apply to what is performed solely for the purposes of being filmed or photographed where the resulting material would not be liable to prohibition (paragraph 11.17).

28. No material or performance should be exempt from the prohibition on the grounds of any intrinsic merit it might possess (paragraphs 10.12 and 11.10).

29. No proceedings should be instituted in respect of a prohibition offence other than by or with the consent of the Director of Public Prosecutions (paragraph 10.20).

30. Prohibition offences should be triable either in the Crown Court or in a magistrates' court, with a maximum term of three years' imprisonment and an unlimited fine on conviction in the Crown Court (paragraph 10.15).

31. The police should have power to obtain a magistrate's warrant to enter and search premises and seize what they believe to be prohibited material kept in circumstances in which they believe an offence is being committed (paragraph 10.17).

32. The court convicting a person of an offence involving prohibited material shall order that any material seized which is in their view prohibited material shall be forfeited (paragraph 10.19).

33. There should be no separate procedure aimed at the forfeiture of prohibited material divorced from criminal proceedings against an alleged offender (paragraph 10.19).

Film censorship

34. Censorship imposed by local authorities on the basis of their powers to licence cinemas should be ended (paragraph 12.20).

35. A statutory board should be set up to take over the censorship powers of local authorities and the functions now exercised by the British Board of Film Censors, but the responsibility for licensing cinemas should continue to rest with local authorities (paragraph 12.29).

36. The Board should be known as the Film Examining Board and should comprise about twelve members chosen to represent a range of interests, including the film industry and local government, and relevant expertise (paragraph 12.30).

37. The Board should be non-profit making and so far as possible self-supporting from the fees charged for examining films; but provision should be made for some financial assistance from public funds (paragraph 12.32).

38. The functions of the Board members should be

(a) to establish the policy and principles of film censorship within the criteria laid down by statute;
(b) to appoint a Chief Examiner of Films and, on the recommendation of the Chairman and Chief Examiner, a small staff of film examiners to take decisions on individual films;
(c) to prescribe procedures for the censorship of films, the fees to be charged and to decide on the waiver of fees where appropriate;
(d) to hear appeals against the decisions of the examiners (paragraph 12.31).

39. When the decision of the examiners is the subject of an appeal by the applicant for a certificate, the Board should be required to view the film before determining the appeal (paragraph 12.31).

40. It should be open to any person to appeal against a particular decision of the examiners, but in the case of an appeal by a person other

than the applicant the Board should have power to reach a decision either after seeing the film or after deciding that the written reasons for the appeal do not justify their taking steps to see it (paragraph 12.31).

41. The Board's examiners should allocate each film examined to one of the following six categories:

(U) Suitable for all ages

(11A) Children under the age of eleven should be accompanied by a responsible adult

(16) No person under the age of sixteen to be admitted

(18) No person under the age of eighteen to be admitted

(18R) For restricted exhibition only. No person under the age of eighteen to be admitted.

Certificate refused
(paragraphs 12.41–43).

42. The category of a film, in the form of an encircled symbol, should be clearly shown in any advertisements for it, at the entrance to the cinema and on the screen immediately before the film is shown (paragraph 12.49).

43. The Board should give to the applicant on request a statement of reasons why a film is refused a certificate or allocated to a particular category, giving sufficient indication of any changes that might be required for it to qualify for a certificate, or for a less restrictive certificate (paragraph 12.45).

44. In formulating its policy on the control of film content, the Board should be required to have regard to the following guidelines:

(a) the issue of certificates indicating a film's suitability or unsuitability for persons under eighteen should take account of the protection of children and young persons from influences which may be disturbing or harmful to them, or from material whose unrestricted availability to them would be unacceptable to responsible parents.

(b) a film should be classified for restricted exhibition only if its visual content and the manner in which it deals with violence, cruelty or horror, or sexual, faecal or urinary functions or genital organs is such that in the judgement of the examiners it is appropriate that the film should be shown only under restricted conditions.

(c) a film should be refused a certificate only if, in the judgement of the examiners, it is unfit for public exhibition. A film unfit for public exhibition should be one that either

(i) contains material prohibited by law; or

(ii) having regard to the importance of allowing the development of artistic expression and of not suppressing truth or reality, is nevertheless unacceptable because of the manner in which it depicts violence or sexual activity or crime.

(paragraph 12.45).

45. A film classified for restricted exhibition should not be shown for gain other than in a cinema designated by the local cinema licensing authority as suitable for the showing of such films. The local authority should have absolute discretion whether or not to approve an application for designation and its decision should be final (paragraph 12.38).

46. An auditorium in a multi-screen cinema complex should be eligible for designation as suitable for the showing of restricted films (paragraph 12.38).

47. A designated cinema should be free to show any film granted a certificate by the Film Examining Board (paragraph 12.39).

48. When exhibiting a restricted film, a designated cinema should be required to make no pictorial display outside the cinema and to display in the foyer a brief synopsis or description of the film prepared by the Film Examining Board (paragraph 12.39).

49. Steps should be taken to bring commercial cinema clubs within the scope of the censorship system by providing an exemption only for film exhibitions not promoted for private gain (paragraph 12.40).

50. A film intended for exhibition in this country should not be seized on importation as a prohibited import without being referred to the Film Examining Board for advice and for decision as to whether, in a cut form, it could qualify for a certificate (paragraph 12.47).

51. It should be an offence to exhibit for private gain any film not possessing a certificate issued by the Film Examining Board (paragraph 12.46).

52. It should be an offence to exhibit any film for private gain other than in accordance with the requirements of the certificate issued to it (paragraph 12.49).

53. It should not be an offence for a person under the age of eighteen to seek to gain entry to a film designated as unsuitable for persons of that age (paragraph 12.51).

54. It should be an offence to advertise a film or exhibit it without complying with the requirements to specify the category of certificate granted to it (paragraph 12.49).

55. The Board should not have a responsibility for prosecuting offenders nor should any individual be free to institute proceedings; prosecutions should be brought by the police or by or with the consent of the Director of Public Prosecutions (paragraph 12.49).

56. Offences concerned with film censorship should be triable only by magistrates. Showing uncertificated films should be punishable by fines of up to £1,000 and imprisonment of up to six months; other offences should be punishable by fines of up to £500 (paragraph 12.49).